CHRISTOCENTRIC COMMENTARY SERIES

A COMMENTARY ON THE

REVELATION
OF JOHN

—⁕—

Jesus Christ:
Victor Over Religion

James A. Fowler

PUBLISHING
P.O. BOX 1822
FALLBROOK, CALIFORNIA 92088-1822

A COMMENTARY ON THE REVELATION OF JOHN

Jesus Christ: Victor Over Religion

~ Christocentric Commentary Series ~

Copyright ©2013 by James A. Fowler

ISBN-10 – 1-929541-49-X
ISBN-13 – 978-1-929541-49-2

All rights reserved. No part of this publication may be reproduced, stored in a retrieval system, or transmitted in any form or by any means (including photocopyings, recording, electronic transmission) without the prior written permission of the author, except for brief quotations embodied in critical articles or book reviews. For information contact the author at C.I.Y. Publishing.

Published by **C.I.Y.** Publishing
P.O. Box 1822
Fallbrook, California 92088-1822

Printed in the United States of America

Scriptural quotations are primarily original translations from the Greek text of the New Testament, but otherwise from the New American Standard Bible, copyrights 1960, 1962, 1963, 1968, 1971, 1972, 1973, 1975, 1977, 1995 by the Lockman Foundation, LaHabra, California.

CHRISTOCENTRIC COMMENTARY SERIES

Cognizant that there are a plethora of New Testament Commentary series available on the market, the question might legitimately be asked, "Why another series of New Testament commentaries?" Although many capable commentators with varying theological perspectives have exegeted the text of the New Testament over the years, seldom do they bring with them into their studies a Christocentric understanding that the Christian gospel is solely comprised and singularly centered in the Person of the risen and living Lord Jesus Christ. The *Christocentric Commentary Series* will exegete and comment on the text of the New Testament from the perspective that the totality of what Jesus came to bring to the world of mankind is Himself – nothing more, nothing less. Having historically died on the cross and risen from the dead, He is not confined to the parameters of the "Historical Jesus," but as the Spirit of Christ He continues to live as He spiritually indwells those who are receptive to Him by faith. This recognition of the contemporary experiential dynamic of Christ's life in the Christian will form the distinctive of the *Christocentric Commentary Series,* bearing out Paul's Christ-centered declaration, "I have been crucified with Christ; it is no longer I who live, but Christ lives in me; and the life I now live in the flesh I live by faith in the Son of God, who loved me and gave Himself up for me" (Gal. 2:20).

All legitimate exegesis of the scriptures must pay close attention to the context in which the texts were originally written. The historical context of a text's *sitz im leben*, the "setting in life" of the author and recipients, is particularly important, for otherwise the interpretation will simply read into the text the presuppositions of the commentator and become *eisegesis* instead of *exegesis*. The *CCS* will carefully consider the historical context as well as the textual context of the scriptures.

Whereas the *CCS* is not intended to be a devotional commentary series or a detailed technical commentary citing all contemporary scholarship, our intent is to steer a middle course that maintains non-technical explanation that is academically viable. Although reference will be made to words from the Hebrew and Greek languages, those words will be converted to Roman lettering, allowing those who do not know the original languages to pronounce them. Citations, quotations, and endnotes will be kept to a minimum.

A diversity of interpretive formats will be utilized in the *CCS*. Some volumes will employ a verse-by-verse exegetical format (cf. *Hebrews* and *Galatians*), whereas others will provide comment on contextual passages (cf. *The Four Gospels* and *Revelation*). Regardless of the interpretive format, the *CCS* will render a "literal interpretation" of the scripture text, that is, in accord with the intended literary genre of the author.

As most biblical commentaries are utilized by pastors and teachers, or studious Christians seeking to understand the scriptures in depth in order to share with others, we join the Apostle Paul in the desire to "entrust these to faithful men (and women) who will be able to teach others also" (II Tim. 2:2). In so doing, may you "do all to the glory of God" (I Cor. 10:31).

PREFACE

When one announces they are going to teach on the book of Revelation there are generally at least three different reactions to such an announcement. (1) Oh no – it is mysteriously confusing, an enigma, a bewildering riddle which no one can understand, so why bother. (2) Oh yes – it is extremely fascinating. These are often the "prophecy freaks" who make it their hobby-horse to engage in fanciful speculations. They bring out their charts, maps, outlines, and study Bibles with extensive notes. (3) Oh no – it is boringly irrelevant. What I need is realism; I need to know how to deal with the present, not fly off into the realm of futuristic science-fiction.

These reactions can be summed up as: (1) avoidance, (2) preoccupation, or (3) apathy. In this document we want to demonstrate that the Revelation is *understandable* – so we should not avoid it; down-to-earth, and presently *practical* – so we do not have to get involved in fanciful speculation; and *realistic and relevant* – so we should not be apathetic about it. Our reaction to the study of Revelation should be: (4) Let us see what God's Spirit has to teach us about Jesus Christ from this portion of His inspired Scripture.

I admit that I avoided the Revelation of John for approximately twenty-five years of my pastoral ministry. Then, in 1993, when I began to select a subject for a doctoral dissertation in Biblical Theology, I determined to face down the nemesis of the last book of the New Testament in order to write a thesis on John's Apocalypse. Though not a traditional verse-by-verse commentary, the objective was to provide a consistent interpretation of the composite of images in the Revelation.

Consistency is a vital interpretive criteria for the understanding of any document of literature. The internal consistency of allowing every portion of the Revelation to be directed at a unified theme is essential. Consistency with the entirety of the new covenant literature of the New Testament is equally important. External consistency of Christian interpretation of the Revelation throughout the centuries of Christian thought appears to be hopelessly impossible. Or is it? In perusing the wide variety of interpretations that have been proffered of John's Revelation, there does seem to be a common thread. The preterist interpreters have identified the primary images of the Revelation (such as the beasts, Babylon, and the whore) with the first century *Dea Roma*, the religious worship of the Roman Empire and emperor, especially Nero. The historicist interpretations have generally sought to identify to identify those same images with the papacy of the Roman Catholic church, or to a lesser degree with the religion of Mohammedanism (Islam). Futurist interpretations of the same images have varied widely, but have often pointed to a revival of the Roman Empire, a "new world order," or a yet to arise politico-religious personage or power. What is the common thread in these far-ranging interpretations? They all seem to point to religious phenomena. Perhaps there is a degree of consistency in the external interpretation of the Revelation throughout Christian history. With that in mind, this study will take the theme of "religion" as the antagonist and adversary of Jesus Christ throughout the apocalyptic imagery of the Revelation.

Our ultimate focus, however, must be on the Victor over religion, the living Person of Jesus Christ. John explained that what he observed was "the revelation *of Jesus Christ*" (1:1). May we ever "fix our eyes on Jesus" (Heb. 12:2) as we exegete the inspired scriptures, and particularly this Revelation.

James A. Fowler (2013)

TABLE OF CONTENTS

Introduction to the Revelation 1

Prologue of the Revelation 25

Religion and the Churches 57

    Religion and the Church at Ephesus 69
    Religion and the Church at Smyrna 79
    Religion and the Church at Pergamum 91
    Religion and the Church at Thyatira 99
    Religion and the Church at Sardis 111
    Religion and the Church at Philadelphia 121
    Religion and the Church at Laodicea 135

Religion and the Seals 147

Religion and the Trumpets 181

Religion and the Beasts 203

Religion and Babylon 233

Religion Goes to Hell 263

Epilogue 297

Application 309

Addenda 315

Bibliography 325

Introduction to the Revelation

The last book of the Bible is the climactic revelation of how Christianity, i.e. the dynamic of the living Christ, is superior to and triumphant over all religion. In a conclusive climax with culminating clarity, the book of Revelation reveals that Christianity is not religion. Instead, Christianity is Jesus Christ who has won the victory over Satan, and presently reigns in His spiritual kingdom, and will ultimately expose and dethrone all religious pretenders inspired by Satan when the victory is consummated and made evident to all upon His return.

Throughout the entirety of the new covenant literature, the New Testament, there is a continuing exposure of the radical difference between religion and the dynamic life of Jesus Christ as it functions within the kingdom of grace. Revelation is the climactic "capstone" that illustrates the triumph of Jesus over diabolic religion.

Throughout the gospel narratives Jesus is constantly countering the religionism of the scribes, Pharisees and Saducees. In the parables Jesus explains that the kingdom He came to bring is entirely different than that anticipated by Jewish religion; His is a kingdom that is not of this world and functions by God's grace. The religious leaders finally realized that Jesus was exposing them in every parable He told (Matt. 21:45).

Introduction

The Acts of the Apostles records the early history of how Christianity was "breaking free from religion," so as to be unhindered by any identification with Judaic religion.

In Paul's letters it is evident that he saw clearly the dichotomy between religion and Christianity. To the Romans Paul explains that righteousness is not in religious rites or the Law, but in Jesus Christ, the Righteous One. In the first epistle to the Corinthians Paul counters the religious excesses that were developing in the young church in Corinth. In the second epistle to the Corinthians Paul differentiates between gospel ministry by the grace of God and the manipulations of religious method. The letter to the Galatians forcefully denies that there is "another gospel" as inculcated by legalistic religion. The gospel is Jesus Christ alone functioning by grace. Writing to the Ephesians Paul contrasts religious exclusivism with the universality of the Christian gospel and explains that in Jesus Christ all men become a new humanity. In his correspondence with the Colossians Paul combats the effects of the regional religionism of Asia, emphasizing the preeminence of Jesus Christ who is the life of every Christian individual.

The writer to the Hebrews explains how the old and the new covenants are differentiated. The old tenets of Judaic religion are replaced by the life of Jesus Christ. James explains that if one is just going through the rituals, such religion is vain. Christian faith is the outworking of the life of Jesus Christ. Finally, then, in the Revelation, John relates in pictorial storyform that religion will try to overcome and secularize Christianity, but Jesus Christ overcomes all the machinations of religion by His life.

For many years preachers, teachers and commentators have bantered and battled, bickered and babbled about what Revelation means. After immersing myself in the new covenant

Introduction

literature of the New Testament for many years, I have come to realize that the Revelation is consistent with the rest of the New Testament in declaring that Christianity is not religion. Christianity is to be contrasted with religion. Christianity is in conflict with religion. This is particularly apparent in the Revelation, where Jesus Christ is portrayed as the victor over all religion.

It is usually conceded that this epistolary, apocalyptic book of prophecy was written late in the first century, probably around 95 AD. Of late there have been attempts to explain that the book was written prior to 70 AD, but this is usually an attempt by certain post-millennialists to justify their preterist interpretation, and their setting of the book in a politically persecutive context. The external evidence of early church writers seems to sufficiently document that the book was written late in the first century. Irenaeus (c. 180 A.D.), for example, indicated that John saw his vision "almost in our day, toward the end of Domitian's reign." Domitian was the Roman emperor from 81-96 A.D.. Despite when it was written; the message is the same, but the historical context of any document is important for it accurate interpretation. The date toward the end of the first century does seem to allow for the perverting and "religionizing" of the churches of Asia, to which the letter is addressed, but "religion" had long plagued the churches of this region. Paul combated "religion" in Ephesus and decided it was best to depart (Acts 19:1-20:1); he cautioned the Ephesian elders about "religionizers" from without and within the church (Acts 20:28-31). In writing to the Colossians, he warns about "man-made religion" (Col. 2:20:23). We will assume that this commentary was drafted toward the end of the first century.

We will also assume that it was written by the apostle John. The author identifies himself as "John" four different times in the book (Rev. 1:1,4,9; 22:8). The best known "John," who would not need to give any other clarification of his identity,

Introduction

would have been the apostle John. The earliest Christian writers accepted the apostle John to be the author.

It has been pointed out that the grammar and vocabulary of the Greek text in which this book is written is very rough and coarse, with what one author called "barbarous idioms." John would have flunked Greek Grammar 101. John's writing in the gospel and the epistles is quite polished, however. Is it because he was getting elderly? He was probably old when he wrote the gospel and epistles, also. Is it because he didn't have a secretary, an amanuensis, out on the island of Patmos, as he seems to have had when he wrote the epistles? Or is it because the vision was so overwhelming and going on all around him, and he was just writing as fast as he could, not worrying about his grammar?

Despite the fact that the Greek grammar is different from the gospel and epistles, and that there are concepts in Revelation not found elsewhere, there are many similarities which tie Revelation with the other Johannine writings: For example, the use of the word *logos* - John 1:1,14; I John 1:1; Rev. 19:13; Jesus as "lamb" - John 1:29,36, 28 times in Rev.; Christ as bridegroom - John 3:29, Rev. 19:7; 21:2; 22:7; Jesus "pierced" - John 19:34, Rev. 1:7; Jesus' overcoming - John 16:33, 6 times in I John, 17 times in Revelation.

Picture-language

The first word in the Greek text of this book is the Greek word *apokalupsis*. Thus it is that the book is often referred to as the Apocalypse. It is often explained that this writing is an example of Jewish apocalyptic literature that was prevalent in the last couple of centuries before Christ and in the first century A.D. Many of the academic attempts to narrowly define apocalyptic literature as distinct from parables, prophecy and allegory are "forced" categorizations. It is better to recognize that it was typical Middle-eastern thinking to teach by "story-telling" in picture-language.

It might be argued that the Revelation is the big, multi-faceted, new covenant parable! A good prelude to studying Revelation would be to study the parables of Jesus, which are the previous picture-language story-telling of Jesus Christ utilizing images and symbols. A study of the parables in the gospels will reveal that Jesus used them as an exposé and critique of religion, in order to explain the difference in the new covenant reality of His life functioning in grace within the kingdom.[1] Jesus uses picture-language in the Revelation in much the same way as He did in the parables.

Just as in the parables, we should not try to force a full-fledged allegorical understanding upon the images. We should not try to figure out the meaning of every detail. The "literalist" who demands a "direct face-value" for every detail in the book is approaching Revelation like a "mechanic" tightening every nut and bolt, rather than an "artist" who wants to "see" the Big Picture. We do not have to get every detail figured out, nailed down. That is the absolutism of understanding that "religion" tries to achieve. Jesus wanted us to think, to ponder, to be discerning; that is why He spoke in parables and picture-language! If Jesus had wanted theological precision or the precision of prophetic calculation, He would have used a different method of teaching, and a precise vocabulary. He would have used plain, straight-foward language!

John was apparently an individual with an artist-mentality. He was a picture-painter with words. He often conveys what he wants to say with images and analogies. In the gospel that he wrote he employs pictorial language: Jesus is the "light of the world" - in contrast to which religion is darkness and blindness

Introduction

(8,12). Jesus is the "good shepherd" - in contrast to the hirelings of religion (15). In his epistles (I,II,III John) he continues to use images of "sons of light" and "sons of darkness;" sons of God and sons of the devil. He saw clearly the either/or antithesis of God and Satan, and pictured such in many ways. When he writes what he saw in the Revelation, it is predominantly picture-language.

John saw the Big Picture and painted it in word-pictures. It is like a cosmic canvas on which he paints. He paints from God's perspective, and it is difficult for us to get far enough back to see the whole picture. We tend to analyze the strokes and the texture. When we come to the book of Revelation, it is so easy to miss the forest for the trees; to miss the message for the minutia of detail and the fanciful interpretation of those details. We do not have to figure out every detail. If any man could do that, he could stack all the factual data of interpretation and put it on the "knowledge" shelf. That is part of the "epistemological heresy" of religion, that reduces Christianity to a mere "belief-system." The life of Jesus Christ cannot be formulized and "put in the box" of doctrinal or eschatological understanding. Who would want such "canned" Christianity? Who would want such a rigid rectification of Revelation?

Therefore, we should attempt to see the message of Revelation in broad sections, rather than analyzing every detail; a macro-vision, rather than micro-vision.

The structure of this recorded vision seems to be something like a "movie in the round." Have you ever been to one of those movies where multiple camera angles recorded the action on every side, 360 degrees around you? When the action starts, you can hardly keep your equilibrium. We do not have eyes in the back of our head, so we cannot see everything at once. To see the whole movie, you would have to re-run it several

Introduction

times and see the different perspectives. The Revelation-vision seems to be like that. John "runs it by again" to view the new covenant reality of Jesus Christ from different perspectives. He turns the gem around to look at different facets of its brilliance.

The Revelation is not so much a time and space, chronological sequence of either history or the future, but is an increasingly intensified recapitulation of the new covenant reality of Jesus Christ. In repetitive parallels John views Jesus from different perspectives, different angles, another picture, another view. It does not seem to be consecutive or contiguous, but rather concyclic or synchronous – the Big Picture in the round!

I will never forget the occasion when I was talking to a young man who was zealous to understand the Bible and spiritual things. He was not well-versed in theological vocabulary, but was trying to use some of the terminology. In referring to the book of Revelation, he meant to refer to it as "apocalyptic," but inadvertently transferred the vowel sounds, and instead referred to it as "a-pickle-optic." I could not help but chuckle to myself when he said it, and the more I thought about it the funnier it became, because I realized that "a-pickle-optic" could be used to describe "apocalyptic." The pictorial imagery that John saw in the vision can indeed be "a pickle of an optic." The interpretation of the symbols has proved to be a difficult "pickle" for Biblical commentators for almost two millennia.

Though the book of Revelation can be "a-pickle-optic," it was meant to be apocalyptic. As previously noted, the book is often identified as the Apocalypse, which is a transliteration of the first word in the Greek text of this book, *apokalupsis*. *Apokalupsis* is derived from two other Greek words, *apo* = from, and *kalupto* = to cover or hide. The Greek word *apokalupsis* meant to uncover, unveil, disclose or reveal. Thus it is that we usually refer to this book in English as the Revelation.

Introduction

The purpose of this book was not to provide a difficult puzzle of images for future expositors to sort out, "a-pickle-optic," but rather to reveal, through the Middle Eastern method of storytelling, the triumph of Jesus Christ.

Varying Interpretations

It will be instructive to consider some of the varying interpretations of Revelation and the interpretive methods they employ. There are hundreds, if not thousands, of varying interpretations of the Revelation, but some of the broader schools of interpretation might be identified as follows: *(cf. chart in Addendum E)*

(1) *Preterist interpretation.* This label is derived from the Latin word *praeter*, meaning "past." This interpretation views the pictures of Revelation as referring to what was happening in the past, in the first century. They see the images as representing governmental persecution during the reign of either Nero or Domitian. Most understand Revelation chapters 21 and 22 as referring to the future, but there are some who "spiritualize" and put all 22 chapters of Revelation back in the past of the first century.

(2) *Historicist interpretation.* This interpretation stretches out the images of Revelation to refer to the history of the Western church. For example, the "fifth trumpet" has been interpreted as the Mohammedans in the 7th century; the "sixth trumpet" has been viewed as the invasion of the Turks. Chapter 10 allegedly refers to the "strong angel" who announces the Protestant Reformation when the "little book" was found, i.e. the Bible. The "seven thunders" are against the Pope. Revelation 11 and the measuring of the temple is interpreted as the Reformation determination of the true church, and the two witnesses have been interpreted as Luther and Calvin against Rome. The ultimate victory is the overthrow of the Roman papacy.

Introduction

(3) *Futurist interpretation*. Revelation 1-3 is recognized to be in the past, but chapters 4-22 are regarded as the record of future events in the seven-year tribulation, leading to the second coming and the millennium. Ryrie, for example, takes 1:19 as the structural "key" for Revelation: (1) "things seen" - 1:9-20 (2) "things which are" - 2:1-3:22 (3) "things which shall take place" (4:1-19:21 in the tribulation; 20:1-15 in the millennium, etc.)

(4) *Triumphalist interpretation*. Sometimes called the idealist or symbolic interpretation, this interpretation usually sees the images of Revelation as explaining the conflict of good and evil, God and Satan, throughout all of time.

The preterist commentator interprets the message of Revelation primarily as in the past. The historicist interprets the message of Revelation primarily as the process of Western history. The futurist interprets the message of Revelation as referring primarily to the future. The triumphalist interprets the message of Revelation primarily as the symbolic representation of the triumph of Jesus Christ in every age.

These varying interpretations are not necessarily issues to fight over. There is value in each of them. From the preterist we can learn that Christianity is contextually rooted in the historical past, and so is the Revelation. From the historicist we can learn that Christianity is continually timely, and so is the Revelation. From the Futurist we can learn that Christianity is confidently hopeful for the future, and so is the Revelation. From the Triumphalist we can learn that Christianity is constantly recognizing Christ's victory, and the book of Revelation certainly reveals such.

Regardless of which interpretive method one employs, one has to admit that there is symbolism in Revelation that pictures

Introduction

the triumph of Christ; the letter was first written to historical churches in Asia in the past, back in the first century; it is a revelation that has had some message for Christians throughout history; and Revelation does speak of the ultimate victory of Christ at the end of time in the future.

In this study we will employ a Christocentic or Christological interpretation that would probably be a sub-category of the Triumphalist or Symbolic interpretation.

The reason I employ the Christocentric-Triumphalist interpretation of Revelation is because it seems to me to provide the best consistency with the interpretation of the rest of the Scriptures. The Bible is consistent in its message from beginning to end, and the Bible is the best commentary on the Bible. The consistency of this interpretation is seen from its:

(1) *Scriptural consistency*. The whole of the revelation of Scripture is to reveal that Jesus Christ is the divine life that makes man man as God intends. Religion will not suffice. The "tree of the knowledge of good and evil" can be viewed as the "religion" tree; the "tree of life" as Christianity. The natural tendency of man is to revert to "religion" man-made religion." (Col. 2:21).

There is a consistency in this interpretation with the Old Testament prophets. They were critiquing "religion" and calling for repentance, using some of the same images.

There is a consistency in the use of picture-language and story-telling. God uses pictures. The entire Old Testament can be viewed as the "picture-book" illustrating what God was to do in Jesus Christ.

Introduction

(2) *New Testament consistency.* The entirety of the new covenant literature, the New Testament, explains the superiority of Christianity over all "religion." Christianity is not religion, it is the vital dynamic of the life of Jesus Christ lived by grace.

The New Testament concept of "prophecy" is primarily that of proclamation rather than prediction; forth-telling rather than foretelling. The prophecy of Revelation is likewise a proclamation of Jesus Christ, rather than the future.

(3) *Internal consistency.* The preterist and futurist interpretations seem to segment the interpretation of Revelation, some in the past, some in the future, with a big chasm in-between in the present. This tends to divide the Revelation into "revelations," as many people inaccurately refer to this book, and create a disjuncture. The Christocentric-Triumphalist interpretation that explains the conflict between Christianity and religion, allows the entire book to remain consistently connected. Chapters 2 and 3 provide the historical setting of "religion" creeping into the churches, so that chapters 4-22 can be pictorially placed alongside to reveal the conflict between Christianity and religion.

It is extremely important that we approach the Revelation, willing to engage in *exegesis*, rather than *eisegesis*. What is the difference? *Exegesis* comes from two Greek words meaning "to lead out." It means that we derive the meaning "out of the text." We do not want to "read into the text" our preconceived ideologies and interpretations. That is *eisegesis*. Too often people come to the book of Revelation with predetermined eschatological opinions, ideological "grids," and they use and abuse the book to try to document what they think they already know, twisting it to fit their presuppositions.

Introduction

Some try to make an issue between "literal" interpretation and "symbolic" interpretation. "Literal" does not mean just a direct, face-value interpretation of the words. "Literal" interpretation refers to an interpretation that is in accord with the literary style and literary intent of the author. If the literature is written in a literary style that uses images and symbols, then "symbolic" interpretation is "literal" interpretation, i.e. it is an interpretation that is consistent with the literary genre of the literature.

Symbolism

Since the Triumphalist interpretation is sometimes called the Symbolist interpretation, I want to amplify what I have already noted about the symbolism employed in the Revelation. Regardless of what interpretive method one uses, there must be the recognition that Revelation is full of pictorial images and symbols. One's interpretation will have to be "symbolic" to some degree. The Middle-eastern mind-set seems to have thought in visual images. They communicated in picture-language and story-telling. There are still many peoples today who still communicate in this way. We of the Western world, with our thinking patterns developed primarily from Aristotelian logic, tend to think in direct, logical categories, rather than in picture-language.

Perhaps the closest thing in our society that conveys ideas in pictures like we have here in the Revelation, might be the editorial cartoons in our newspapers. For example, the President might be pictured as an eagle, with his face attached, and his antagonist as a rodent. Sometimes it is difficult even now, for readers to see what the cartoonist means to convey by the pictures. Just think what it would be two thousand years from now, to look at the pictures and try to see what they mean. Thankfully, the picture-language of the Revelation is not

Introduction

trapped in a particular historical setting as the editorial cartoons usually are; the images of Revelation are "timeless" pictorializations, not trapped in history, not trapped in the future, but forever applicable.

The parables and the Revelation are cast in images that create "pictorial ponderables." They employ "round-about" thinking. They are problematic and puzzling. There are strange, bizarre, weird images that seem at times to be "past finding out." I think that Jesus spoke in such picture-language, both in the parables and in the Revelation, so that we would have to think and ponder and discern. If you have religiously dissected and determined every detail of the Revelation, then you have taken away all the value of the personal spiritual discernment of individual Christians in every age. That has been the "religious" tendency. These images should remain "dynamic," for they refer to the spiritual conflict that takes place throughout time. They are not static statements. They are spiritual truths that must always be spiritually discerned. As we ponder the pictures, the divine perspective begins to "sink in" so that it "colors" how we think. The images are like a dum-dum bullet that goes into our brain, and therein explodes religious misconceptions in order to bring about God's perception.

The real issue is not whether we "*get it*" that is, get the Revelation all figured out. The real issue is whether He "*gets us*," and we discern what He, as Lord, wants to be and do in our lives, by His grace. The issue is not whether we *know* the combatants in the pictured battles, but rather whether we *know* the One who is the Victor – whether we "*know*" Jesus Christ.

Introduction

Conflict

Perhaps the major symbol or metaphor that is a motif throughout the Revelation is the idea of a conflict. You cannot read the Revelation without recognizing that there is a conflict. There is a war going on! There are adversaries and antagonists battling against one another. But one realizes from the outset that there is no dualism here; there are not two equal forces with an indeterminate ending as to who will win over the other. There is no doubt who has the greater power, and who the Victor will be!

It is a battle between the Divine kingdom and the demonic kingdom, between good and evil, between God and Satan, between Christianity and religion. This is a theme that runs throughout the new covenant literature of the New Testament. (Matt. 16:23; John 8:44; 12:31; 13:27; 16:11; Acts 5:3; Rom. 8:39; II Cor. 4:4; 12:7; Eph. 6:16; Col. 1:13; II Thess. 2:7-10; I Tim. 1:20; Heb. 2:14; James 4:7; I Pet. 5:8; I John 2:22; 3:8,10; 4:3; II John 7, etc.)

An apt title for the Revelation might be "Kingdoms in Conflict." Chuck Colson, the Watergate conspirator who was gloriously regenerated, and thereby transfered from one kingdom to another (Col. 1:13), has a book by that title, wherein he contrasts the Kingdom of God and the kingdom of politics. Some of what he has to say applies to the "kingdoms of conflict" in the Revelation, though:

> "In the process of announcing the Kingdom and offering redemption from the Fall, Jesus Christ turned conventional views of power upside down. When His disciples argued over who was the greatest, Jesus rebuked them. 'The greatest among you should be like the youngest, and the one who rules like the one who serves.' Jesus was as good as His words - He washed His

Introduction

own follower's dusty feet, a chore reserved for the lowliest servant of first-century Palestine. ..Servant leadership is the heart of Christ's teaching.[2]

"Nothing distinguishes the kingdoms of man from the Kingdom of God more than their diametrically opposed views of the exercise of power. One seeks to control people, the other to serve people; one promotes self, the other prostrates self; one seeks prestige and position, the other lifts up the lowly and despised. ...It is crucial for Christians to understand this difference. For through this upside-down view of power, the Kingdom of God can play a special role in the affairs of the world.[3]

"His Kingdom has come, in His people today, and it is yet to come as well, in the great consummation of human history."[4]

The world is concerned with power and control. Religion thinks and acts in accord with the ways of the world, because it is aligned with the "god of this world" (II Cor. 4:4). Religion is the most subtle and insidious form of Satan's activity, in a kingdom that attempts to manipulate people and events using the social theory of "power-plays" and political persuasion.. Disguised as an "angel of light" (II Cor. 11:14), diabolical religion counterfeits the church and masquerades as Christianity. C.S. Lewis puts into the mouth of Screwtape, the devil, "it will be an ill day for us if what most humans mean by 'religion' ever vanishes from the Earth... Nowhere do we tempt so successfully as on the very steps of the altar."[5] Blaise Pascal wrote, "Men never do evil so completely and cheerfully as when they do it from religious conviction."[6]

Throughout the centuries, religion has succumbed to the lust for power. In the first century, the religion of Judaism expected God to act with militaristic power against the Romans. "Beat 'em, bash 'em, knock 'em dead!" Religion adopts the world's view of straight-line, strong-arm, clenched-fist power. The

Introduction

misnomer of "Christian religion" has abused power likewise: the Crusades, the Inquisitions, for example. We have observed so-called "Protestants and Catholics" fighting with guns and bombs in Northern Ireland, while "religionists" have bombed abortion clinics and murder doctors in the U.S. The Islamic "religionists" battle with tanks and jet fighters and the most sophisticated "fire-power" in the Middle-East. The "power-plays" of the religious power-brokers never seems to cease! But they will some day, as the Revelation reveals to us.

Religion often tries to help God out, apparently because He appears so impotent. "Why isn't God doing something? Why is God delaying? If God is so powerful, why doesn't He knock a few heads together? ...smash a few obstacles? ...level the enemies? We want to see some visible action that will impress people. So let's conceive big things and achieve big things, 'for God.' Let's 'go to bat' for God. Let's plan, get organized and make it happen. Onward Christian soldiers! Let's conquer for Christ." Remember Constantine, the Roman Emperor, who allegedly saw a "cross" in the sky and heard a voice say, "By this sign, conquer"? Historically, that was one of the greatest perversions of Christianity into religion. But religion in every age engages in "activism," encouraging people to "involvement" and "commitment" to "make things happen." "We are saved to serve," they tell us. They plan their programs and their pogroms. "We shall overcome!" is their battle cry. Whatever it takes to win; the end justifies the means; might is right; a "just war." So it is that "religion" plays its power-games!

On the other hand, in the Kingdom of God, although God is All-powerful He does not exert power just to force the issues. God's power is an ultimate authority that is rooted in His character. That is why Chuck Colson quotes Max Weber as saying that "power involves the use of coercive force to make others yield to one's wishes even against their own will. Authority is

Introduction

achieved by virtue of character that others are motivated to follow willingly."[7] God always acts in accord with His character, and exercises His "Lordship" accordingly.

Isaiah 55:8,9 explains that "God's thoughts are not our thoughts, and His ways are not our ways." That is certainly true when it pertains to how God exercises His Power. Jesus was tempted in the wilderness in the wilderness by the devil, but He refused to exercise power as the world does.

Zechariah 4:6 is a key verse to understanding the theme of the Revelation. In the context of a rebuke of religion, Zechariah exclaims, "Not by might nor by power, but by My Spirit, says the Lord of hosts." The passage in Zechariah seems to provide both the setting and the subject-theme of the Revelation. The "setting" illustrated by the seven lamps, which are identified in the Revelation as the seven churches; and the "subject-theme" being the recognition that God acts "not by might nor by power, but by His Spirit," in His own way and in accord with His character.

When the final view of the consummated victory of Christ is given in Rev. 19:11-21, there is no battle. God's army is dressed in wedding garments. The beast is subdued without a struggle revealing his "pretense of power." Satan's greatest temptation is to sucker Christians into playing his "power-games," fighting on his field and using his techniques.

History of the Conflict

The great conflict between God and Satan, between the divine kingdom and the demonic kingdom, between Good and Evil, as it relates the created order of mankind, commenced in the Garden of Eden as recorded in Genesis chapter 3. In the form of a serpent Satan approached the first couple offering

Introduction

them the "lie" of life apart from God's function within their spirit. By their decision of sin, they did indeed die that day as God had promised (Gen. 2:17). They and their offspring were spiritually "dead in trespasses and sins" (Eph. 2:1,5; Rom. 5:12-21).

Throughout the old covenant period recorded in the Old Testament, mankind is forced to recognize that he does not have what it takes to be man as God intended man to be apart from the presence of God in the man. Religion will not suffice, with its legalism, sacrifices, involvement, commitment and obedience to law.

The only solution to man's problem is that God would take the initiative in accord with His character of graciousness, to send His Son, Jesus Christ (John 3:16), as the God-man (John 1:14). As man, He then subordinated Himself perfectly to the indwelling presence of God the Father (John 14;10), and thereby could be the substitutionary sinless sacrifice for the sins of mankind, in order to take the death consequences of our sin.

From the cross He exclaimed, *"Tetelestai"* "It is finished! Mission accomplished! The victory is won over the Evil One!" (John 19:30; 17:4) By His resurrection, ascension and Pentecostal outpouring, His very resurrection-life dynamically actuated by the Spirit of Christ is available to all men who will receive such by faith in order to be restored to humanity as God intended, allowing the indwelling life of Jesus Christ to live out the character of God in our behavior to the glory of God.

The consummation of Christ's victory, whereby it will be evident to all, and the entirety of the created order will recognize Christ as Victor, is yet to come. There will come a time when "every knee shall bow and every tongue confess that Jesus Christ is Lord" (Phil. 3:10,11).

Introduction

Meanwhile we live in the interim between the accomplishment of Christ's victory and the consummation of Christ's victory. This complete intervening period (represented by the numerical imagery of 1000 years in Rev. 20) between Christ's first advent and His second advent presents Christians with somewhat of an enigma which is difficult to understand. The Revelation addresses this enigmatic situation, but the symbolic imagery is also difficult to understand, thus often increasing the enigma of the present anomaly of Christianity in the present world. Why does Christianity not seem to work? Why is there no "peace on earth"? Why is there not the perfect loving community of Christians in the Church?

The first disciples of Jesus faced the "enigma of the interim" between Good Friday and the resurrection on Sunday. How victorious did Jesus appear to be at that time? They had heard His words, "It is Finished," but they surely sounded then like words of defeat and despair. Only after the resurrection could they begin to appreciate the victory of the resurrection of Jesus Christ. Even then they found themselves in an "enigma of the interim" between the resurrection and the *parousia* when the victory would be consummated and made evident for all to see.

That enigmatic interval has extended for almost two millennia now, and generation after generation of Christians have lived in the enigmatic tension of a discipleship that is tested by the enigma of an unconsummated accomplishment, alongside of an apparent situation in the tangible and visible realm where Satan's world-system and his false-religion appear to be so successful and victorious in defeating God's purposes, even to the extent of persecuting and martyring Christians.

The defeated "god of this world" (II Cor. 4:4) exercises His diabolic power in every conceivable way to dissuade men from believing the victory of Christ in the crucifixion and resurrec-

Introduction

tion, and receiving the Victor and His life by faith. Furthermore, the devil attempts to dissuade Christians from reckoning on the victorious resurrection-life of Jesus Christ in order to allow that Christ-life to be lived out to the glory of God. Then, to add insult to injury, the Evil One attempts to persuade Christians to adopt his tactics of warfare within the counterfeit of "religion," which appears to be doing battle against the "bad" and the "evil" in the world. In so doing, Christians try to do what Christ has already done in conquering evil, and try to do by their own self-effort what Christ wants to do through them now by His grace.

Balanced Perspective of Victory

The Revelation shown to John and recorded by John is the revelation of the victorious life and work of Jesus Christ, past, present and future. (*See chart in Addendum C*)

(1) *The victory of His historical redemption*, which Christians must constantly remember, especially when His visible presence is not with us during the interim between the ascension and the *parousia*. The victory has been won on the cross! "It is finished!" (John 19:30). Mission accomplished! The work has been accomplished! (John 17:4). The price has been paid in full! (I Cor. 6:20; 7:23).

(2) *The victory of His continuing reign in the Kingdom*. Jesus Christ does reign as Lord and King in the lives of His people, Christians in every age throughout the interim. We can "reign in life" through Him (Rom. 5:17,21), despite the testings, tribulations and trials that confront us.

(3) *The victory of His consummating return*, when the victory will be made evident for all to see most vividly. At the parou-

sia, the second coming, the victory of Christ will be eternally etched upon the consciousness of all mankind who ever lived.

Jesus Christ is *Christus Victor*.[8] He has...He does...He will conquer Satan, evil and religion. Christians must recognize His past, present and future activity of victory.

This is the main difficulty in the interpretation of the Revelation; always trying to keep a balanced perspective of Christ's victory as it has been accomplished in the "already," as it is enacted in the "now," and as it will be consummated in the "not yet." This is like juggling three balls ("already," "now," and "not yet") all the way through the interpretive process of this book.

What happens when such a balanced perspective is not maintained? If any of the aspects of Christ's victory are over-emphasized to the diminishing of the others, then aberrations of theological and practical emphasis will result:

(1) If the "finished work" of Christ in His accomplished victory on the cross is over-emphasized, then one's Christian teaching often takes the form of "triumphalism" with some variety of "perfectionism." The practical outcome of such is often passivism and pacifism.

(2) If the present victorious reign of Christ is over-emphasized, then a mis-emphasis on participation in "spiritual warfare" often results, sometimes taking the form of "liberationism" or "exorcism." Christians have often developed a "siege-mentality" which led in the past to such aberrations as the Crusades and the Inquisitions, and lends itself to leadership efforts to recruit Christians to an activistic cause, to "fight for the right."

Introduction

(3) If the future consummation of Christ's victory is over-emphasized, then Christians may focus on expectations not yet fulfilled, and become so fixated on "futurism" that they fail to recognize the present sufficiency of Christ. Such can be an "escapist" approach focused on the deliverance of the future or on a heavenly "pie-in-the-sky-bye-and-bye."

Likewise, on the other hand, a failure to emphasize any of these three aspects of Christ's victory adequately will lead to aberrations in theological understanding and practical Christian living:

(1) Failure to emphasize the "finished work" of Christ's redemptive victory on the cross is to undermine the entire historical and theological foundation of the Christian gospel. It may lead to the instability of existential mythologizing which disregards the historical Jesus, or to subjective experientialism which determines reality by psychological impact.

(2) Failure to emphasize the present reign of the victorious risen Lord Jesus may lead to the ambivalence and apathy of *laissez-faire* with no direction or involvement. Christians may conclude that their past is forgiven and their future is assured, but the present is unbearable, so they lapse into fatalism.

(3) Failure to emphasize the future consummation of Christ's victory is to undermine God's direction and destiny for Christians and for the entire created order. Ever so subtly this leads to hopelessness and despair.

The importance of keeping a balanced perspective of Christ's victory in the "already," the "now," and the "not yet," cannot be over-emphasized. One can analyze the popular eschatological systems of interpretation and discover their primary emphases as well as their subsequent failures to keep a balanced empha-

Introduction

sis in all three areas. Dispensationalism, for example, employs the futurist method of interpretation and tends to over-emphasize the future consummation of Christ's victory, often to the neglect of understanding the "finished work" of Christ, and with either a denial or a decidedly pessimistic understanding of Christ's victorious reign today. Historical pre-millennialism, like Dispensational pre-millennialism, also has a futuristic focus on Christ's expected victory at the end of time, but usually retains a better foundation in the "finished work" of Christ on the cross, with a more optimistic realization of Christ's reign in the already realized kingdom. Post-millennialism places primary emphasis on the victory of Christ in the present, but there is often very little understanding of the already realized victory of Christ, as they engage in the activism that seeks to enact Christ's victorious kingdom on earth so as to "make it happen" and "usher in" the consummated kingdom at Christ's second coming. Amillennialism sometimes engages in the Post-millennial mis-emphasis, but often over-emphasizes the "finished work" of Christ's victory on the cross so as to engage in a triumphalistic perfectionism which becomes passivistic. It is imperative that Christians maintain a balanced perspective of Christ's victory in the past, present and future; the already, the now and the not yet. Such should be our objective as we study and seek to interpret what Christ was saying in the Revelation, and this is why we will employ the triumphalist method of interpretation that seeks to maintain a balanced perspective of the triumphant victory of Jesus Christ in the already, the now and the not yet.

The particular emphasis of the Revelation is to encourage the Christians at the end of the first century and in every intervening century thenceforth until the second coming of Jesus, to recognize the victory of Christ on Calvary (past), to reckon on that accomplished victory despite all appearances to the contrary, to recognize the ongoing conflict of God and Satan in the

Introduction

contrast of Christianity and "religion, and to repent of any and all tendencies and occasions of having succumbed to Satan's religious trap (present), as we all await the expected return of Jesus Christ (future).

The message of the Revelation is indeed "good news." The gospel is clearly presented throughout the imagery of this book, so as to encourage Christians to live by God's grace in accord with His character whatever the outward circumstances of the physical world might be. It is the message that the Christians at the end of the first century needed to hear. It is the message that the Christians at the end of the twentieth century need to hear. "He who has ears to hear, let him hear what the Spirit says to the churches."

ENDNOTES

1. cf. Capon, Robert F., *The Parables of the Kingdom* (1985). *The Parables of Grace* (1988). *The Parables of Judgment* (1989). Grand Rapids: Wm. B. Eerdmans.
2. Colson, Charles, *Kingdoms in Conflict*. Grand Rapids: Zondervan Pub. 1987. pg. 272.
3. *Ibid.*, pg. 274
4. *Ibid.*, pg. 371
5. Lewis, C.S., *The World's Last Night and other Essays*. "Screwtape Proposes a Toast." New York: Harcourt Brace Jovanovich. 1960. pg. 70.
6. Pascal, Blaise, as quoted by Colson, *op. cit.*, pg. 43.
7. Colson, Charles, *op. cit.*, pg. 275
8. Aulen, Gustaf, *Christus Victor*. London: Society for Promoting Christian Knowledge. 1934.

Prologue

Revelation 1:1-20

The first chapter of the Revelation serves as the prologue wherein the apostle John explains the location, occasion, commission and objective of his committing what he saw into writing. Some interpreters refer only to the first nine verses of the first chapter as the prologue, and identify verses nine through twenty as introductory to the first vision concerning the seven churches. This study will treat the entire first chapter as the prologue since John explains throughout the chapter the initial setting wherein he viewed the entire revelation.

A phrase-by-phrase commentary style will be employed for the study of this first chapter, in order to explain the setting and the use of imagery with more precision. Thereafter we will utilize a less formal literary style in order to grasp the larger perspective of the vision that John observed.

(1) ***The revelation*** - singular, not plural "revelations." (preterist and futurist interpretations tend to disjoin and make into "revelations.") Greek word, *apokalupsis*, from *apo* - "from" and *kalupto* - "to cover or hide." Uncovering, disclosure, unveiling, that which releases from concealment, revelation. Some get caught up in seeing a certain type of literature, a genre of Jewish literature, called "apocalyptic." Such is a limited

1:1

and "forced" understanding. Some think of violent destruction and doom and gloom, like in the movie "Apocalypse Now." It simply means "a revealing of...". A friend of mine inadvertently transferred the vowel sounds and referred to "apocalyptic" as "a-pickle-op-tic." The Revelation has been a "pickle of an optic" to interpret, but it is meant to reveal and disclose Jesus Christ.

...of Jesus Christ - The genitive can mean "*by Jesus Christ*," meaning that Jesus is the instrument by means of which the revelation was given; the conduit or channel or vehicle. Or it can mean "*about Jesus Christ*," meaning that Jesus is the subject or the content of the revelation. Jesus is more than just the impersonal object of the information in the Revelation. He is personally the One revealed. The genitive can mean "*which belongs to Jesus Christ*," meaning that Jesus is the possessor of the revelation, and can thus "show" or give it to John. Or it can mean "*which is comprised of Jesus Christ*," meaning that Jesus is the reality of the revelation. The being and essence of the life of Jesus Christ is the reality of the revelation. The latter interpretation maintains the ontological connection of Jesus Christ as the revelator and revelation, the subject and the object of the revelation, but there is a sense in which we can recognize that the phrase pertains to "all of the above."

Notice, it is not the "revelation of past history," nor the "revelation of the future," nor the "revelation of the second coming," but the "revelation of Jesus Christ." Jesus is the one who is revealed. (The polemic revelation of the defeat of "religion" is only secondary.) We must always recognize the Christocentric or Christological focus of this revelation. We want to see Jesus!

Jesus is the One who makes all things new! (21:5). "Old things pass away, behold all things become new" (II Cor. 5:17). The "new wine" cannot be put in the old wineskins of "religion" (Judaism) - Matt. 9:17; Mark 2:22). There is a "new creation" (II Cor. 5:17; Gal. 6:15; Rev. 21:1).

..which God gave Him to show to His bond-servants. Jesus is always the revelator of God, the one who reveals the Divine. He takes the things of God and reveals them to man. Matt. 11:27 - "no one knows the Father, except the Son, and anyone to whom the Son wills to reveal Him." John 1:18 - "He has explained Him". (cf. John 5:19-23; 12:49; 17:8). Jesus is the "mediator" between God and man. (I Tim. 2:5)

Notice the sequence: God the Father, Jesus Christ, angels, bond-servant John, bond-servants. Some think the final "bond-servants" are other Christian prophets who would in turn proclaim Jesus; "faithful men who will teach others also" (II Tim. 2:2). More likely, the final "bond-servants" refers to all Christians who have submitted to the Lordship of Jesus Christ, "bondslaves of God" (I Peter 2:16).

As the subject and the object of the revelation, Jesus "shows" it to His bond-servants, first of all to John. What a "show!" – the great "movie in the round." Glimpses of glory that are beyond human expression, "glory that is to be revealed to us" (Rom. 8:18); "glory far beyond all comparison" (II Cor. 4:17); even "Christ in you, the hope of glory" (Col. 1:27).

...the things which must shortly take place; - Does this mean an "imminence" that must be narrowly defined as the immediate near future of the first century? Preterists seem to think so, yet they decry such when the futurists speak of such "imminence" in reference to the second coming. Some have seen an allusion here to Daniel 2:28, "what will take place in the latter days." (This will depend on how you understand "latter days.")

The most probable meaning of "shortly take place," is not so much to a specific chronological time, but to emphasize the impending crisis and ordeal and tribulations that are foreseen. There should be a sense of urgency and watchfulness among Christians, for such things will "come to pass" without delay. There is a certainty of such, an inevitability; they are "bound to happen." Indeed they have happened to the Christians of the first century and to every time period thereafter. Luke 18:7,8 -

"Now shall not God bring about justice for His elect, who cry to Him day and night, and *will He delay* long over them? I tell you that He will bring about justice for them speedily. However, when the Son of Man comes, will He find faith on the earth?" Romans 16:20 - "the God of peace will soon crush Satan under your feet." There is obviously an "already" and a "not yet" understanding to the "shortly take place" expression. Such a combination of awareness should be retained throughout.

..and He sent and communicated by His angel - God sent and signified the revelation. The Greek word for "communicated" is *semaino* which is best translated "signified" (John 18:32), for it is the basis of the word *semeion*, which is the word John uses for "sign" through his gospel, indicating the "significance" of that which is seen (John 20:30,31). The "sign" or the "symbol" is not the focus, but that which is "signified." The revelation is full of symbolic significance.

Angels are sometimes to be understood as "messengers." Throughout the Revelation they are often the "scene-shifters" on the stage of this cosmic drama.

...to His bond-servant John. - The author identifies himself merely as "John." He does so four times in this book - 1:1,4,9; 22:8. There has been much speculation as to whether this is the apostle John who was one of the twelve disciples of Jesus, or whether it is another man named John. The traditional understanding has been that this is the apostle John. John was probably one of the youngest of the disciples, the "kid," and by this time was an old man.

(2) ***who bore witness to the the word of God*** - John is fond of the word "witness;" the Greek word is used twice in this verse, for both "witness" and "testimony". The Greek word is *martureo, -ia* and is the word from which we get the English word "martyr." To be a Christian and a witness for Christ was "to lay down one's life" for Jesus, to invest it entirely for Him. John may have had a premonition that he would indeed be doing so as a physical martyr, as historical tradition indicates he did.

John also likes to refer to the "word of God." The Greek word is *logos*, and it is used in John 1:1 - "in the beginning was the Word, and the Word was with God, and the Word was God." John 1:14 - "the Word became flesh." I John 1:1 - what we beheld concerning the Word of life." Rev. 19:13 - "His (Jesus') name is the Word of God." The "word of God" can be understood as the

1:2

message of the gospel, but what is the message of the gospel, but Jesus Christ, so it is best to recognize the ontological reality of Jesus Christ whenever the "word of God" is referred to, and to thereby retain a Christocentric emphasis. It is not a reference to the book called the "Bible."

...and to the testimony of Jesus Christ - Again, the genitive can interpreted as "by, about, of." The Greek has a double usage of the same word - "John *martureod* of the *marturia* of Jesus Christ. We could say "John testified of the testimony of Jesus Christ," but John is referring to more than a verbal proclamation about Jesus. John had "laid down his life" for the One who "had laid down His life" for mankind. It is more than just an epistemological "message" that John proclaimed. In the Christian gospel, the Man (Christ Jesus) is the message! The ontological connection must be maintained.

Early Christians were very aware that to receive Jesus Christ in them, was to receive the martyr-Man. They would be "hated on account of His name," His presence in them (Matt. 10:22; John 15:18). Their own lives would likely be "laid down" even in physical death. Rev. 12:11 - "the word of their testimony, and they did not love their life even to death." Also 12:17. Rev. 20:4 - "those who had been beheaded because of the testimony of Jesus and because of the word of God."

...to all that he saw. - He certainly "saw" a cosmic panorama! John is sometimes referred to as "the Seer," in light of "all that he saw." Numbers 12:6 - "if there is a prophet among you, I shall make Myself known in a vision...." I Samuel 9:9 - "a prophet was formerly called a seer."

(3) ***Blessed is he who reads and those who hear the words of the prophecy,*** - This is the first of seven beatitudes in the Revelation. (1:3; 14:13; 16:15; 19:9; 20:6; 22:7,14). This does not mean that one will be "blessed" because they know history better or know the future better because of the way they interpret the Revelation. Such would be a gnostic "blessing" of knowledge. Christians are only "blessed" because they know Jesus! We are "blessed with every spiritual blessing in heavenly places in Christ Jesus" (Eph. 1:3). Those who hear and heed the Revelation will be "blessed" with Christ, having chosen Christ over "religion."

This Revelation was sent as a letter to the churches. "He who reads" is probably a reference to the "reader" who would read the letter aloud in the assembly of the church. Many of the early Christians were illiterate. It was the custom to "read aloud" in the early Christian gatherings, as it was in the Jewish synagogues. Nehemiah "read from" the Law (Neh. 8:2,3), and the Thessalonians were told to "have the letter read to all the brethren" (I Thess. 5:27). Modern Christians misunderstand what John wrote if they think that they are "blessed" because they read their Bibles, or more particularly the last book.

The Revelation is referred to as a "prophecy." Prophecy means "to speak before," but this can mean both "...before the time," or "before people"; it can be both predictive and proclamatory; it can mean both to "foretell" or "forth-tell." In the new covenant literature of the New Testament, the word "prophecy" is used primarily of proclamation rather than prediction. It conveys the sense of "thus saith the Lord," implying that it is a divine revelation, not just human information. Consistent with this primary purpose of prophecy in the New Testament, the prophecy of the Revelation is more of a proclamation of Jesus Christ than a prediction of the future; a fact not understood by many interpreters.

...and heed the things which are written in it, - This is not just a Revelation to ponder on, or argue about the interpretation of. It must be acted upon. We are "blessed" with the life of Jesus Christ, as the activity of His life is lived out in our behavior. Luke 11:28 - "Blessed are those who hear the word of God, and observe it." The gospel, the only "good news" is the ontological life of Jesus Christ, the Word of God.

How can Christians heed what is written in the Revelation? They must recognize and be discerning about the spiritual conflict of God and Satan, avoid the diabolical techniques of religion, and live by the life of Jesus Christ expressing His character. It would be difficult to "heed" warnings about Roman emperors (preterist interpretation), or references to the invasion of the Turks (historicist interpretation), or even that which will likely not take place in your lifetime (futurist interpretation).

...for the time is near. - The Greek word for "time" is *kairos*. This does not necessarily mean that the precise chronological time for the fulfillment of all that is symbolized in this Revelation was "imminently" soon or near. (Preterists and futurists both like to emphasize such, but with different time-lines in mind). More likely it means that there was an "impending" time of crisis and decision, wherein the life of Jesus Christ would need to be lived out in their lives. Such is true for all Christians in every age. The application of the out-lived Life of Jesus Christ in the Christian is always "at hand" and "near." Luke 1:15 - "the kingdom of God is at hand." Rom. 13:11 - "knowing the time, that it is already the hour for you to awaken from sleep; for now salvation is nearer to us than when we believed." Rev. 22:10 - "the time is near." The "time" for God to work out the "saving life" of Christ in our lives is always "near." We must not try to pin-point this chronologically on an historical time-line.

(4) *John, to the seven churches that are in Asia:* - The author again identifies himself as John as in 1:1. He is writing an epistle, a letter, to the seven churches in Asia, listed more specifically in verse 11, and addressed individually in chapters 2 and 3. The location of these seven cities was in the Roman province of "Asia," sometimes referred to as "Asia Minor," on the western coast of what is now Turkey. Why are these seven churches selected? There were more than seven churches in the area, for there was a church in Troas (Acts 20:5), Colossae (Col. 1:2), Hierapolis (Col. 4:13) and probably elsewhere. Since the number "seven" is often used in the Revelation to refer to "completeness," it is likely that these seven churches are representative as a "cross-section" of all churches. Based on his personal knowledge of the condition of these churches in the region where he, the apostle John, had ministered, he could use them by the inspiration of the Spirit to portray how insidiously "religion" threatens the Church of Jesus Christ in different ways, and how we must "battle" against such by allowing the life of Jesus Christ to prevail. It has been suggested that the sequence of the seven churches might have been the order in which this letter was dispatched, in a big arc, which may have been the "postal circuit" of the day.

1:4

Grace to you and peace, - This is a typical salutation from Christian letters of that day, as can be seen throughout the letters of Paul. "Grace" is more than a wish for God's graciousness and mercy. In Christian usage it is God's activity by the risen Lord Jesus, in accord with His character. It is the operative dynamic of Christianity, in contrast to the human performance of "religion," with its "works" of self-effort. "Peace" is likewise more than just a "shalom" greeting. Christ is our peace, as He provides the functionality of God at work in man and among men. It is the "peace of God that surpasses all comprehension" (Phil. 4:7), in contrast to the frustration of "religion."

from Him who is and who was and who is to come;- This is a common designation throughout the Revelation (1:8; 4:8; 11:17; 16:5), referring to the eternality of God, who is the eternally present "I AM" (Exodus 3:14). Likewise, Jesus Christ as God is the same "Yesterday, today and forever" (Heb. 13:8). God is changeless and immutable.

...and from the seven Spirits who are before His throne; - Who are these "seven Spirits" that John keeps referring to? (3:1; 4:5; 5:6). Jewish tradition spoke of seven angel-spirits; seven archangels. On the other hand, they referred to the seven-fold work of the Holy Spirit based on Isaiah 11:2-4 - "the Spirit of the Lord will rest on Him, the spirit of wisdom and understanding, The spirit of counsel and strength, The spirit of knowledge and the fear of the Lord...He will judge with righteousness." This is referring to the Spirit of the Lord in the work of the Messiah, Jesus Christ. So is is likely that the numerical symbolism of the number seven is again referring to the fullness and completeness of the work of the Holy Spirit. The capitalization of the word "Spirits" in the NASB would seem to evidence that the translators understood this to be deity. A trinitarian derivation from "Father, Spirit and Son" is retained by this interpretation.

(5) *and from Jesus Christ,* - This completes the trinitarian derivation in the salutation of the letter. Obviously, John recognizes the presence of the risen Lord Jesus, who is both revelator and revelation.

the faithful witness, - Jesus is identified as the One who "laid down His life" in faithfulness. See also 3:14. He is the One who "has been through it." He is credible, reliable, the standard of integrity, the guarantee. Yes, He is God and thus a "faithful witness" (Ps. 89:37); the One whose "faithful mercies" (Isa. 55:3,4) can be "banked upon." But as a man He was "faithful" in subordination to the Father, "even unto death" (Phil. 2:8), in giving His own life. You can count on Jesus despite your present problems; He will not deceive you or lie to you. He is the "faithful witness" as He Himself declared as He faced crucifixion (John 18:37 - "I have come into this world to bear witness to the truth."). In His crucifixion Jesus bore witness to the faithfulness of God's ways as contrasted with the ways of "religion," inspired by the devil: strength out of weakness; glory out of shame; joy out of suffering; life out of death.

..the first-born of the dead, - Jesus had accepted death, the genuine and ultimate test of faith and obedience. Christians can appreciate that when they too are persecuted and face death. But the victory was in the resurrection when Jesus rose from the dead, the "first-born from the dead." Paul also referred to Jesus as "the

1:5

first-born from the dead" (Col. 1:18). Jesus was the first man to have experienced the spiritual death of separation from God (Matt. 27:46 - "My God, My God, why has Thou forsaken Me?"), and to be restored to spiritual life with God's presence in the man. His resurrection was a "birth" - Acts 13:33 - "God fulfilled this promise...when He raised up Jesus...'Today I have begotten Thee.'" Thus Jesus became the "first fruits of those who are asleep" (I Cor. 15:20), "so that in Christ all shall be made alive" (I Cor. 15:22); Jesus is the "first-born among many brethren" (Rom. 8:29), in the "church of the first-born" (Heb. 12:23). Christians are spiritually born out of spiritual death in identification with Jesus Christ "the first-born from the dead," and born with the very resurrection-life of the "first-born of the dead." That gives Christians hope when they face physical death, that there is indeed life out of death.

...and the ruler of the kings of the earth. - The authority of Jesus is asserted in this designation. This is one of the important motifs of the Revelation; the superiority of Christ's authority and rule over the "power" of the earthly rulers. The victory of the divine kingdom over the demonic kingdom, of Christ over religion, is expressed from the very beginning. There is no dualism of equal powers with a question of who will prevail. This is the revelation of Jesus Christ as the Victor.

The sequence of identification of Christ as "first-born" and "ruler" may be an allusion to Psalm 89:27 - "I shall make him My first-born, the highest of the kings of the earth." The Messianic Psalm 2:7-9 refers to Jesus as "begotten" and having the "nations as thine inheritance." Psalm 110:2 refers to "ruling in the midst of enemies."

The "kings of the earth" is a phrase that is often used in the Revelation. (1:6; 6:15; 17:2; 18:3,9; 19:19; 21:24; cf. 16:14; 18:3,11,23). It might refer to any type of earthly and worldly "power-brokers," those who rule nations, organizations, religions, etc. The Pope, for example, might be seen as a royal ruler of the earth, along with other ecclesiastical hierarchical heads. "Religion" is the most subtle and insidious form of satan's lust for power and control of people.

Jesus Christ exercises the ultimate divine authority and power. He has won the victory over all satanic and earthly kingdoms. He is the "King of Kings" (17:14; 19:16; cf. Dan. 2:47). The earthly powers, of course, are not aware of Christ's victory, but the ultimate consummation of such will become evident, as the Revelation shows.

To Him who loves us, - God in Christ continually loves us all the time. That is His character (I John 4:8,16). In fact, God's power is in His love – far more powerful than all the manipulations of earthly powers. But when Christians are in tribulations and being persecuted, it is sometimes difficult to remember God's love. The visible threats loom so large, and it is then that we must recall God's invisible love.

and released us from our sins by His blood. - The recognition of God's love is best remembered when we look back to the cross and resurrection. He "loved us and gave Himself for us" (Gal. 2:20). The "blood of Christ" should not be taken as a magical fetish, but as referring to the substitutionary death of Christ on our behalf, "having made peace through the blood of His cross" (Col. 1:20). From the cross Jesus exclaimed, "It

1:6

is finished! - Mission Accomplished!" (John 19:30). The redeeming work of Christ was completed, and the resultant restoration of all things in Christ is set in motion toward its inevitable consummation and fulfillment. Christians who have accepted the redeeming work of Christ are "released," freed, liberated, emancipated, so as to be free to be man as God intended man to be, divinely indwelt humanity expressing the character of God. (The KJV use of "washed" instead of "released" is an apparent misunderstanding of *lusanti* for *lousanti*.)

1:6 (6) ***and He has made us to be a kingdom,*** - That Christ is the victor is clear from the beginning of the Revelation. Because of Christ's death, the victory has been won! There are still "kingdoms in conflict," but the outcome is not in doubt.

Those who have identified with Christ "have been transferred into the kingdom of the Son" (Col. 1:13). Granted, His kingdom is "not of this world" (John 18:36), but He reigns "within us" (Luke 17:21), and we "reign in life" through Him (Rom. 5:17), and we "shall reign with Him" (II Tim. 2:12) in the consummated kingdom. Even now as "citizens of heaven" (Phil. 3:20; Eph. 2:19; Heb. 12:23), we share Christ's authority by His indwelling in us (Rev. 2:26; 3:21: 5:10; 20:6).

priests to His God and Father; - Peter refers to this combined privilege of "kings" and "priests" by explaining that Christians are a "royal priesthood" (I Peter 2:9). Later in the Revelation we are referred to as "a kingdom and priests to our God" (5:10). God's intent for His people from the beginning was that they might be "a kingdom of priests and a holy nation" (Exodus 19:6), and the prophecy of Isaiah was that those in Christ would be "called the priests of the Lord" (Isa. 61:6). The intent of God was not to develop a "religious" hierarchical order of priests with special privileges, but that His People might be "the priesthood of all believers," with access to the presence of God, sacrificing themselves (Rom. 12:1) in praise (Heb. 13:15), and ministering to others. The "priesthood" is a "holy priesthood" (I Peter 2:15), and demands that Christians be available to God's Holy character, thus "serving Him day and night in His Temple" (Rev. 7:15).

to Him be the glory and the dominion forever and ever. Amen. - God, by His glorious character and glorious work in Christ, is to be glorified, but can only be glorified by the active expression of His character in His creatures. He does not give His glory to another (Isa. 42:8; 48:11). His "dominion" and ruling authority will indeed be expressed and exposed "unto the ages," forever and eternally. Such will be revealed pictorially throughout the Revelation. So be it! - Amen.

(7) ***Behold, He is coming with the clouds,*** - This may be an allusion to Daniel chapter 7 where the imagery of "beasts" is used and the "ancient of days" slays the beasts, and Daniel says, "Behold, with the clouds of heaven One like a Son of Man was coming, ..and He was given dominion, glory and a kingdom" (Daniel 7:9-14). (Note connection of "kingdom, glory and dominion" from previous verse.) Jesus quotes these verses from Daniel in identifying Himself as the Messiah (Mark 14:62), so Daniel seems to be referring to the "coming" of Christ in the incarnation. The Greek word, *erchomai*, used here for "coming" is used elsewhere in the New Testament for the "coming" of the incarnation, cf. "Jesus has come in the flesh" (I John 4:2,3).; and

1:7

also of Jesus' coming at Pentecost, cf. "If I go, I will come again" (John 14:3,23; 15:26; 16:7,8). The use of the present tense rather than the future tense here in 1:7 has led some to interpret this as the present experiential "coming" of the presence of God by His Spirit in Christian lives. Though such may be a viable interpretation, the predominant understanding is to interpret this "coming" as the future coming of Christ, the *parousia*, the second coming, which the Revelation most certainly refers to in the later chapters. At His ascension Jesus was taken into a cloud (Acts 1:9), and the angels indicated that He would "come in just the same way" (Acts 1:11), which is probably what Jesus was referring to when He seems to quote Daniel 7 in Matthew 24:30.

Christians of every age must recognize that their "hope" is in Jesus Christ (I Tim. 1:1), and expectantly look forward to the consummation of the victory that Christ has already achieved. Once again we see the "already" and the "not yet" of Christ's coming. Though the victory is achieved and complete, the consummated expression of such is yet to become evident in the ideal of God's perfect and heavenly order.

"Clouds" are often used to refer to the Divine presence. (Exod. 13:21; 16:10; Matt. 17:5).

and every eye will see Him, - They will recognize and perceive who Jesus is, the Almighty God, and they will have to "bow down and confess" (Phil 2:10,11) who He is. (cf. Rom. 14:11). The triumph of Jesus Christ will be evident to all.

even those who pierced Him; - John is the only New Testament writer who employs this Greek word, doing so in John 19:37 and in this verse. In both locations it appears to be an allusion to Zechariah 12:10 - "I will pour out on the house of David...the Spirit of grace..so that they will look on Me whom they have pierced; and they will mourn for Him." Those instrumental in the death of Christ will recognize that they "murdered the Righteous One" (Acts 7:52) and crucified Him who is Lord and Christ (Acts 2:23,36). In one sense, of course, we are all guilty of so doing.

and all the tribes of the earth will mourn over Him. - All men will recognize that it was their sin that sent Jesus to the cross. This does not necessarily mean that all will "repent," but that those who did not receive Him in faith will have "remorse" over having rejected the only One who could be their Savior.

Even so. Amen. - It is expected. It is inevitable and must come to pass. There is a sense of certainty.

(8) "***I am the Alpha and the Omega,***" ***says the Lord God,*** - First we recognize the identification with the Divine "I AM" of Jehovah (Exodus 3:14). The "I AM" always conveys the ontological connection of God with His creation, to avoid the deistic detachment so often present in "religious" understandings of god.

Using the first and the last letters of the Greek alphabet, God identifies Himself as everything from A to Z, the first and the last and everything in between, the starter and the finisher and the sustainer of everything in between. God is the commencement and the objective, the derivation and the destiny, the Creator and the Judge. A comprehensive signature, indeed!

1:9

Isaiah often referred to God as "the first and the last" (Isa. 41:4; 44:6; 48:12), which is repeated in the Revelation (1:17; 2:8). The same thought is present in the designation "the Alpha and the Omega" (1:8; 21:6; 22:13).

who is and who was and who is to come, - The eternality of God is expressed by this phrase, as in vs. 4. and 4:8; 11:17; 16:5). The immutability of the unchangeable God is also implied, as with He who is the same "Yesterday, today and forever" (Heb. 13:8).

the Almighty. - Christians who are awaiting the consummation of Christ's victory need continually to recognize the "pantocracy" of the all-powerful God. Despite the appearances of "power" amongst the earthly and religious authorities, God is sovereign, supreme, omnipotent. Our God is victorious! Our God reigns!

1:9 (9) *I, John, your brother* - The author again identifies himself simply as John (1:1,4,9; 22:8). He was most likely the apostle John who was a disciple of Jesus. He identifies with the readers as "your brother." "I am one of you; we are in this together." Christian "brother" indicates that they are in the same "family;" they are related to Christ and to one another as Christians. Cf. Heb. 2:11 for sense of being "brethren" with Christ. John was probably well-acquainted with many of them, having ministered in that region for many years.

and fellow-partaker in the tribulation and kingdom and perseverance - Continuing his identification of kinship with the readers, John indicates that he is a co-sharer in their spiritual privileges and what they are going through on earth. He is not "off on the sidelines" telling them what to do, coaching them from a position of immunity.

The Christians to whom he was writing were undergoing "tribulation" of some kind. (cf. 2:3,9-10,13; 3:10). Tribulation may include pressure, distress, troubles, afflictions, suffering, persecution, ostracism, slander, humiliation, threat of death, etc. Jesus told His disciples that "in the world you have tribulation, but take courage, I have overcome the world" (John 16:33). Paul, likewise explained that "all who desire to live godly in Christ Jesus will be persecuted" (II Tim. 3:12). Such "tribulation" and persecution is to be expected for those who are in the "kingdom" of God. Paul explained that "through many tribulations we must enter the kingdom of God" (Acts 14:22). This is obviously not a reference to the "great tribulation" expected as a special "dispensation" by the Dispensationalists.

John was a "*partner*" in the "kingdom" with the Christians to whom he was writing. All Christians have been "transferred to the kingdom of His beloved Son" (Col. 1:13). Previously, in vs 6, John noted that "He has made us to be a kingdom." It is the "kingdom which is not of this world...realm" (John 18:36). It is the spiritual kingdom wherein we "reign in life through Christ Jesus" (Rom. 5:17,21), while still looking forward to the consummation of "the kingdom promised" (James 2:5). In that interim where the "kingdom" is already, but not yet, John wants to encourage Christians to continue to recognize the authority of Jesus Christ as Lord and King of their lives, and to reckon upon the dynamic of His life and strength.

In other words, John encourages Christians to "persevere," and identifies with them in such "*perseverance*." (cf. 2:3,10,19; 3:10). The sufficiency of Christ's life will be tested: "Does it work? Is it the life that wins?" The victory of Christ is not always apparent or visible. John encourages Christians to persevere, to "abide under" (*hupomone*) the situations which confront them. John likes to use the word "abide" - cf. John 15:1-6; I John 2:24). While "citizens of the heavenly kingdom" (Phil 3:20), we encounter earthly tribulations, and our endurance and steadfastness and perseverance evidences that we know Who the Victor really is. Paul explained that "tribulation brings about perseverance..character..hope" (Rom. 5:3-5). We are to "persevere in tribulation" (Rom. 12:12). To the Corinthians, Paul writes of "enduring the sufferings...being burdened excessively...so that we despaired even of life...that we should not trust in ourselves, but in God who raises the dead...on whom we have set our hope" (II Cor. 1:6-10). Such is the thrust of John's encouragement in the Revelation. Jesus promised that "by your perseverance you will win your souls" (Luke 21:19), and Paul referred to "perseverance unto glory and honor and immortality" (Rom. 2:7).

The trilogy of "tribulation, kingdom and perseverance" is also found in II Thess. 1:3-5, where Paul writes of "your perseverance...in the midst of persecutions and afflictions...so that you may be considered worthy of the kingdom of God, for which you are suffering."

Living in the spiritual kingdom of Christ's authority as Lord, and yet at the same time in the midst of earthly tribulations, we are to endure and persevere, refusing to give in under pressures, eager to show the credibility of how Christ's life works even when the going gets tough, always alert to deception, discerning of the temptation to fear and anxiety and doubt, the temptation to revert to "religion" and its tactics, and willing to forgive the perpetrators of our trials. The strength and dynamic for such is only derived from Jesus Christ within us, so that we experience the "upside-down" reality of strength out of weakness, joy out of suffering, life out of death.

which are in Jesus, - Those who are "in Jesus" will experience the tribulations, the kingdom and the perseverance. Jesus said, "If they persecuted Me, they will also persecute you" (John 15:20), and "you will be hated by all on account of My name" (Luke 21:17). Note, though, that the perseverance is also "in Jesus," who endured to the end, "even unto death" (Phil. 2:8).

was on the island called Patmos, - When John received this Revelation he was on a small island in the Mediterranean Sea southwest of Ephesus, a part of the Dodecanese islands. (*cf. map Addendum A*) It was a small outcropping of rock, approximately 8 miles long and 4 miles wide. The traditional explanation is that John was exiled or banished to the island, imprisoned in a Roman penal colony which labored in the rock quarries. The Roman historian, Tacitus, (also Juvenal) indicates that there was such a penal colony on Patmos.

Some have questioned whether John wrote the letter later after he was released from Patmos, based on the past tense usage of "was on the island," but vs. 11 seems to stress the immediacy of the occasion for writing.

because of the word of God and the testimony of Jesus. - John thus explains why he was on Patmos. It is doubtful that he merely traveled out there for personal worship and meditation. He was there because of his identification with Jesus Christ, "the Word of God" (John 1:1,14); his identification with the gospel, which is the person of Jesus Christ. Here, as throughout the new covenant literature, "word of God" does not refer to the Bible. John expands his explanation for his presence on Patmos by indicating that it was because of "the testimony of Jesus." Most likely this means that his witness for Jesus, his "laying down his life" for Jesus, in some way caused him to be sent to Patmos. Later John will refer to Christians who were martyred "because of the word of God and the testimony of Jesus" (6:9; 20:4), so it is likely that John was on Patmos as a punitive consequence of his Christian witness.

(10) *I was in the Spirit on the Lord's Day,* - What does it mean to be "in the Spirit"? Does it mean he was feeling spiritual? Does it mean he fell into a trance of ecstasy? Does it mean that he was open, available and receptive to the Spirit? Does it mean that he was under the influence and control of the Holy Spirit? Probably the latter. Ezekiel writes of being "lifted up" by the Spirit when he heard from God (Ezek. 3:12,14). Some commentators take the four occasions where John refers to being "in the Spirit" (1:10; 4:2; 17:3; 21:10), and use them for the structural outline of the Revelation. Such is to be questioned.

"The Lord's Day" probably does not refer to the prophetic "Day of the Lord," but rather to the Christian designation of the first day of the week as "the Lord's day," since Jesus rose from the dead on that day (Luke 24:1; John 20:19). The Christians began to meet on the first day of the week (Acts 20:7; I Cor. 16:2).

and I heard behind me a loud voice like the sound of a trumpet, - John may have thought of Moses and the sound of the trumpet when God was calling him to Mt. Sinai (Exod. 19:16,19). The imagery may refer to a voice that was loud, piercing, and unmistakable, announcing the presence of someone important. The sound of the trumpet is also mentioned concerning yet future announcement and calling of the Lord (Matt. 24:31; I Cor. 15:52; I Thess. 4:16).

(11) ***saying, "Write in a book what you see,*** - John was commissioned to write what was revealed to him on a papyrus scroll. There were no "bound books" like we have today. It is not improper to refer to "the Book of the Revelation." **1:11**

and send it to the seven churches: - As in 1:4 these "seven churches" are likely a complete representative "cross-section" of all the churches in Asia Minor and everywhere.

to Ephesus and to Smyrna and to Pergamum and to Thyatira and to Sardis and to Philadelpha and to Laodocea. - These particular seven churches in seven cities of Asia Minor were the original recipients of the Revelation. It has been speculated that the order of the seven may indicate the order of visitation by the courier of the letter. Thus the Revelation would have been an "encyclical" letter. (*Cf. map, Addendum A*)

(12) ***And I turned to see the voice that was speaking with me.*** - Obviously one cannot "see a voice," but John turned to see the one who was speaking. "No one has seen God at any time", but John saw the visionary revelation that Jesus Christ gave to him. **1:12**

1:13

And having turned I saw seven golden lampstands;- In the language of symbolism, the number "seven" often refers to completeness, and "golden" to a thing of value. Because of his Jewish heritage John may have thought of the Jewish menorah, a "lampstand of pure gold..with seven lamps" (Exod. 25:31-38). There is a definite similarity to the vision that Zechariah saw of "a lampstand of gold..with seven lamps" (Zech. 4:2). The Zechariah prophecy may serve as the model for the "setting" of the Revelation, for Zechariah continues to say, "Not by might nor by power, but by My Spirit, says the Lord of hosts" (Zech. 4:6), which is in accord with the theme of the Revelation also.

The image seems to have changed from a single lampstand with seven branches to seven lampstands or candelabra, with no reference to the number of lights. It is possible that this was designed to show that the Church of Jesus Christ is the "new Israel" (Rom. 9:6: Gal. 6:16), and that each congregation is an expression of the Church in its fullness.

1:13 (13) *and in the middle of the lampstands* - It is obvious that the following reference is to Jesus Christ. Jesus Christ is central to His Church, represented by the lampstands. Though Jesus has ascended, He is still in the midst of the churches. He is not absent or withdrawn, distant or detached, operating the church by "remote-control" or by "virtual reality." His life is ontologically vital to the churches and the Christians which comprise such. The Christians in Asia Minor in the first century and Christians everywhere in every age thereafter, need to realize that Jesus Christ is present in the midst of His church, and especially so as they encounter difficulties and tribulations. He does not "leave or forsake" us (Heb. 13:5). He dwells within His temple, individually (I Cor. 6:19) and collectively (I Cor. 3:16; II Cor. 6:16).

one like a Son of man, - The images used to describe Jesus Christ here in vss. 13-16 are similar to those used to describe God in the Old Testament. They obviously attribute deity to Jesus. They are images of indescribable splendor, wonder and authority. They are not photographic descriptions. Since they are metaphors and picture-language, we should not try to "pin them down" in exact comprehension of interpretation. There is no way to make precise determination of the significance of the symbols. Attempts to do so take away the Spirit's right to bring individual personal spiritual discernment. What is obvious is that John saw God in Christ. Jesus is the fulfillment of the "law and the prophets," the "Amen" of God's promises (II Cor. 1:20).

The imagery employed has a definite allusion to that employed by Daniel in his vision. Daniel 10:5,6 - "I lifted my eyes and looked, and behold, there was a certain man dressed in linen, whose waist was girded with a belt of pure gold...His body was like beryl, his face had the appearance of lightning, his eyes were like flaming torches, his arms and feet like the gleam of polished bronze, and the sound of his words like the sound of a tumult."

"Son of man" (14:14 also), identifies Jesus as a human figure, for He was the incarnate Son of God. Luke uses "Son of Man" as a designation for the humanity of Jesus, but the designation here used is different. Old Testaments prophets had referred to one like a "Son of man" (Dan. 7:13; cf. 8:15; 10:16; Ezek. 1:26; 8:2).

1:14

Matthew refers to Jesus as the "Son of Man coming in His kingdom" (16:27,28).

clothed in a robe reaching to the feet, - John might have thought of Exodus 28:4, 39, and the "robe,..and sash" of the priest. Kings and priests wore robes, so this image may indicate a person of importance, distinction and authority.

and girded across His breast with a golden girdle. - This may have been more like a scarf or sash around the shoulder and across the breast. The priest of the Old Testament wore such, Exod 28:39; 29:9. Later in Rev. 15:6, the seven angels have on such a garment.

1:14 (14) ***And His head and His hair were white like white wool, like snow;*** - John may have remembered Isaiah 1:18 that refers to "white as snow...like wool" when he employed this double description. Daniel 7:9 also refers to "hair on His head like pure wool." The whiteness of head and hair may refer to wisdom, purity, integrity and dignity.

and His eyes were like a flame of fire; - This same description is repeated in 2:18 and 19:12. It probably describes the searching and penetrating vision and insight of Jesus Christ, from whom there is no concealment. In his gospel, John explained that Jesus "knew what was in man" (2:25). The writer of the Hebrews refers to Jesus as "able to judge the thoughts and intentions of the heart" (4:12), as "all things are open and laid bare to the eyes of Him with whom we have to do (4:13).

(15) ***and His feet were like burnished bronze, when it has been caused to glow in a furnace.*** - This is repeated in 2:18. cf. Ezek. 1:7 and Dan. 10:6. The symbolism may refer to strength, stability, perfection, etc.

and His voice was like the sound of many waters. - One would expect God to speak with awe-inspiring authority. "More than the sounds of many waters..the Lord on high is mighty" (Ps. 93:4). Ezekiel, likewise, describes a voice "like the sound of many waters" (Ezek. 43:2). John uses similar imagery in 14:2 and 19:6.

(16) ***And in His right hand He held seven stars;*** - cf. 1:17; 2:1; 10:5; 13:16; 20:1,4. The "right hand" often pictures favor, power or protection, so this image may refer to Christ's authority and sovereignty.

and out of His mouth came a sharp two-edged sword; - cf. 2:16; 19:15,21. Isaiah pictures the one who will bring "salvation to the ends of the earth" as having a "mouth like a sharp sword" (Isa. 49:2). A two-edged sword is highly effective. Heb. 4:12 refers to the effectiveness of Christ, "sharper than any two-edged sword." Some have interpreted the "two-edged sword" as representing judgement.

and His face was like the sun shining in its strength. - God is often pictured by the "shining sun" to indicate His transcendent glory and radiance. The Psalmist said, "The Lord God is a sun" (Ps. 84:11). Remember, John was at the transfiguration event where Jesus "was transfigured..and His face shone like the sun" (Matt. 17:2); he surely had not forgotten what he saw there.

1:17,18

1:17 (17) ***And when I saw Him, I fell at His feet as a dead man.*** - Is this the prostration of reverence and respect? Or is this indicating that he was "bowled over" or "knocked down" in the sense of being overwhelmed and overcome by the majesty of Christ? The latter most likely. Ezekiel was overwhelmed (1:28; 3:23; 43:3; 44:4). Paul was overwhelmed (Acts 9:3,4; 22:6,7).

And He laid His right hand upon me, - Yes, He already had "seven stars" in His "right hand" (1:16), but this is imagery. The picture is that of protection.

saying, "Do not be afraid, - The quotation marks that begin here, do not conclude until 3:22, indicating that this is a single, unified message.

Many times God tells men who encounter Him to "not be afraid" (Isa. 44:2; Dan. 10:8-12). At the transfiguration, John heard Jesus say, "do not be afraid" (Matt. 17:7); he knew that voice! cf. Rev. 2:10; 19:10; 22:8.

I am the first and the last, - Jesus identifies Himself, first as the "I AM" in accord with Exodus 3:14. John had heard Him say, "Before Abraham was born, I AM" (John 8:58). Isaiah explains that God is "the first and the last" (Isa. 41:4; 44:6; 48:12). God is eternal, before all things and after all things. cf. 2:8; 22:13.

1:18 (18) ***and the living One;*** - As God, Jesus had "life in Himself" (John 5:26), and said "I AM the way, the truth and the life" (John 14:6). He is one with the "Living God" (Ps. 42:2). Particularly, on the basis of the resurrection, Jesus could explain that He was the Living One, as He goes on to indicate.

and I was dead, - As a man, Jesus died on the cross by crucifixion. From that cross He exclaimed, "*Tetelestai*," "It is finished; Mission accomplished; the work is completed" (John 19:30; 17:4).

and behold, I am alive forevermore, - The battle is won! The victory of Jesus Christ over all forces of evil is assured and guaranteed. Jesus is alive forevermore! cf. 4:10; 10:6.

and I have the keys of death and of Hades. - "Keys" represent authority and control. "Death and Hades" are the expression of the devil's power. "Hades" was equivalent to the grave, the place of departed spirits (Acts 2:27,31). Jesus has rendered powerless the one "having the power of death, is the devil" (Heb 2:14), destroyed the works of the devil (I John 3:8). "Oh death, where is your victory?" (I Cor. 15:55). In explaining His forthcoming victory to His disciples, Jesus explained that "the gates of Hades would not overcome" the church, but that He would give to them "the keys of the kingdom of heaven" (Matt. 16:18,19). The symbol of the "keys" is also present in Rev. 3:7; 9:1; 20:1, and the defeat of "death and Hades" in 20:11-14.

(19) ***Write therefore the things which you have seen,*** - Again, John is commissioned to "write" what he has seen, the vision of the triumphant Christ, the whole of the Revelation.

and the things which are, - in order to give to the Christians who were to be the recipients of this letter, a correct appraisal of the present situation, so as not to be deceived or feel defeated. "The things which are" be-

1:20

tween the first coming and the second coming of Jesus Christ.

and the things which shall take place after these things. - the future consummation of Christ's victory, which is the confident expectation of all Christians. This does not necessarily imply an "imminent" expectation of the Second Coming of Jesus, either for the first-century Christians, or for Christians today.

Some premillennialist and Dispensationalists have taken the three-fold statement of this verse as an outline of the Revelation. Such an arbitrary structuralization is referred to by Caird as a "grotesque over-simplification."[1]

1:20 (20) ***As for the mystery of the seven stars which you saw in My right hand, and the seven golden lampstands:*** - These images are a "mystery," a symbolization that signifies something that must be made known by God Himself. On "mystery" cf. 10:7; 17:5,7.

the seven stars are the angels of the seven churches, - Much speculation has been generated by the reference to the "angels" of the churches. Does each church have a "guardian angel"? Are these "angels" to be understood merely as "messengers" (Lk. 7:24; 9:52)? Are the "angels" referring to physical leaders, bishops, pastors, delegates of the churches? Is this a general reference to the Holy Spirit at work in the churches (cf 1:4). It was important that the early Christians at the end of the first-century, as well as Christians of every age, recognize that though Christ has ascended, we have not been abandoned. We have not been left to our own devices and effort. We are still in Christ's "right hand' of favor and protection, "protected by the power of God" (I Peter 1:5).

and the seven lampstands are the seven churches.
- The local congregations are to be the visible manifestation of Christ, the "light of the world" (John 8:12; 12:35; Matt. 5:14; 13:43). In 2:5 Christ threatens to "remove their lampstand" in Ephesus, but such would not remove the Church of Jesus Christ from the world, for it cannot be overpowered (Matt. 16:18).

ENDNOTE

1 Caird, G.B., *A Commentary on the Revelation of St. John the Divine*. London: Adam and Charles Clark. 1966. pg. 26.

Religion and the Churches

Revelation 2 and 3

The second and third chapters of the Revelation provide the setting for the whole of the Revelation. In setting forth the historical context, they also serve to introduce the subject-theme to be dealt with in the Revelation. Both of these, the setting and the subject, are established within a structured sequence of epistolary exhortations to seven churches. It behooves us, therefore, to consider the *setting*, *subject* and *structure* of what Jesus Christ has to say to the churches as recorded in the second and third chapters of Revelation.

Setting

The stage for the great panoramic picture-show must be set. Otherwise we will not understand the context of all the action that is portrayed. In chapters two and three of Revelation, Jesus tells John to write to seven churches and directs him what to write. Thereby He establishes the historical setting, the exegetical setting and the theological setting for the whole of the Revelation.

The historical setting is important. The time when this was written was in the last decade of the first century A.D., about 95 A.D. The location was in Asia (also called Asia Minor) on the east side of the Aegean Sea, on the west side of what is now Turkey. There were numerous churches in the communities of this region, but Jesus instructs John to write to seven of them,

2 – 3

which probably indicates that these seven were indicative and representative of all churches in that region and elsewhere.

The apostle John was well-acquainted with these churches and the Christian people who comprised them. He had probably been ministering in this region for 20-25 years prior to his banishment to the isle of Patmos, that as a punitive consequence for his testimony to Jesus Christ. The risen Lord Jesus, of course, was even more aware of what was happening in those churches, and it is He who addresses them and exposes them. John becomes the secretary, the amanuensis, but he is aware of, and familiar with, what Jesus is referring to.

As they neared the end of the first century, the churches of Asia Minor had sufficient time to be tempted by the tempter to pervert the gospel of the dynamic life of the risen Lord Jesus into static and self-oriented forms. There had been plenty of time to "religionize," to revert to man's activity instead of Christ's activity. (This is the subject-theme that will be discussed later.)

By noting the historical setting of the writing of the Revelation in the latter part of the first century, and directed toward particular historical churches in Asia Minor, we do not want to imply that the entirety of its intent and application was only, or even primarily, for these first-century Christians. The Revelation is "rooted" in that historical setting, but not "trapped" there. The message of the Revelation is for all Christians in all churches in all ages.

The exegetical setting provided by chapters two and three of Revelation is also important. By providing the historical and theological setting in these early chapters, it is incumbent upon any legitimate exegete of the Revelation to maintain continuity with that setting and subject throughout his/her exegesis, in order to maintain a consistent and valid interpretation of the book. Chapters two and three are a springboard for understanding the rest of the Revelation. If continuity with the setting and subject of chapters two and three is not maintained, the interpreter will inevitably end up with a detached, disconnected and disjointed understanding of the Revelation, divorced from its context and interpreted "out of context."

When such discontinuity is employed the Revelation becomes a segmented series of "revelations," as it is often mistakenly referred to. These "revelations" are then interpreted as referring to time periods divided by thousands of years. The preterist interpretation, for example, tends to "trap" the intent of the majority of the Revelation back in the first century, and then jump ahead thousands of years to apply the final chapters to the future. The historicist school of interpretation divides the Revelation into application for successive periods of Western church history. The futurist interpretation makes a big division between chapters three and four, recognizing the first-century historical setting of chapters two and three, but interpreting chapter four and following as referring to the future tribulation period and beyond, creating a gap which extends to almost two millennia now. Continuity with the exegetical setting and subject do not seem to be maintained in these interpretations.

The Revelation is an indivisible unity. The same unified Revelation that Jesus Christ gave to John which had a consistent message applicable to the first century Christians, is the same unified and consistent message applicable to Christians in every age and location.

Chapters two and three provide the historical setting and the theological subject of the conflict between the dynamic of Christianity and religious attitudes and methods. Chapters four and following are then parabolically placed alongside to picture the spiritual conflict that continues to take place in the "enigma of the interim" between the first and second physical comings of Jesus Christ to earth. Christians of all time are reminded of the triumph of Jesus Christ over all of Satan's schemes by His "finished work" of redemption and restoration, as they look forward to the consummation of that victory made evident to all in the future at the end of time. This is the basis of the Christocentric-Triumphalist interpretation that we are employing in this study.

Subject

The subject-theme established in chapters two and three might also be referred to as the "theological setting" for the Revelation. It has been previously mentioned within the discussion of the historical setting that the issue within those seven historical churches in Asia Minor was the tendency to revert to religion instead relying completely on the life of Christ.

Those Christians in the first century, and many Christians in every age since then, have understood the spiritual victory won by Jesus Christ in His death, burial, resurrection, ascension and Pentecostal outpouring. They have looked forward with hope to the ultimate consummation of that victory as promised. But now, in the present, in the "enigma of the interim" between His first and second physical advents, how is the victorious reign of Jesus Christ played out? The victory does not often appear evident. By most appearances "man-made religion" (Col. 2:23) seems to predominate, even among those who verbalize identification with Jesus as Christians. With self-established statistical "success" factors, religion employs "power-plays" and ploys that are not energized by the power of the risen Christ.

By the end of the first century Satan had already infiltrated the churches with his counterfeit religion. He diabolically masquerades as an "angel of light" (II Cor. 11:13-15), aligning with what is relatively "good," and encouraging Christians to fight against the "bad" and the "evil." What he solicits Christians to engage in is contrary to and a counterfeit of the dynamic life and activity of Jesus Christ, and is therefore the working of "anti-Christ," which John informs us in his epistle is "already in the world" (I John 2:18,22; 4:3). Religion is anti-Christ!

The Christians of Asia in the first century were bombarded with religion. There was a whole pantheon of mythological Greek gods. Numerous temples were constructed in all of the cities: temples to Artemis, goddess of the moon; temples to Cybele, goddess of nature; temples to Zeus, the chief of gods; temples to Dionysus, god of wine; temples to Aesculapius, god of healing; etc. Alongside these Greek religious temples were temples of Roman emperor worship, the religion of *Dea Roma*. The Roman emperors (some more than others) desired to be worshipped and to have people bow down and declare "Caesar is lord." Temples to particular emperors such as Augustus and Tiberius were constructed in some of the cities. In addition to these there were local religious cults which developed in these cities. Religion was a favorite hobby in this region. This area was a breeding ground for new religions. Trade guilds, superstitions, anything could be made into a religion. If that were not enough, they also had the synagogues of the Jewish religion. By the end of the first-century it was well established that Christianity was not to be identified with Judaism. The Christians of this area were living in a "religious swamp," all the while trying to maintain that Christianity was not another religion, but that it was the vital dynamic of the life of the risen Lord Jesus who had conquered all evil and sin and death.

It certainly did not look that way by outward appearances! "If Jesus is the victor, then what is all this spiritual conflict and all this religion that we see?" "What kind of war is this where we do not even seem to fight on the same plane?" Paul told the Ephesians, "Our struggle is not against flesh and blood, but against rulers, against the powers, against the world forces of this darkness, against the spiritual forces of wickedness in the heavenlies" (Eph. 6:12). Christians are to "stand firm" in Christ (Eph. 6:13), not using the overt power procedures of the world, but trusting that God is working by His grace through the risen Lord Jesus and the power of the Holy Spirit. After several decades (and for us, after many centuries), some of these Christians were surely beginning to wonder, "Is Christianity really just another religion of man?" "Is this fledgling Christian enterprise just a dying cause? Is it going to die out like a flash in the pan?" Some of them knew it was a "dying cause," for they were dying physically as martyrs for their faith in Jesus Christ.

Satan was right there to tempt them to revert to his religious attitudes and methods. "Everybody's doing it, you know!" The effectiveness of his diabolic solicitations is revealed as the living Lord Jesus exposes how the various churches had lapsed into religious practices.

The historical and theological setting in which the Revelation was written allows the Revelation to be applicable to Christians in every age. Jesus Christ, through the apostle John, encourages the Christians of Asia in the first century, and the Christians of every location in every time:

(1) *to remember the victory of Jesus Christ* in His death, burial, resurrection, ascension and Pentecostal outpouring.

(2) *to resist the temptation to succumb to religion,* for (as will be pictured) such is involvement with the religious Beast rather than the Lamb, Jesus Christ; such is connection with the religious Harlot rather than the Bride; such is to dwell in religious

Babylon instead of the New Jerusalem.

(3) *to repent of any and all occasions of thus lapsing into religion* and failing to live by the dynamic of the life of Jesus Christ, as all of the churches addressed seem to have done.

(4) *to reaffirm the hope that is ours in Jesus Christ* of the consummation of Christ's triumph made evident to all for eternity when Christ comes again.

It is imperative to a proper understanding of the Revelation to have a well-established foundation of understanding of the setting and the subject that are laid out here in chapters two and three.

Structure

There is a uniform structure to these letters in which the setting and subject is set forth. As Jesus dictates to John what he should write to the churches, He employs a repetitive structure. The chart in *Addendum D* graphically illustrates how the sections of each letter fit the seven-fold structure.

(1) The first feature of each passage in chapters two and three is the *commission* Jesus gives to John to write a letter to a church at a particular *address*. These were local churches in seven communities of Asia Minor. They were not the only churches, but they were representative of all the churches that existed then and all the churches that have existed throughout church history, and indicative of how religion infiltrates the churches of Jesus Christ.

Jesus addresses each letter to the "angel" of the church in each location. What is the meaning of this angel? Does every congregation of the church of Jesus Christ have a guardian angel? Sometimes the Greek word *angelos* simply means "messenger." Was Jesus addressing the preacher of each church; the "messenger" who delivered the message? Was He addressing the leadership of elders or bishops?

Previous reference has been made to "seven Spirits" (1:4), which referred to the fullness of the work of the Holy Spirit, and to "seven stars" (1:16) which are subsequently identified as "the angels of the seven churches" (1:20). As our identity as Christians in the church of Jesus Christ is based on our spiritual union with the Spirit of Christ, and the Holy Spirit is the spiritual messenger to our individual hearts, and to the leadership of the local congregation, perhaps the risen Lord Jesus is addressing the Holy Spirit in each church. The Holy Spirit becomes the spiritual "messenger" to Whom we are to listen in order to hear the revelation of Jesus Christ. Such an interpretation emphasizes the ontological association of the Holy Spirit, the Spirit of Christ, with each individual Christian and with the collective congregation of Christians in the local church. Such an emphasis was a needed message for the Christians of the first century and for Christians ever since then, as it is contrary to religious tendencies.

(2) Second, Jesus declares a particular facet of His *personal identity* to each congregation. His self-designation of identity appears to be specifically tailor-made for that particular congregation, to reveal that He is the necessary remedy to their particular religionizing tendencies. The ontological presence of the risen Lord Jesus serves as the divine reality that overcomes religion in every form. Taking the assertion that Jesus makes to each congregation concerning who He is, it is possible to note the contradictory religious tendency that may have been present in that church.

(3) In each of the letters, Jesus then makes some *observations* about the situation that existed in that particular church. In every case these observations begin with Jesus saying, "I know..." this or that about you. The all-knowing, omniscient, risen Lord Jesus knows the situation in every church, in every part of His Body. No Christian and no congregation escapes His attention or "pulls the wool over His eyes." He knows even the motivation of everything we do.

What Jesus knows about the particular church sometimes elicits praise and commendation. His knowledge of the situation sometimes brings His expression of sympathy. In several cases Jesus' supernatural knowledge brings forth a censure that exposes their religious perversion.

(4) Fourth, Jesus makes some specific *charges* against the churches, often by noting, "I have this against you..." In so doing He usually exposes their particular religionizing tendencies. The charges seem to be imbedded within the observations and commands to the churches at Sardis and Laodicea. Two of the churches, Smyrna and Philadelphia, do not have specific charges brought against them, but this does not mean that they are not just as guilty of reverting to Christ-less religion. The religionizing of these two churches is exposed in the other comments Jesus makes to them.

(5) The fifth thing Jesus does in each letter to the seven churches is to issue a particular *command* (or series of commands) to the people of the church being addressed. These commands call upon the Christians in the churches to "wake up" (3:2) from their apathy, to "remember" (2:5; 3:3) all they have received in Jesus Christ, to "be faithful" (2:10) in persevering, to "hold fast" (2:25; 3:11) to the sufficiency of Jesus Christ. In other words, the Christians in the churches are commanded to "repent" (2:5,16,21,22; 3:3,17). They are not merely

encouraged to have remorse or regret and consider changing their ways. The only appropriate response to God in light of the sin of failing to allow Jesus to be all and do all as the living Lord in the life of a Christian is repentance!

Repentance is a "change of mind (*metanoia*) that leads to a change of action." The "change of mind" is the recognition that "I can't; only Christ can" live the Christian life. The "change of action" is then to allow for that Christ-function, the outworking of the saving life of Jesus Christ in and through our behavior. This is one of the basic objectives of the Revelation, to call Christians in all the churches in every age to repentance for the sin of religiosity, the substitution of man's actions instead of God's action.

Of all the writers of the new covenant literature in the New Testament, John seems to have seen most clearly that man's spiritual condition and behavioral expression are to be viewed in the polarized dichotomy of an either/or. In his first epistle he explains that "the children of God and the children of the devil are obvious" (I John 3:10). In his gospel he records Jesus telling the Jewish religionists that they were "of their father, the devil" (John 8:44); their father was not of the God of Abraham as they religiously claimed. John saw clearly that all men are identified either with God or the devil. They function either by Christ or by Satan. They are either for Christ or against Him (Matt. 12:30). They are either "sons of God" or "worshippers of the Beast," participating and living either in Babylon or the New Jerusalem, related and interacting either with the Harlot or with the Bride, as John uses the images later in the Revelation. We participate in either Christianity or religion – either/or! That is why religion cannot be tolerated in the church of Jesus Christ. We must not be fraternizing with the enemy, and employing his techniques and tactics.

(6) The sixth element of each letter is the *call to discernment*. In every case Jesus says, "He who has an ear, let him hear what the Spirit says to the churches." Jesus wants Christians to listen, to be spiritually attuned, to what He, the Spirit of Christ, is directing in their lives, so as to be all and do all in them.

Jesus is encouraging obedience, the "obedience of faith." Obedience in the new covenant means to "listen under," derived from the Greek word *hupakouo*. We are to "listen under" the guiding direction of the Spirit of Christ, and respond with faith which allows for the receptivity of His activity in our behavior.

To the original disciples in the Upper Room, Jesus indicated that He would send the Holy Spirit, and "the Holy Spirit will teach you all things, and bring to your remembrance all that I said..." (John 14:26; cf. I John 2:27); "the Spirit will guide you into all truth...He will take of Mine and disclose it to you...He will glorify Me" (John 16:13-15). Paul explained to the Corinthians that we "have received...the Spirit who is from God, that we might know the things freely given to us by God...taught by the Spirit...spiritually appraised" (I Cor. 2:12-14).

Jesus calls Christians to be spiritually discerning, particularly to the Satanic subtlety of allowing religion to be substituted for, and to usurp the vital dynamic of the life of Jesus Christ in Christians. Frankly, there is not much discernment among Christians today! Most Christians cannot even tell the difference between Christianity and religion.

Note also that Jesus tells the Christians in each church to "hear what the Spirit says to the churches" (plural). They are not just to listen to the particular message directed at the revealing of their own religiosity, but to listen to all that the Spirit says to all the churches, so as to be discerning about other forms of religion also. As the seven churches are representative of all churches in every age, this is a call for all Christians to be spiritually discerning concerning the radical difference between religion and Christianity.

(7) Finally, Jesus makes a *promise* (or promises) to each church addressed, based on their willingness to identify with Him, the Overcomer (John 16:33), and thus to "overcome the Evil One" (I John 2:13) and to overcome the temptation to succumb to Satan's seditious substitute of religion. Even in the promises Jesus reveals that He knows what the real need of each church is, and He seeks to counter their particular propensity for religiosity by promising what they really need.

What we really need, of course, has been provided in Jesus Christ Himself. We do not need anything more. All the promises of God are affirmed and fulfilled in Jesus Christ (II Cor. 1:20). Although we have the promises of God in Jesus Christ and can participate in the spiritual realities of those promises presently, there is also a "not yet" unhindered experience of those realities for which we hope and expectantly await in the future. The verbs used in most of the promises to the churches are in the future tense.

The contingency for full participation in the promises is the obedient faithfulness which repents of looking to and relying upon anything other than Jesus Christ for our sufficiency of living and for the operation of the church. In such repentance we will overcome the temptation to revert to religion and will depend upon Jesus Christ alone as the King who reigns within us (Luke 17:21) and within His church.

2:1-7

Religion and the Church in Ephesus

Revelation 2:1-7

Ephesus was the most important city in the region of Asia Minor in the first century. That is probably why Paul went there as part of his mission strategy to reach the population centers. He stayed longer in Ephesus than in any other city, approximately two and half years (Acts 19:8-10).

The city of Ephesus was located at the mouth of the Cayster River and was a seaport city, serving as the primary commercial center of the region. It was a beautiful city. One of the seven wonders of the ancient world was located in Ephesus, the temple of Artemis (or as it was called in Latin, the temple of Diana). Artemis or Diana was the goddess of fertility, depicted as a female with many breasts. The people of Ephesus were really proud of this beautiful temple, and many made their living off the idolatrous trade associated with the temple. When Paul's preaching of the gospel began to impinge upon their trade, a silversmith named Demetrius organized a protest that started a riot and led to Paul's departure from the city (Acts 19:24–20:1). Religion was a powerful force in Ephesus!

The church in Ephesus was apparently founded by Paul when he visited there on both his second and third missionary journeys (Acts 18:18-21; 19:120:1). As

2:1

usual, Paul clearly differentiated between the dynamic gospel of the indwelling life of the Spirit of Christ and the legalistic performances of religion. Paul's younger disciple, Timothy, later ministered in Ephesus (I Tim. 1:3). The apostle John lived and ministered there in the latter decades of the first century.

2:1 What is the message that Jesus had for the church in Ephesus? He identified Himself as *"the One who holds the seven stars in His right hand, the One who walks among the seven golden lampstands"* (2:1). The risen Lord Jesus is indicating that He is the One who has divine authority. "All authority is given to Me in heaven and in earth" (Matt. 28:18). He is the One who controls the Church. "He is the head of the Body, the church" (Col. 1:18). "He put all things in subjection under His feet, and gave Him as Head over all things to the church, which is His Body, the fulness of Him who fills all in all" (Eph. 1:22,23). The work of the Holy Spirit in the church is the work of the Spirit of Christ. He walks among the churches. In the old covenant God had said, "I will walk among you and be your God, and you shall be My People" (Lev. 26:12). The living presence of the Lord Jesus is to be the dynamic action of God in the churches. He is not just an object of belief or assent.

Why does Jesus identify Himself like this to the Ephesians? Because religion has this haughty tendency to think that they are in control, that authority is invested in their hierarchical leaders, that they are the ones who "run the business," and that they will do whatever is necessary to be successful in such "churchy busyness" (despite how contrary it might be to God's business).

Jesus makes His observation of the church in Ephesus in verses two and three. "*I know...*" In His gospel record John writes that Jesus "knew all men" (John 2:24), and records Peter saying to Jesus during his being questioned about his love, "You know all things..." (John 21:17). Jesus knew that the Ephesian Christians had "tested the spirits to see if they were from God" (I John 4:1), and had detected false prophets and apostles who were "wolves in sheep's clothing" (Matt. 7:15). Paul had warned the Ephesian elders that "savage wolves will come in among you not sparing the flock" (Acts 20:29). They had been on the lookout for these "false teachers...secretly introducing destructive heresies" (II Peter 2:1), "false prophets" representing "the spirit of the anti-Christ already in the world" (I John 4:1-3). They had persevered and endured and not grown weary. Jesus knew this about them.

2:2,3

"*BUT...*" the charge against them is in verse four. "*I have this against you...you have left*, you have forsaken, *your first love.*" The honeymoon is over!

2:4

The Ephesian Christians had been commended for their love when Paul wrote to them explaining that he had heard of their "love for all the saints" (Eph. 1:15). What had happened? Apparently their love for Jesus Christ and subsequently for one another had waned. "We love because Christ first loved us" (I John 4:19), and because the "love of Christ is shed abroad in our heart by the Holy Spirit whom He has given us" (Rom. 5:5). The "fruit of the Spirit is love..." (Gal. 5:22). John, the apostle of love, had recorded in his gospel the words of Jesus when He said, "By this all men will know that you are My disciples, if you love one another" (John 13:35). But the Ephesian Christians had lost the fervent devotion of their early Christian experience (cf. Jere. 2:2-5). The passion, the zeal, the intimacy had faded.

How does that happen? Perhaps the previous observation of verses two and three gives us the clue to why the Ephesian Christians are guilty as charged. Heresy-hunting can put you in a religious frame of mind very quickly. If you are constantly on the lookout for ideological falsehood, you usually become critical and suspicious. You are looking for heretical aberration under every bush (or idea). You set out on an inquisition, and everyone is a suspect. This can definitely kill your love for Christ and for one another. Enthusiasm for orthodoxy can dull all desire for intimacy with Jesus Christ and with others.

Then when you think you have developed good skills at this kind of doctrinal discernment, it breeds pride and arrogance. Religion boasts of having everything figured out. "We know what is right and what is wrong." "We can do this detective work." Success in discernment and perseverance can lead to an attitude of self-sufficiency and superiority. The "father of lies" (John 8:44) is so deceptive as he attempts to cause sincere, loving Christians to lapse into religion, which inevitably turns one's love to something or someone other than Jesus Christ, and those in whom Jesus lives, i.e. Christians. Religion will create a primary love for orthodoxy and correct doctrine, for good feelings and entertainment, for productivity and the success factors of buildings, budgets and baptisms, for prestige, position, and power. Religion will make you critical and suspicious and judgmental of others, even other Christians, because religion has lost any connection with the dynamic love of Jesus Christ.

What does Jesus command the Ephesians to do? In verse five He commands them to (1) remember, (2) repent, and (3) re-enact.

First, "*remember from where you have fallen.*" Remember all that has been provided to you in Jesus Christ when He came to dwell in you and to be your life. The prodigal son in Jesus' parable remembered all that he had back at his father's house.

Second, the Ephesians are commanded to "*repent.*" Repentance is a "change of mind that leads to a change of action." The "change of mind" is the recognition that "I cannot, only Christ can live the Christian life." The "change of action" is the receptivity of Christ's activity that allows Christ to function in our behavior in accord with His character.

Thirdly, the Ephesians were to "re-enact." "*Do the deeds you did at first.*" They were to re-engage in the first-deeds that issued out of their first-love. We were "created in Christ Jesus for good works, which God prepared beforehand that we should walk in them" (Eph. 2:10). "Faith without works is dead" (James 2:26). "God is able to make all grace abound to you, that always having all sufficiency in everything, you may have an abundance for every good deed" (II Cor. 9:8). "God... will equip us in every good thing to do His will, working in us that which is pleasing in His sight" (Heb. 13:20,21). This was not a command like that so prevalent in religion, "Get to work for Jesus!" or "Do these deeds and you will be righteous." Not at all. The deeds that Jesus demands are always derived from the dynamic of His own deity! It was such divinely energized "good deeds" that Christ wants them to re-enact.

2:6

The failure to thus live out of the dynamic of Christ's life and activity can result in the "*removal of the lampstand from its place.*" That does not mean that the church universal will be overcome. Jesus said, "Upon this rock (of faith in Jesus Christ), I will build My church, and the gates of Hades will not overpower it" (Matt. 16:18). But local churches have been and are removed for their misrepresentation. The premier exhibit of such is that there is no church in Ephesus today!

Religion fails to recognize that permanency is only in Jesus Christ; when we are deriving from Christ by faith. This is true both individually, as well as ecclesiastically. Religion operates on the premise that permanency is achieved by prolonged programs, by historical heritage, or by perpetual endowments and entitlements.

The attitude of Jesus Christ is that it is better to have no church, no group calling itself the "church of Jesus Christ," than to have an aberration, a misrepresentation, a religion which has no love, a religion that does not manifest His character and activity.

2:6 Jesus makes one more observation of the Ephesian church in verse six, noting that they have "*hated the deeds of the Nicolaitans.*" Who were these Nicolaitans? We shall observe that they were in Pergamum also (2:15). Some have suggested that the Nicolaitans were somehow identified with one of the seven servers mentioned in Acts 6:5 - "Nicolas, a proselyte from Antioch." This is very doubtful, and has no evidence to substantiate such. The Nicolaitans can probably better be identified by the etymology of the name. Two Greek words are joined together: *nike* meaning "victory" (such is the basis of Nike brand shoes), and *laos* meaning "people" (from which we get the word "laity"). The Nicolaitans are those who "conquer the people." This is indicative of religion. It is an organized attempt to manipulate and control the people, to make them into unthinking pawns and followers who will do whatever they are told to do by the religious leaders (especially to give up their money and time). Religion is afraid of Christians who live by the freedom of God's grace, allowing the Spirit of Christ to direct their lives and manifest His character. You cannot control those kind of people. They believe that Jesus Christ is their Priest and their Lord, and they will not bow down to any other, or be controlled or conquered by any other.

At least the Ephesians had rejected the religion of the Nicolaitans which "conquered people." They still needed to be discerning to what the Spirit, the Spirit of Christ, was saying to the churches, especially in the avoidance of all kinds of religion by depending upon Jesus Christ alone. *"He who has an ear, let him hear what the Spirit says to the churches"* (2:7).

The promise to those who would overcome the temptation to revert to religion by deriving all from Christ the Overcomer (John 16:33), was that they could "eat of the tree of life, which is in the Paradise of God" (2:7). To understand this promise we have to go all the way back to the first book of the Bible, to Genesis. In the garden of Eden God placed the "tree of life" right in the middle (Gen. 2:9), encouraging free access to eat from it (Gen. 2:16) while Adam and Eve were still in their sinless state. What did that "tree of life" represent? It represented the choice that the first man had to allow for the divine outworking of the divinely inbreathed life of God in man. God had breathed into man the divine

2:7

breath (spirit) of His life (Gen. 2:7). As man partook of the "tree of life" he would have been functioning as God intended in the sanctification process, allowing the life of God to be expressed in the behavior of man, to the glory of God. After the first pair sinned by eating of the "tree of the knowledge of good and evil," they were denied access to the "tree of life" (Gen. 3:24), lest they become perpetual sinners.

In the Proverbs, the "tree of life" is identified with wisdom (3:18), righteousness (11:30), fulfilled desire (13:12) and gracious speech (15:4). Jesus Christ in the Christian is our wisdom and righteousness (I Cor. 1:30), the fulfillment of all our God-given desires, and the basis of all gracious speech (Eph. 4:29). There is a sense in which Christians presently partake of the "tree of life" in the sanctification process whereby we allow the life of Christ to be expressed through us.

Later in the last chapter of the Revelation, Jesus pronounces the last of the beatitudes, saying, "Blessed are those who wash their robes, that they might have the right to the tree of life, and may enter by the gates of the city" (Rev. 22:14). Some have seen in that verse the sequence of justification (sins washed away and made righteous), sanctification (tree of life), and glorification (entering the glorious city). The final reference to the "tree of life" in Revelation 22:19 cautions that anyone who does heed the words of this Revelation, and instead "takes away from the words of the book of this prophecy, God shall take away his part from the tree of life and from the holy city..." This seems to imply that Christians who will not learn from the exhortations against religion in the Revelation are in jeopardy of losing sanctification and glorification. It may indicate that there is a "not yet" participation in the "tree of life" as well as the present participation which the Christian "already" enjoys.

There is much that every Christian in every age and every location can learn from what Jesus speaks to the church in Ephesus. We are to "hear what the Spirit says to all the churches," and not lapse into the diabolical counterfeit of religion.

2:8-11

Religion and the Church in Smyrna

Revelation 2:8-11

Smyrna, like Ephesus, was a sea-coast city with a natural harbor on the West side of the Aegean Sea. In terms of natural beauty, Smyrna was the "jewel" of all the cities in the region. Apollonius of Tyana mentioned the "crown of porticoes" which circled the summit of Mount Pagos in Smyrna, creating a particularly beautiful center point of the city.

The Greek word *smyrna* is the same word translated "myrrh" in reference to an aromatic spice brought to Jesus by the Magi (Matt. 2:11), and used in His embalming (John 19:39). Smyrna is the only location of those mentioned for the seven churches, where there is still a city. The modern city of Izmir, Turkey is at the same site as Smyrna of the first century.

Like all of the cities at the end of the first century, idolatry was rampant in Smyrna. Not only did they indulge in the Greek gods, such as Dionysius, the god of wine, but the citizens of Smyrna were at the forefront of Roman emperor worship. The first temple of *Dea Roma*, dedicated to the worship of the goddess of Rome, was constructed at Smyrna. There was also a temple to honor the Emperor Tiberius. This emphasis on worshipping the Roman emperor as "savior" and "lord," led to intensified persecution of the Christians

2:8

who worshipped Jesus Christ alone as "Savior" and "Lord." Being a Christian in Smyrna at the end of the first century was not easy; in fact, it was risky!

2:8   In addressing Himself to the Christians at Smyrna, Jesus identifies Himself as *"the first and the last"* (2:8), just as he had identified Himself to John earlier (1:17). Jesus is the beginning and the end and everything in between. He is the source of all things and the summation of all things. Why would Jesus identify Himself like this to the church at Smyrna? Religion has a tendency to think that everything begins and ends, starts and finishes, with their religious activities and program. There is always an inherent self-sufficiency to religious thought, wherein all activity is considered in the context of their own self-effort. Jesus wants Christians to understand that all activity that can be called "Christian" must have its derivation and destination in Him.

Jesus goes on to explain that He *"was dead, and has come to life"* (2:8). The risen Lord Jesus who is addressing these Smyrnean Christians identifies Himself as the same Jesus who was historically crucified at Golgotha and subsequently rose from the dead three days later. Religion so quickly loses the connection between the historical Jesus and the eternally risen Lord Jesus. Some interpreters focus on the historical Jesus and fail to understand the resurrected Christ in His spiritual form. In so doing they often have no concept of the believer's resurrection out of spiritual death and the dynamic of the resurrection-life of Jesus Christ in the Christian. Other religious aberrations have denied the historical elements of the crucifixion and resurrection of Jesus, relegating them to mere "myth-stories," and focus on a spiritualized and subjective, existential experience with the Spirit of Jesus. Jesus says that he "was dead, and has come to life," and all that He does now by His Spirit is connected to and based upon what He did then! He is the risen Lord Jesus! Christianity recognizes that everything issues forth from the resurrection. Ever so subtly, some have religiously emphasized the cross and the crucifixion death of Jesus rather than the resurrection, making Jesus into a martyr-model, and encouraging masochistic self-crucifixion amongst Christians rather than living by the resurrection dynamic of Christ's life. The death on the cross was the remedial act whereby Jesus took our deserved death, but the resurrection is the basis of the glorious restoration of God's life to man, life out of death. The Christians at Smyrna apparently needed to be reminded of the risen Lord Jesus.

The observations that Jesus makes about the church at Smyrna are found in verse 9. The all-knowing Christ says, "I know..." this about you. There is not anything He does not know about us! Of the Smyrnean Christians, Jesus says, "*I know your tribulation and your poverty.*" There was much pressure upon the Christians in Smyrna to capitulate to the Roman emperor religion. Their poverty probably was a result of being economically ostracized and boycotted for their obstinate refusal to recognize Caesar as lord, ever affirming that "Jesus is Lord." This was in addition to the pressures brought to bear upon them by Greek religion, regional religions, Jewish religion, etc. They knew well the tribulation and the poverty that can be imposed by religious oppression.

Religion has a tendency to look at the observations that are made of the believers in Smyrna, and conclude

2:8

that they were obviously not "right with God." Religion reasons, "Are you having trials, troubles, temptations, tribulations? Then you are not 'right with God.' Are you poor, deprived, economically disadvantaged, merely middle-class? Then you do not have enough faith to realize and enjoy the prosperity that you deserve and which is your 'divine right,' which can be demanded of God in faith." The religious "health and wealth" gospel could never accept the "tribulation and poverty" of the Christians in Smyrna. Yet, Jesus does not fault the Smyrnean Christians for such; He merely observes that this is the situation in which they find themselves, and encourages them to recognize another perspective of prosperity.

Jesus says to them, "***you are rich.***" Not materially or monetarily rich, but spiritually rich. The abundance of life does not consist in possessions (Luke 12:15); "the man who lays up treasure for himself is not rich toward God" (Luke 12:21), Jesus had previously proclaimed. "Lay up for yourselves treasure in heaven" (Matt. 6:20). The apostle Paul wrote of "having nothing, yet possessing all things" (II Cor. 6:10). The writer to the Hebrews mentions their having "accepted joyfully the seizure of their property, knowing that they had a better possession, and an abiding one" (Hebrews 10:34). What kind of riches did the Christians of Smyrna have? The "riches of God's grace" (Eph. 1:7,18; 2:7), the "unfathomable riches of Christ" (Eph. 3:18); spiritual riches rather than physical riches.

Religion does not understand the spiritual riches in Christ. They are "banking on the wrong things." Because of misplaced religious teaching, many Christians have "sold themselves short," thinking themselves to be bankrupt, when in reality they are spiritually rich in Jesus Christ. Jesus says to the Christians of Smyrna and to Christians of every age, "You are rich."

The Smyrnean Christians were also suffering persecution at the hands of religionists of another kind. Jesus refers to *"the blasphemy of those who say they are Jews and are not, but are a synagogue of Satan"* (2:9). Religion of every kind tends to be persecutive toward Christians. Why is this so? Because religion is the devil's playground. Religion is Satan's diabolic parody of the relationship between God and man through Jesus Christ. That is why religion will always "bad mouth," speak evil of, and blaspheme Christianity. Satan is a slanderer. He is the "accuser of the brethren" (Rev. 12:10). The very name "Satan" means adversary or opponent.

The Jewish religion likes to play upon people's sympathies with a persecution complex that portrays them as always having been "victimized." They have, no doubt, been persecuted at different times in their history, but they have doled out religious persecution on others as well, and those who claim to be Jews are still doing so today.

Those who were persecuting the Christians in Smyrna claimed to be Jews. They probably were Jews by all outward criteria of race and religion – tithing members of the local Jewish synagogue. But Jesus indicates that they were not really Jews. What does the word "Jew" mean? Originally it referred to those of the tribe of Judah, one of the sons of Jacob. The name means "to the praise of God." Later the word became the designation of all Israelite peoples. Although the physical, racial

83

2:9

Jews of the old covenant were to be the pictorial prototype of the "people of God," they were unfaithful and failed, as a whole, to believe in the Messiah, God's Son, Jesus Christ. It was to Jewish religionists that Jesus explained that they were not of their father, Abraham, as they claimed to be, but "You are of your father, the devil" (John 8:44). Despite his previous pride in Jewish heritage (Phil. 3:4-6), Paul explained to the Romans that a real Jew was one who was so spiritually. "He is a Jew who is one inwardly" by the "circumcision of the heart" (Rom. 2:28,29). These persecutive Jews in Smyrna claimed to be Jews, but they were not real Jews, not spiritual Jews. They were not real "People of God" or they would not be persecuting God's People, the "People of God's own possession", the "chosen race" (I Peter 2:9,10), the people who are now true Jews spiritually, that is Christians.

These so-called "Jews" in Smyrna were not functioning "to the praise of God," which can only take place "in Christ" under the new covenant. Their synagogue may have read the Torah every Sabbath, but Jesus says it was a "synagogue of Satan." Satan was functioning in these religious people as he does in all religious people. Their gathering place was the dwelling place of Satan. Satan is the adversary of all that God does in Jesus Christ. He is the source of all religion and the blasphemous attacks of religionists against those who are "in Christ." The Christians in Smyrna were being blasphemed by these religious, racial Jews, who were spiritual non-Jews, whose activity was being energized by the devil.

In response to their situation, Jesus commands the Smyrnean Christians to "fear not" and to "be faithful"

(2:10). These two commands constitute a negative and a positive admonition positioned together, as seen elsewhere in Scripture (cf. Rom. 12:2; Eph. 5:18). To obey the positive command is to fulfill the negative and make the negative a moot issue. Religion, of course, tends always to emphasize the negative commands, stressing the performance of abstinence and suppression.

Jesus tells the Christians of Smyrna, "*Do not fear what you are about to suffer. Behold the devil is about to cast some of you into prison, that you may be tested, and you will have tribulation ten days*" (2:10). Decades earlier Jesus had told the twelve disciples, "Do not fear those who can kill the body, but are unable to kill the soul; but rather fear Him who is able to destroy both soul and body" (Matt. 10:28). In his epistle, John wrote, "perfect love casts out fear" (I John 4:18). Since God is perfect love (I John 4:8,16), when He is functioning in us by the grace of Jesus Christ, we have nothing to fear; we are safe "in Christ." He is the basis of our security.

Religion, on the other hand, perpetuates fear. It motivates people with fear and shame and guilt. There is the continuing fear of having violated God's will, of having committed the "unforgivable sin," of not having done enough to please God. There is fear of the spiritual enemy and of his conspiracies, and of how Christianity is being bombarded and overcome. Religion plays off of these fears to get the people to do what the leaders want. Sometimes Christian people even have cause to fear their own church leaders, and what they threaten to do to them. Despite what religion does, Jesus says, "Do not fear..."

2:10

Jesus tells the Christians in Smyrna that they are going to be tested for a brief period of time. It will be of limited duration. The pressure will be on for only "ten days" (a time period that can be taken literally or figuratively). The devil is going to cause some of the Smyrnean Christians to be cast into prison, probably at the instigation of some of his religionist agents. All of this will be an opportunity for these Christians to be "tested" and to demonstrate that Christ's life works even when the going gets tough. God does not promise Christians that there will always be easy and pleasant circumstances in life. He did not promise a rose garden, a red-carpet treatment, smooth sailing on the seas of life. Jesus said, "In this world you will have tribulation" (John 16:33), and Paul proclaimed that "through many tribulations we must enter the kingdom of God" (Acts 14:22).

In the midst of these tribulations Christians are tested to see whether they will allow the character of Jesus Christ to be manifested in their behavior to the glory of God, to demonstrate that His life works, to express His sufficiency in the midst of any situation. James explains that "the testing of your faith produces endurance" (James 1:3), and says, "Blessed is the man who perseveres under trial, he will receive the crown of life" (James 1:12), which Jesus likewise here promises to those of Smyrna. Peter explains that Christians "though distressed by various trials...their faith, even though tested by fire, may be found to result in praise and glory and honor at the revelation of Jesus Christ" (I Peter 1:6,7).

Religion does not have the resources to handle hardship like this. Religion does not have the sufficiency of God's grace in Jesus Christ. So when the trials and the tough times comes, religionists often become pessimistic "doomsday sayers," fatalistic Stoics, or escapists seeking deliverance from all tribulation. Of course, there is the other religious extreme that thinks that the more one suffers the more "spiritual" that person is, so they masochistically seek suffering situations. Only in Jesus Christ do we have the sufficiency of God's grace for every situation that God providentially allows in our lives.

"Be faithful unto death" (2:10), Jesus says to the saints in Smyrna. We can avoid fear, anxiety and worry by allowing for the receptivity of God's divine activity in Jesus Christ. Faith is the antidote for fear. We are to live in faith until we die, and particularly in situations that might take us unto the point of dying. The "sting of death" (I Cor. 15:55,56) is gone. Christians have the life of Jesus Christ, which is eternal.

Religion knows nothing of this type of faithfulness. The religious concept of being "faithful" is being faithful in attendance at religious meetings, faithful in giving to religious causes, and faithful in serving where requested, i.e. faithful to the well-being of the organization and the human authorities thereof.

Neither does religion understand the Christian having no fear of physical death. Religion attempts to avoid death or deny death. The Christian knows that Jesus has "rendered powerless the one having the power of death, that is, the devil" (Heb. 2:14), so we rest assured in the victory that is ours in Christ Jesus, delivered from any bondage to "the fear of death" (Heb. 2:15).

2:11 This is why Jesus promises that faithful Christians "*shall not be hurt by the second death*" (2:11). Physical death for the Christian is just passing through an open door into continued eternal participation in Christ's resurrection-life (Rev. 20:6), with no fear of the perpetual absence of, and separation from, the life of God forever in the "second death." Only those who have refused to receive Jesus will experience the ultimate destruction in the "second death" of hell and the "lake of fire" (Rev. 20:14; 21:8).

Christians will proceed to participate in the victory already won by Jesus Christ, realizing the consummation of that victory by the receipt of the victory "*crown of life*" (2:10). The Greek language has at least two words for "crown." The crown promised by Jesus to the Smyrnean Christians, and subsequently to all Christians, is not the royal crown (*diadema*), but the victory crown (*stephanos*). We already participate in Christ's life and Christ's victory, but the crowning consummation of such is yet to be experienced when we receive the imperishable victory wreath (I Cor. 9:25), the "crown of life" (James 1:12). Paul explains that "in the future there is laid up for me the crown of righteousness...for all who have loved His appearing" (II Tim. 4:8).

Religion usually has a mercenary and materialistic understanding of future, heavenly "rewards." They argue over how many and how valuable are the jewels they expect to receive in their royal crown (*diadema*), based on their religious performances. Such is not the kind of crown Jesus refers to in this passage. The crown Jesus refers to is the "crown of victory" for faithfully resting in, and participating in, Christ's victory.

Jesus Christ urges the Christians in Smyrna and in every age and place to be spiritually discerning about what *"the Spirit says to the churches"* (2:11). The Spirit of Christ is cautioning the churches to *"overcome"* all tendencies to revert to naturalistic, diabolic religion. By faithful receptivity of Christ's life, we shall receive the "crown of life" (2:10) and *"not be hurt by the second death"* (2:11), functioning meanwhile by His sufficient life.

Religion and the Church in Pergamum

Revelation 2:12-17

Pergamum was the capital city of the Roman province of Asia. This political connection was an incentive for the citizens of Pergamum to remain loyal to Rome. Emperor worship was part of this loyalty, and a large temple dedicated to emperor Augustus was located in Pergamum.

The city itself was built on a rocky hill approximately one thousand feet tall in the Caicus valley. The name of the city, Pergamum, is derived from the Greek word *purgos* meaning "tower." Pergamum sat like a citadel towering above the valley. On the top of the thousand foot tall acropolis was the temple of Zeus, the highest of the Greek gods. Archaeological remains of the temple of Zeus in Pergamum can be viewed in the Berlin Museum today.

The temple of Aesculapius, the Greek god of healing, was also located in Pergamum. People came from all around to seek healing at this temple, crying "*Aesculapius soter*," i.e. "Aesculapius is our savior." This site became the "Lourdes" of ancient Asia. The idolatrous insignia of this temple was an emblem of a serpent entwined around a staff, which medical physicians still use to this day.

2:12

Pergamum was also the intellectual center of Asia. Its library was second in size and renown only to that of Alexandria in Egypt. A dispute between the two libraries led to Egypt's imposing an embargo on all papyrus, the reed sheets which were developed and manufactured in Egypt and used for writing scrolls, preventing them from being sent to Asia. The library at Pergamum had to develop a new writing material made of animal skins, which was called the "Pergamene sheet," or as it is better known, "parchment," which became the medium of choice for written documents for many centuries thereafter.

The church in Pergamum was probably established through outreach endeavors from Ephesus, as most of the churches in the region were. Luke reports that while Paul ministered in Ephesus, "all who lived in Asia heard the word of the Lord, both Jews and Greeks" (Acts 19:10).

2:12 Jesus identifies Himself to the Christians in Pergamum as *"the One who has the sharp two-edged sword"* (2:12). In thus identifying Himself, Jesus is exclaiming that He, as the risen Lord Jesus, has an effective power that is above any other, certainly more powerful than earthly government authorities like those of Rome. Jesus, is the "Word of God, living and active and sharper than any two-edged sword, piercing... and able to judge the thoughts and intents of the heart" (Heb. 4:12).

Those within religion often assume their own power, and fail to recognize the effectiveness of God's power and God's judgment. They fail to realize the divine ability to distinguish what is of God and what is not, and to effectively judge that which is derived from diabolic source.

"*I know...,*" Jesus observes, "*where you dwell, where Satan's throne is...*" (2:13). The satanic activity of religion was indeed entrenched in Pergamum. Emperor worship was practiced at the temple of Augustus Caesar. The highest of the Greek gods, Zeus, was worshipped at the temple on top of the mound. The serpent himself was the emblem worshipped at the temple of Aesculapius. Later in the Revelation, Jesus will refer to "the serpent of old who is called the devil and Satan, who deceives the whole world" (12:9; 20:2), identifying him with the satanic serpent in the Garden of Eden (Gen. 3:1-5). In some sense, Pergamum was especially and particularly the "throne of Satan," Hell's Headquarters, the Devil's Den.

Religion incorporates the highest level of diabolic reign and activity. Within religion the devil's ways are enthroned and falsely identified as God's methods. In religion Satan parodies God and brings people so close, and yet so far, from what God wants in their lives. Satan does indeed "dwell" in religious people, "working in the sons of disobedience" (Eph. 2:2).

In continuing His observations, Jesus commends the Pergamene Christians by saying, "*You hold fast My name, and did not deny My faith...*" (2:13). Having confessed Christ, received Christ, and been identified as "Christ-ones," Christians, these Pergamene believers had held fast even in the midst of persecution. They had apparently fulfilled Peter's admonition, "if anyone suffers as a Christian, let him not feel ashamed, but in that name let him glorify God" (I Peter 4:16). They had not

2:14

denied their faith in Jesus Christ, and they had done so ***"even in the days of Antipas, My witness, My faithful one, who was killed among you, where Satan dwells"*** (2:13). We know no other details about this person named Antipas, who was probably one of the Christian believers from the church in Pergamum, and was apparently martyred for his faithful witness to Jesus Christ, at the instigation of Satan and his religious henchmen there in Pergamum.

2:14 Jesus had observed their situation and their faithfulness, but then comes that looming transitional "but..." ***"But I have a few things against you,"*** He charges, ***"because you have there some who hold the teaching of Balaam, who kept teaching Balak to put a stumbling block before the sons of Israel, to eat things sacrificed to idols, and to commit immorality"*** (2:14). Apparently the church in Pergamum was tolerating some religionists, who like Balaam of the old covenant, were a scandal to God's righteous action. The record of Balaam's pronouncements to Balak is found in Numbers 22-24. Balaam tried to have it both ways at once, to play both sides against the middle. His was the way of pragmatic expedience and appeasement to do whatever worked to save his own skin. The "error of Balaam" (Jude 11) led to the "wages of unrighteousness" (II Peter 2:15) because "the counsel of Balaam" caused the Israelites "to trespass against the Lord" (Numbers 31:16). Balaam's accommodation caused the people "to play the harlot with the daughters of Moab" and to "bow down to their gods" (Numbers 25:1,2). Adultery and idolatry were the result, as Jesus intimates.

The religionizing tendencies of Balaam were present in Pergamum. Religion survives on pragmatic expedience, compromise, accommodation and appeasement. The "end justifies the means" in religious practice, so whatever corrupt beguilement, deceit or treachery that might be deemed necessary to the end desired is employed. They will not stand up for God's way alone in accord with God's character, but religion capitulates to the prevailing powers that be, with an attitude of "If you can't beat 'em, join 'em." Such is not the way of God, who never compromises His character.

When religion engages in such permissive appeasement with the world and its ways, activated by "the god of this world" (II Cor. 4:4), the resultant perversion of the populace is predictable. They revert to their naturalistic tendencies of idolatry and immorality. Religion perpetuates and promotes idolatry. Noting the idolatry of the Athenians, Paul cited them for being very "religious" (Acts 17:22), or more literally, having "great respect for demons." Writing to the Corinthians, Paul also explained that "sacrifice to idols..." was "sacrifice to demons" (I Cor. 10:19-21). Religion inevitably pursues idolatrous false-gods, rather than submission to the One true and living God in Jesus Christ. Religion also permits immorality and adultery by failing to measure all things by the faithful character of God, and the expression thereof by the Spirit of Christ.

Jesus continues His charge against the Pergamum church by charging, "***You also have some who in the same way hold the teaching of the Nicolaitans***" (2:15). This type of religious perversion was previously mentioned in the letter to the Ephesians (2:6). The label "Nicolaitans" is etymologically derived from the Greek words *nike*, meaning "to conquer" or "to be victorious," and *laos*, meaning "people." Nicolaitan religion "conquers the people." It is but another variation of Balaamite religion, for the name Balaam is derived from two Hebrew words, *bala*, meaning "to devour" or "to consume," and *am*, meaning "people." Religion devours and consumes the people. It uses and abuses them. It "eats them alive," swallowing up all that they have in order to appease its insatiable appetite for personal enrichment and institutional advancement. Religion does not seek the highest good of men, but it is men seeking their own personal benefit.

2:16 In consequence of the charges against the church at Pergamum, Jesus commands them to *"**Repent therefore, or else I am coming to you quickly, and I will make war against them with the sword of My mouth**"* (2:16). Repentance is what any church needs when it has tolerated religion. A change of mind about who is capable, and a change of action that is available to God's ability to enact all things in accord with His character.

There is an "or else" ultimatum that Jesus makes to the Pergamene Christians. If repentance is not forthcoming, Jesus indicates that He will **"*come quickly, and make war against them,*"** apparently meaning "against the Balaamite and Nicolaitan religionists." His "coming quickly" does not seem to refer to the second physical advent of Jesus Christ to earth, but rather to His providential action in judgment whereby He will "make war" exercising His divine power and authority against all satanic activities in government, religion or elsewhere.

It is important to note that it is Jesus who "makes war." Religion often engages in the activism of what they like to call "spiritual warfare," but it is merely humanly activated assault against demons, against government policies, or against social causes such as immorality, pornography, abortion, etc. Such religious activity is usually totally ineffective, if not counter-productive, because they are trying to achieve what only divine power can accomplish. It is Jesus who "makes war" because He personifies the "sword" of divine power. Christians are to "stand firm" in their faith in Jesus Christ, rather than fighting ineffectively in activistic wars and crusades "full of sound and fury, signifying nothing," and accomplishing nothing.

Christians of every age must be spiritually discerning to *"hear what the Spirit says to the churches"* (2:17). We do not want to be deceived into employing Satan's tactics and techniques which he so subtly introduces into religious activity. Rather, we want to "overcome" all tendencies to religious activity.

2:17

The promise that Jesus makes to the Christians of Pergamum who will faithfully derive all from Him, is two-fold. *"I will give of the hidden manna." "I will give him a white stone, and a new name written on the stone which no one knows but he who receives it"* (2:17).

God was faithful to provide physical sustenance to the Israelite people in the wilderness. "It was like coriander seed, white; and its taste was like wafers with honey" (Exod. 16:31), and they "ate the manna for forty years" (Exod. 16:35). The physical manna was but a pictorial representation of the spiritual sustenance that Christians have in Jesus Christ. Jesus explained the significance of the manna and related it to Himself when He said,

2:17

"I am the bread of life. Your fathers ate the manna in the wilderness, and they died. This is the bread which comes down out of heaven, so that one may eat of it and not die. I am the living bread that came down out of heaven; if any man eats of this bread, he shall live forever" (John 6:31-35; 48-51). Our spiritually sustaining nourishment for living as Christians is to be found in Jesus Christ alone. Religion often offers a substitute diet whereby people can get "fed" on a particular creedal doctrines and supposedly orthodox expositions of Scripture. Christians must never settle for anything less than the sustaining of the "hidden manna," the "bread of life," the dynamic provision of the life of Jesus Christ by His Spirit. The fulfillment of this promise of spiritual nourishment and sustenance is experienced only by those who partake only of Jesus Christ.

What is the white stone with a new name written on it, which Jesus promises? Whereas religion extends "stones instead of sustenance" (Matt. 7:9), and they always attempt to "make a name for themselves," Jesus promises faithful Christians godly character bearing the name of Christ. The prophet said we would "be called by a new name" (Isa. 62:2; 65:15). Indeed we are! We are called Christ-ones, Christians, and no one understands what that means unless they have received the life of Jesus Christ into their spirit. A Christian is not an individual who has "got religion," or "joined a church" or repeated a creed. Rather, a Christian is a person who has received the Spirit of Christ into their spirit (Rom. 8:9), and then lives by that indwelling Christ-life, manifesting the character of God in their behavior to the glory of God. That is what Jesus wanted to see in the Christians of Pergamum and in Christians of every location in every age.

Religion and the Church in Thyatira

Revelation 2:18-29

Thyatira was the manufacturing and trade center of the region of western Asia. It was located approximately fifty miles northeast of Smyrna in a valley which was a branch of the Hermus River. The city had no natural fortification and had been conquered by numerous different kings and armies throughout its history.

The people of Thyatira were just hard-working people making a living by the work of their hands. There were tradesmen, craftsmen, and artists. There were leather-workers, bronze-smiths, potters and bakers. A particularly active trade in Thyatira was that of garment-making from wool and linen. A "Turkish red" dye made from the madder root was distinctive to the region, and used to dye fabrics for garments.

When Paul first went into the region of Macedonia on his second missionary journey, his first convert in Europe was a woman name Lydia. Acts 16:14 records that "a certain woman named Lydia, from the city of Thyatira, a seller of purple fabrics, a worshiper of God, was listening; and the Lord opened her heart to respond to the things spoke by Paul." Lydia may have been an importer of "purple fabrics" from her home-town of Thyatira back in Asia, which she then marketed in Philippi; a first-century female entrepreneur.

2:18

As with all the other communities where Jesus addresses a local church in the region, religion was rampant in Thyatira. A unique form of local religion prospered in this trade-center. The tradesmen and craftsmen in each particular type of trade formed guilds or unions. Each trade-cooperative identified with a particular pagan deity, trusting that deity to preserve their prosperity. The unions became a tight social structure with political and religious connotations. Banquets were held at which they ate the meat of animals which had been sacrificed to their idolatrous protective gods.

The Christians of the church in Thyatira were faced with a difficult social, political, and vocational problem. How could they continue to practice their trade and make a living if they excluded themselves from these tight idolatrous associations? It was very plain that the leaders of the early church had decreed that all Christians should "abstain from things sacrificed to idols" (Acts 15:29). The Thyatiran Christians were tempted to compromise their exclusive faith in Jesus Christ. Their pragmatic motto might have been: "A man has to make a living!" This is certainly representative of Christians in every age who have allowed illicit religious and business associations to draw them away from unadulterated faith in Jesus Christ.

2:18 Jesus identifies Himself to the Christians in Thyatira as "*the Son of God, who has eyes like a flame of fire, and His feet are like burnished bronze*" (2:18). John may have remembered back to when he first heard Peter utter that great confession of Jesus, "Thou art the Christ, the Son of the Living God" (Matt. 16:16). Jesus now declares Himself the "Son of God" with "eyes like a flame of fire." Such was His self-description to John in 1:14 and is repeated as a description of Christ in 19:12. The penetrating vision of Jesus cannot be hidden from. "All things are open and laid bare to the eyes of Him with whom we have to do" (Heb. 4:13), for He is "able to judge the thoughts and intentions of our heart" (Heb. 4:12). Perhaps those who were succumbing to religion in Thyatira needed to remember the omniscient awareness of the risen Lord Jesus Christ. He knew what they were doing! So often religious leaders think that they "know it all," that they have the methodologies all figured out, and that they can engage in illicit activities that God is not aware of. Not so! Jesus has "eyes like a flame of fire" that penetrate with an all-knowing insight even unto the motivations of our actions.

Jesus continues to explain that "His feet are like burnished bronze," apparently indicating His strength and stability. He cannot be shoved around and manipulated. Did He thus identify Himself to the Thyatiran Christians because some of the religionists thought they could "use" Jesus for their own ends? Religionists often think that strength and stability are to be found in their procedures and programs, and the natural results thereof. Jesus indicates that the strength and stability of the church are in Him alone.

Making His observation of the church at Thyatira, Jesus says, "*I know your deeds, and your love and faith and service and perseverance, and that your deeds of late are greater than at first*" (2:19). This is quite an affirmation of their faithfulness. Their deeds were apparently "manifested as having been wrought in God" (John 3:21). The "love of God" had apparently been poured out to others by the Holy Spirit given to them (Rom. 5:5). They had been receptive to God's activity

2:20

in a faith that was worked out in the tangible work of ministry and service to the building up of the body of Christ (Eph. 4:12). They were abiding under the situations of life in perseverance that demonstrates proven character (Rom. 5:4). In so doing they were progressing unto maturity and their "deeds of late were greater than at first." It is always a sign of healthy Christianity when people understand that Christian living is progressive, that it is a lifetime growth process. Religion often tempts us with some form of "instant spirituality," or some spectacular emotional experience whereby we are allegedly sanctified entirely and think that we have arrived at the pinnacle of Christian experience. Beware of the religious "get spiritual quick" schemes and scams! Paul explained that he had not "already obtained it" or "already become perfect" or "laid hold of it," but he "pressed on toward the goal for the prize of the upward call of God in Christ Jesus" (Phil. 3:12-14). Thus we continue to "grow in the grace and knowledge of our Lord and Savior Jesus Christ" (II Peter 3:18), as the Thyatiran Christians seem to have been doing.

2:20   "*But,*" Jesus charges them in verse 20, "*I have this against you, that you tolerate the woman Jezebel, who calls herself a prophetess,...*" Who was this woman, Jezebel, who was allowed to operate in the context of the church at Thyatira? In the old covenant King Ahab married a woman named Jezebel who was the daughter of the king of Sidon. She was an evil woman who encouraged idolatry and immorality, and "killed the prophets of the Lord" (I Kings 18:4). Her name became a proverbial name for feminine wickedness. A domineering, evil woman is often referred to as "a Jezebel" to this very day. Whether there was actually a woman with the name Jezebel living there in Thyatira, or whether this

2:20

is the name by which she is designated because of her actions, we cannot be certain. Not many families have named their daughters Jezebel since the time of the Old Testament. What we can be sure of is that a particular woman there in Thyatira claimed to be a "prophetess" and was teaching and leading Christians astray unto immorality and idolatry, just like the Jezebel of old.

There is a variation in one of the older manuscripts of the Revelation which reads, "I have this against you, that you tolerate your wife Jezebel..." In that case it might have been the preacher's wife who was the wicked woman leading others astray. History is certainly replete with other examples of pastor's wives who have become "Jezebellian" in character and usurped authority that was not theirs, but we must admit that this is not the reading of the majority of the best manuscripts.

Whoever this Jezebel woman was she was outside of God's order for the church. Scripture is quite clear that the leadership of the church of Jesus Christ is to be comprised of faithful men who serve as elders of the church (I Tim. 3:2; Titus 1:6). It is not that women are not as competent as men in positions of leadership, or that women are "second class citizens" of the kingdom of God, for Paul clearly indicates that "male and female, all are one in Christ Jesus" (Gal. 3:28). It is merely a practical matter that retains the order that God intends. In contradiction to this church order, religion has often tolerated and encouraged strong-willed and assertive women to take control and "call the shots" in the church. Even within the early church of the first-century, there were feminist movements which attempted to usurp the leadership responsibility in the church. When some of the early Christian women began

2:21

to understand the emancipation that was theirs in Jesus Christ, they began to take it too far. That seems to be the issue Paul was dealing with in I Corinthians chapter seven. Likewise, he addresses similar problems in the first and second epistles to Timothy. Such problems have resulted throughout the history of the church when women have claimed to be prophetesses, when they assumed ecclesiastical positions of elders and pastors, and have even proceeded to found new denominations. The contemporary trend where an increasing number, even a majority, of students in the Bible schools and theological seminaries are women is a perpetuation of this religious phenomena that does not bode well for the Church of Jesus Christ.

2:21 The Jezebel of Thyatira encouraged immorality and idolatry just like the Jezebel of the Old Testament. These characteristics have been indicative of some types of religion throughout the centuries of mankind. Natural man gravitates toward religion that has a pleasure-orientation, and which tolerates or encourages sexual permissiveness, promiscuity and immorality. There are many religious groups today wherein the "deeds of the flesh" are evidenced in "immorality, impurity, sensuality, idolatry, etc." (Gal. 5:19,21). The Greek word used in verses 20 and 21 and translated "immorality" is *porneia*, from which we derive the English word "pornography." It refers to any sexual activity outside of the marriage relationship that God intended between husband and wife. The word for "commit adultery" in verse 22 is the Greek word *moicheuo* which also refers to sexual relations outside of marriage. Most likely there was sexual promiscuity taking place in the church at Thyatira, but some would interpret these words only of spiritual adultery and unfaithfulness.

Jesus threatens to *"cast her (Jezebel) upon a bed of sickness, and those who commit adultery with her into great tribulation, unless they repent of her deeds"* (2:22). This may be a play on words. If it is a bed that Jezebel wants, then she will get a bed. The punishment will fit the crime. The bed of lust (Greek *koite*; from which we get the English word "coitus"; cf. Rom. 13:13; Heb. 13:4) will be replaced with a bed of sickness (Greek *kline*, from which we get the English word "clinic"). If Jezebel is intent on going to bed, God will send her to a hospital bed.

2:22

Does God do that sort of thing? Are there really personal punitive consequences for sin? Yes, Scripture indicates that God can and does take physical action to chastise and control sinful action. Paul explains to the Corinthians that because of their actions at the Lord's Supper, "for this reason many among you are weak and sick, and a number sleep" (I Cor. 11:30), meaning some have died. God is in control and there are punitive and disciplinary consequences for sinful activity. Some regard the A.I.D.S. epidemic to be such a divine response.

Jesus continues to explain that *"those who commit adultery with Jezebel will be cast into great tribulation, unless they repent of her deeds, and He will kill her children with pestilence..."* (2:22,23). This is not referring to the "great tribulation" that some eschatological speculators expect. It refers to God's disciplinary and punitive action toward sin. God hates religion, and those who participate in it as "children" and adherents will receive the consequences thereof. The prophet Isaiah similarly warned the people of Israel of being "offspring of an adulterer and a prostitute" (Isa. 57:3) who had "made their bed" (Isa. 57:7) and would suffer

2:23

2:23

the consequences thereof, for "there is no peace for the wicked" (Isa. 57:21).

The Lord Jesus Christ knows what is going on. No one is pulling the wool over His eyes. His "eyes are like a flame of fire" (2:18); He *searches the minds and the hearts* " (2:23) of His people. Jeremiah the prophet spoke for God previously saying, "I, the Lord, search the heart, I test the mind, even to give to each man according to his ways, according to the results of his deeds" (Jere. 17:10). Jesus' words here in verse 23 echo what He had spoken through Jeremiah long ago. God in Christ knows what we are doing, and there are consequences "according to our deeds." This is the plain teaching of Scripture: Christ has taken the judgment for our sinfulness, but we will still be judged according to our deeds. The "Son of Man will recompense every man according to his deeds" (Matt. 16:27). "God will render to every man according to his deeds" (Rom. 2:6). "Each man's work will become evident" and he will "receive a reward" or "suffer loss" (I Cor. 3:13-15). "Each one will be recompensed for his deeds in the body, according to what he has done, whether good or bad" (II Cor. 5:10). All will be "judged...according to their deeds" (Rev. 20:13). To the extent that we have faithfully allowed our deeds to have been "wrought in God" (John 3:21) activated by the grace of God (II Cor. 9:8) in accord with what "God prepared beforehand, that we should walk in them" (Eph. 2:10), allowing for the outworking of the life of Jesus Christ in our behavior by our receptivity of His activity, we need not have any concern over God's evaluation of our behavioral deeds. Only when we have pursued our own selfish ways and participated in the activism of religion do we need to be fearfully concerned about the consequences of God's judgment of our deeds.

Thus it is that Jesus continues in verse 24, "***But I say to you, the rest who are in Thyatira, who do not hold this teaching (of Jezebel), who have not known the deep things of Satan, as they call them I place no other burden on you.***" "If you have not succumbed to Jezebellian religion, then do not worry about My threats, just continue to allow My life and character to be manifested in your behavior," Jesus seems to say.

2:24

Whatever the religion of Jezebel included in Thyatira, it apparently had been labeled as "the deep things of Satan" by those involved therein. Why is it that men always want to consider "deep things" which pander to their natural quest for knowledge? Deep musings of the human mind are often not of God, but of Satan. God has made His "good news" for man gloriously simple in the person of His Son Jesus Christ. It is religion that seduces men with "deep things" of Gnostic knowledge, promising esoteric understanding of spiritual secrets. Even the subjective seeking of a "deeper life" in Christ can be a satanically inspired selfish pursuit for "deep things" that are in addition to Jesus Christ Himself.

The command of Jesus to those in Thyatira who were engaged in Jezebellian religion was that "***they repent of her deeds***" (2:22). They needed a change of mind that recognized their inability to please God by their religious efforts, and a change of action that was based on their receptivity of Christ's activity in their behavior.

To those who had resisted the false teaching and behavior of Jezebel, Jesus commands, "***Nevertheless***

2:25

2:25-27

what you have, hold fast until I come" (2:25). To all Christians in the enigma of the interim between Christ's first and second coming the command is to hold fast to that which we have in Jesus Christ. All things belong to us in Christ (I Cor. 3:21,22), "everything pertaining to life and godliness" (II Peter 1:3), "every spiritual blessing in heavenly places" (Eph. 1:3). Despite the appearances of the demise of Christianity, we must "hold fast our confession" (Heb. 4:14), by holding fast to Him and all that we have in Him (3:11). This we must do "until He comes" in His physical return to earth at the second advent.

Religion realizes that to encourage people to "hold fast" and persevere in the midst of all circumstances is not a message that people want to hear. They gain far more followers by offering people an "easy way out." It is the false-teaching of religion that promises deliverance from all problems and escape from all suffering, and the avoidance of all inconvenience. Jesus says, "Hold fast to what you have in Me!"

2:26 The promises to those who overcome the temptation to revert to religion by "holding fast" to the Overcomer (John 16:33) and *"keep His deeds until the end"* by allowing Him to work out His life and deeds in them are explained in verses 26 through 28:

2:27 First, Jesus promises what was promised by the Psalmist long ago in the Messianic Psalm: *"To Him I will give authority over the nations; and he shall rule them with a rod of iron, as the vessels of the potter are broken to pieces"* (2:26,27 from Psalm 2:8,9). The Christians in Thyatira and throughout Asia were being oppressed by the Roman authorities, and it might not have appeared that Christ had much authority, much less that they had any authority. Jesus reminds them that He "*has received authority from His Father*" (2:27); "All authority has been given to Me in heaven and on earth" (Matt. 28:18). The promise is that those who are identified with and united "in Christ" shall exercise authority with Him over the nations of mankind, "reigning with Christ" (20:4). As "kings and priests they will reign upon the earth" (5:10), even "judging angels" (I Cor. 6:3).

Not content to understand spiritual authority in Christ, religion has historically asserted its own ecclesiastical and governmental authority. Indeed, religion has gained "authority over the nations" as it developed church/state liaisons and established state churches. Powerful authority structures have been formed in the institutional churches. The authority of priests, pastors and shepherds has been asserted in the local churches. Such ecclesiastical authority with its power to manipulate others is not the kind of authority that Jesus promises to Christians in these verses.

Second, Jesus promises the faithful Christians of Thyatira, and of every location in every age, that He will "*give them the morning star*" (2:28). What is this "morning star?" At the very end of the Old Testament, Malachi prophesies that "the sun of righteousness will rise with healing in its wings" (Malachi 4:2). Zacharias, the father of John the Baptist, prophesied that "the Sunrise from on high shall visit us" (Luke 1:78), referring to the incarnation of Jesus Christ. The second epistle of Peter indicates that "we have the prophetic word...until the day dawns and the morning star arises in your hearts" (II Peter 1:19). Then, at the conclusion

2:29

of the Revelation, Jesus says, "I am...the bright morning star" (Rev. 22:16). Shedding light over a world of death and darkness, Jesus did come as the Sunrise of the "Sun of righteousness." "The life was the light of men" (John 1:4). After the dark night of religious domination and worldly degradation, Jesus will come again as the "morning star" to remind us that all light and all life is in Him, and that He will reign forever in the eternal and heavenly "daytime, where there is no night" (Rev. 21:25), and we with Him. This is a promise that the Thyatiran Christians and Christians in every age expect to see fulfilled. We look forward in expectant anticipation of hope to the dawning of that eternal day of heavenly glory when Christ shall reign unhindered, and we shall reign with Him forever.

2:29 Meanwhile Jesus calls us to discernment by saying, ***"He who has an ear, let him hear what the Spirit says to the churches"*** (2:29). The message of Jesus to each church is applicable to us all.

Religion and the Church in Sardis

Revelation 3:1-6

Five centuries before Christ, Sardis had reigned as one of the greatest cities in the world at that time. By the end of the first century when Jesus addressed the Christian community at Sardis, the residents of the city were living with a pride of their past history and glory. They were arrogant, wealthy and immoral.

Sardis was located about 50 miles east of Smyrna in the valley formed by the Pactolus River. Five roads converged in a junction in this valley. A jagged rock outcropping with steep cliffs on three sides rose about 1500 feet above the valley on the edge of Mt. Tmolus/Boz. This became the acropolis of the city of Sardis. The site was nearly impregnable and inaccessible. So the Sardisians thought, but twice in their history their city had been captured because of their over-confidence when they had allowed enemies to infiltrate. This happened in 549 B.C. when the Medes overcame the city, and in 218 B.C. when the Cretans conquered them.

Toward the end of the first century Sardis still remained a wealthy city. Gold had been discovered in the river valley, and Sardis may have been the first city to ever have used gold coinage. Wealth often leads to the pretense of self-sufficiency, and such seems to have been the case in Sardis.

3:1

The wide variety of religious offerings were present in Sardis as in the other cities of the region. There was a temple of the fertility goddess, Cybele. Archaeologists have uncovered an extremely large temple that was an imitation of the great temple of Artemis at Ephesus, but it was apparently never finished due to an earthquake in 17 A.D.

Jesus begins His address to the church in Sardis by identifying Himself as **"He who has the seven Spirits of God, and the seven stars"** (3:1). What is Jesus trying to say to the Christians of Sardis by thus identifying Himself?

Throughout the Revelation (1:4; 3:1; 4:5; 5:6) reference to "the seven Spirits" appears to be a symbolic allusion to the completeness of the work of the Holy Spirit. The Sardisian Christians were apparently "resting on their laurels" again, and their "deeds were not completed in the sight of God" (3:2) because they were not allowing the Holy Spirit, the Spirit of Christ, to complete His work in them. When the "seven Spirits" are identified with "seven eyes" later in the Revelation, the implication is that the Holy Spirit is omniscient and sees all that is going on in the church at Sardis.

By indicating that He is the One who "has the seven stars" (1:17; 1:20; 2:1; 10:5; 13:16; 20:1,4), Jesus is telling the Christians of Sardis that He is the One who has the authority and is in control. Earlier Jesus had explained to John that "the seven stars are the angels of the seven churches" (1:20). Sometimes the human leadership of a local church concludes that they have the authority and are in control of the church. Religion has this natural tendency to establish hierarchical authority structures, complete with "flow charts" of political authority and administrative responsibility. In so doing they usually bypass the authority of Christ who is the "head of the Church"(Eph. 5:23; Col. 1:18) and fail to submit to His leadership and guidance of His church. Jesus identifies Himself to the Christians at Sardis as the One who knows what is going on, the One who is in control, and the One who intends to complete His work in them.

Jesus' observation of their condition there in Sardis is expressed when He says, "*I know your deeds, that you have a name that you are alive, and you are dead*" (3:1). They had a reputation that they were spiritually "alive." There was an alleged vitality, but it was "in name only." They were only nominally vibrant Christians. There was some hypocritical play-acting going on. The risen Lord Jesus charges the Sardisian Christians with an externality that appears to be alive, but in essence they are "dead." Jesus had exposed the hypocritical Pharisees similarly when He said, "You are like whitewashed tombs which on the outside appear beautiful, but inside they are full of dead men's bones and all uncleanness. You outwardly appear righteous to men, but inwardly you are full of hypocrisy and lawlessness" (Matt. 23:27,28). Those in the church at Sardis were like zombies operating in a lifeless church. It was "Tombstone Territory."

It has been said that "Few things are better organized than graveyards, but there is little life there." So it is that few things are better organized than religious programs and activities, and there is little life in them. A church may be very busy and very active, and it will appear to undiscerning people that such a church is really

3:2

"alive," but despite the frenetic activity of performance and productivity that church might be very "dead," because they are not deriving what they do from the life of Jesus Christ.

Life is in Jesus Christ alone. Jesus said "I am the resurrection and the life" (John 11:25); "I am the way, the truth and the life" (John 14:6). Paul explained that "for me to live is Christ" (Phil. 1:21); "Christ is our life" (Col. 3:4). Unless our activity, whether individually or collectively, is the "manifestation of the life of Jesus" (II Cor. 4:10,11), then it is not the expression of life. Activities that are not derived from the life of Jesus Christ are but the expression of "dead works" (Heb. 9:14); they "bring forth death" (James 1:15).

Religious activities may appear to be so "alive" with enthusiasm and excitement, but if they are not activated by the life and character of Jesus Christ Himself by His Spirit, they are a "dead loss." Religion propagates a pseudo-life that appears to be "alive," but is actually dead because it is devoid of the divine life of God in Christ. Lifeless religion is so deceiving because the undiscerning think it is alive, when it is really dead.

3:2 Jesus continues to charge the Christians in Sardis when He says, ***"I have not found your deeds completed in the sight of My God"*** (3:2). We were "created in Christ Jesus for good works, which God prepared beforehand, that we should walk in them" (Eph. 2:10), and these Christians had some unfinished works. They had disallowed Jesus to do what He wanted to do in their lives and in their church. They had "quenched the Spirit" (I Thess. 5:19). To thus quench the manifestation of Christ's life and ministry can have serious consequences. Jesus told the parable of the vineyard keeper who did not find fruit on his fig tree, and ordered it to be "cut down" (Luke 13:6-9). God's purpose is to have the fruit of His character to be expressed in the behavior of His people unto His own glory, and the failure to allow for such is a misuse of humanity.

To remedy the situation in the church at Sardis, Jesus issues several commands. There are five imperative verbs in verses two and three which command the Sardisians to respond: "be watching, strengthen, remember, keep and repent."

First, Jesus tells them to "*be watching.*" What are they to be watching? They are not to "be watching" the statistics on the attendance board or their place in the denominational polls. They are to "be watchful" of how Satan can so subtly deceive them into religious practices, rather than living out the life of Jesus Christ. Peter advised Christians to "be watching" because "your adversary, the devil, prowls around like a roaring lion, seeking someone to devour" (I Peter 5:8). Jesus told His disciples, "Keep watching and praying, that you may not enter into temptation; the spirit is willing, but the flesh is weak" (Matt. 26:41). Paul encouraged us to "Be watching, stand firm in the faith..." (I Cor. 16:13). We are to be "on watch" against ungodly forces, and the religious methodologies that Satan inspires.

Jesus goes on to explain the consequences of not "standing watch." "*If you will not watch, I will come like a thief, and you will not know at what hour I will come upon you*" (3:3). This may have had a particularly pointed implication for the people of Sardis, for twice previously in their history their city had been

3:3

captured because of their failure to "keep watch." They thought they were physically strong and secure, and in their over-confidence they were conquered. When Jesus warns that their failure to watch will result in His coming upon them "like a thief," it means that He will come suddenly, unexpectedly, unannounced and without forewarning. Although the same imagery is used of Jesus' coming at His second advent (I Thess. 5:2; II Peter 3:10), it does not appear that this is the "coming" that Jesus is referring to in His warning to the Christians in Sardis. The final Parousia is not dependent on the watchfulness and repentance of the Sardisian Christians. Jesus is simply indicating that their failure to respond in repentance will result in His coming unexpectedly to bring some kind of physical consequence of judgment or discipline.

Secondly, Jesus commands them to "*strengthen the things that remain, which were about to die*" (3:2). Establish what you do have "in Christ," and build stability on the foundation of Christ. Paul exhorted the Thessalonian Christians to "comfort and strengthen their hearts in every good work and word" (I Thess. 2:17), and then turned around and wrote, "The Lord is faithful, and He will strengthen you" (I Thess. 3:3). So it is that Jesus is not asking the Christians in Sardis to do anything that He is not willing to do in them, if they are willing in faith. "The Lord of all grace...will establish you" (I Peter 5:10; Rom. 16:25).

The third command of Jesus to the Sardisian Christians is to "*remember what you have received and heard*" (3:3). What had they received and heard which they are now to remember? Had they received an ideological belief-system, or a morality code, or membership in an organization, or a ticket to heaven? No, that is what religion offers. These Christians had received Jesus Christ by faith (John 1:12; Col. 2:6), and heard His call upon their lives. They were to "remember Jesus Christ, risen from the dead" (II Tim. 2:8).

The fourth imperative imposed upon the Christians in Sardis was to "*keep*" what they had received and heard. Having received Jesus Christ, they were to "keep His word" (I John 2:5), "keep themselves in the love of God" (Jude 21), and "keep the faith" (II Tim. 4:7).

The fifth command was to "repent." If they were going to get out of their lifeless spiritual graveyard there had to be repentance, a change of mind that led to a change of action. Their complacent and self-sufficient thinking would have to be exchanged for the recognition that only the activity of Christ in them was pleasing to God. Whenever religion has permeated the life of a church there must be repentance to reverse the direction of the church and allow them to return to faith.

"*But,*" Jesus observes, "*you have a few people in Sardis who have not soiled their garments; and they will walk with Me in white; for they are worthy*" (3:4). In almost every church situation there are the "faithful few," who have continued to walk in the purity of Christ, "hating the garment polluted by the flesh" (Jude 23) and "keeping themselves unstained by the world" (James 1:27). When we become Christians we "put on the new man" (Eph. 4:24; Col. 3:10) and are clothed in His righteousness, holiness, love, joy, peace, etc. Whenever we revert to the practice of religion we are clothed instead with self-effort, self-justification and self-adulation. Such behavioral garments are soiled, stained and

3:5

polluted by the satanic motivation of the flesh in conjunction with his world-system.

Those who repudiate such soiled garments of religion are promised by the Lord Jesus Christ that they "will walk with Him in white, for they are worthy" (3:4). They will allow the purity of Christ's character of godliness and holiness to be expressed in their behavior. It is not that they are "worthy" because of any meritorious action on their own part, but they are "worthy" because they are relying on the "Worthy One," Jesus Christ, to be operative in them. Only thus can any Christian "walk in a manner worthy of the Lord, to please Him in all respects, bearing fruit in every good work" (Col. 1:10), "walk in a manner worthy of the God who calls us into His kingdom and glory" (I Thess. 2:12), "walk in a manner worthy of the calling with which we have been called" (Eph. 4:1), and be "considered worthy of the kingdom of God..." (II Thess. 1:5).

Religion often considers "worthiness" to be based on natural talents and the performance of service and contribution. A person is then considered "worthy" of being considered for a higher position in the church and "worthy" of being honored before men. They know nothing of the "worthiness" that is derived only from the "Worthy One" living in and acting through the Christian.

3:5   The promise of Jesus to the church at Sardis is continued with a three-part promise: *"He who overcomes shall thus be clothed in white garments; and I will not erase his name from the book of life, and I will confess his name before My Father, and before His angels"* (3:5).

Christians who overcome the temptation to revert to religion by maintaining their association with the Overcomer (John 16:33) will be clothed in "white garments," representing the purity of the character of Christ. Religion, on the other hand, concerns itself with external activity and clothing rather than the character of Christ. Pre-occupied with ecclesiastical robes and garments and with people wearing "Sunday-go-to-meeting" clothes, religion inevitably emphasizes the external rather than the internal. Jesus is concerned that we be clothed internally with His character.

Jesus also promises that overcomers will not have their names "erased from the book of life." The obvious implication is that it is possible to have one's name erased from the book of life, or else the statement would have no meaning whatsoever. The Psalmist had requested that the unrighteous "be blotted out of the book of life, and not be recorded with the righteous" (Ps. 69:28). The "book of life" seems to represent the register of heavenly citizenship. As Christians "our citizenship is in heaven" (Phil. 3:21); we are part of "the church of the first-born who are enrolled in heaven" (Heb. 12:23); and we "rejoice that our names are recorded in heaven" (Luke 10:19,20). We are "those whose names are written in the Lamb's book of life" (Rev. 20:15; 21:27). But when we substitute religion for the Savior we are liable to having our names erased and blotted out of the book of life. God will not and cannot tolerate diabolic religion contrary to His character and grace. The security of heavenly citizenship is not in religious doctrines of "eternal security" and "once saved, always saved," but in dynamic dependence upon the function of the Savior living out His life in us. Religion

3:6

offers a false-security, and religionists are in danger of having their names erased from the book of life.

The third part of Jesus' promise is that those who overcome the temptation to revert to religion will be privileged to have Jesus serve as their advocate and "confess their name before His Father, and before His angels." Jesus had previously said to His disciples, "Everyone who shall confess Me before men, I will also confess him before My Father who is in heaven" (Matt. 10:32), and "before the angels of God" (Luke 12:8). As our behavior "confesses," "agrees with," "says the same thing" as the character of God because He is energizing such by His grace, Jesus will in turn "confess" us before God and the angels as being "in agreement" with Him.

3:6   All of what Jesus promises can only transpire by our listening carefully with spiritual discernment to what Jesus is saying by His Spirit. *"He who has an ear, let him hear what the Spirit says to the churches"* (3:6). Such "listening under" the Spirit of Christ will issue forth in obedience that glorifies God as the life of Jesus Christ is lived out through us.

Religion and the Church in Philadelphia

Revelation 3:7-13

The city of Philadelphia was located approximately 60 miles east of Smyrna. It was built on a plateau which was about 700 feet above the Hermus River valley. The area was very fertile and there were many vineyards planted in that vicinity. It is not surprising, therefore, that there was a temple to the Greek god, Dionysius, the god of wine, located in Philadelphia.

The Greek influence in Philadelphia was quite evident. The city was originally founded in the second century B.C. when Attalus II imported a number of Macedonian veterans to the site in order to build a city that would become the "gateway to the East." Attalus was a Pergamene king who was known as Attalus Philadelphus. The surname "Philadelphus" was added because he was very loyal to his brother, Eumenes II. So the name of the city, "Philadelphia," named after its founder, Attalus Philadelphus, means "lover of a brother," or "the city of brotherly love."

This particular city seems to have been quite enamored of seeking identification with important people and changing its name to reflect such. Early in the first century, in 17 A.D., a particularly severe earthquake had devastated the city. Tiberius was the Roman Caesar at the time and contributed funding to rebuild the city.

3:7

In appreciation the citizens of Philadelphia changed the name of their city to Neoceasarea, meaning "the new city of Caesar." Later, when Flavius Nespasian was emperor of Rome, they changed their name to Philadelphia Flavia. In the third century A.D., they changed their name to Philadelphia Neokoros, indicating that they were the "keepers of the temples" which honored the Roman emperors. The temples that had been erected to the Roman emperors and the Greek gods had become so numerous and such beautiful structures that Philadelphia became known as "the little Athens."

Near the end of the first century when Jesus addressed the church in the city of Philadelphia, the city was an important trade center which was quite prosperous. Religious temples were continually being built to honor Roman emperors and Greek gods. The Jewish religion had a synagogue in Philadelphia. The prevailing religious attitude toward Christians who refused to worship any God other than the Lord Jesus Christ, was not one of friendly co-existence.

3:7 Jesus identifies Himself to the Philadelphian Christians as "*He who is holy, who is true, who has the key of David, who opens and no one will shut, and who shuts and no one opens*" (3:7). In the midst of the many religious offerings in Philadelphia, Jesus indicates that He is the One who is "set apart" from all others as having the character of holiness. Religion is more concerned with hierarchy, heritage and heresy, than they are with holiness. Jesus also says He is the One who is the true God, the reality of deity that gives meaning to all of creation. Whereas religion engages in the mere shadows of reality, Christ is the substance. Later in the

Revelation the Christian martyrs will refer to Jesus as the "Lord, holy and true" (6:10).

Jesus also explains to the Christians of Philadelphia that He is the One who "has the key of David." This is an obvious reference to King David of the Old Testament. God spoken through the prophet Nathan saying, "I will establish the throne of his (David's) kingdom forever" (II Sam. 7:13). It was a Messianic prophecy. The prophet Isaiah said concerning the coming Messiah, "There will be no end to the increase of His government or of peace, on the throne of David and over His kingdom" (Isa. 9:7). Later God says through Isaiah, "I will set the key of the house of David on his shoulder; when he opens no one will shut; when he shuts no one will open" (Isa. 22:22). This latter prophecy of Isaiah seems to be that which Jesus claims to fulfill in His self-identification to the Christians in Philadelphia. The angel had already declared at His birth that "the Lord God will give Him (Jesus) the throne of His father, David, and He will reign over the house of Jacob, and His kingdom will have no end" (Luke 1:32). At the end of the Revelation, Jesus explains, "I am the...offspring of David" (22:16).

What does it mean to have "the key of David?" The one who has the key has authority. The one who has the key controls ingress and egress, those who go in and those who go out, those who enter and those who exit. Jesus Christ is the One who has sovereign authority over God's kingdom which was pictorially pre-figured in the physical kingdom of David. Jesus Christ is the sole basis of access and life and residency in the Kingdom of God, the divine household, the new city of David, the "New Jerusalem." When He opens access

3:8

through Himself, no one can shut that door. When He shuts it, no one can open it. Religionists set up their own little false-kingdoms in the institutional churches. They want to be in control of who goes in and who goes out, of who may enter and who will exit by excommunication. They want to have the authority to invite or debar, to determine who is in and who is out. Jesus asserts that He is the only One who has authority over the Kingdom of God, and He is "faithful over God's household" (Heb. 3:6), and "head over the Church" (Eph. 1:22).

3:8 Jesus proceeds to make His observation of the church in Philadelphia, saying, *"I know your deeds. Behold, I have put before you an open door which no one can shut, because you have a little power, and have kept My word, and have not denied My name"* (3:8). The observation Jesus makes of the Philadelphian Christians is generally favorable. This is one of only two of the seven churches of which Jesus makes no direct charges of misconduct (the other was Smyrna). This does not mean the Christians in Philadelphia were perfect in their faithfulness, but that there was not any direct reversion to religion that Jesus saw need to point out. He knew their deeds, as indeed He knows all of our deeds and the motivations inspiring such, and apparently the deeds of the Philadelphians were being "wrought in God" (John 3:21), activated by His grace (II Cor. 9:8).

Again Jesus indicates that He "had put before them an open door which no one could shut." Isaiah had prophesied that God would "open the gates, that the righteous nation may enter" (Isa. 26:2). Jesus came and opened the door to the presence of God, to the Messianic kingdom of God. He is that "door" (John 15:7). He is "the way, the truth and the life" (John 14:6), the "new and living way" to enter the holy place of God (Heb. 10:19,20). The Christians of Philadelphia had entered through the door of Jesus Christ, as have Christians throughout the world in every age since then, and there is no one more powerful than Jesus Christ to shut them out.

That no one else has the power to shut them out is evidenced by the fact that the Philadelphian Christians "had little power, and yet they kept Christ's word and did not deny His name" (3:8). Religionists were doing all they could to shut down Christianity in the region, but the few Christians in Philadelphia remained faithful. They did not have much power. They did not have political clout. They were probably a small congregation who relied on Christ's strength to be exercised in their weakness (II Cor. 12:9). Religion today looks down their noses in disdain at a small congregation of Christians which focuses on the sufficiency of Jesus Christ in their lives. They are regarded as unsuccessful, having little power or impact upon society. But if they have entered through the door of the Person and work of Jesus Christ into the kingdom of God, then no one can shut them out despite the worldly expectations of religion.

Continuing His observation of the situation in Philadelphia, Jesus says, "**Behold I will cause those of the synagogue of Satan, who say that they are Jews, and are not, but lie – behold, I will make them to come and bow down at your feet, and to know that I have loved you**" (3:9). The Jewish religionists in Philadelphia at the end of the first-century were as persecutive of the early Christians as were the other forms of religion. Historically the adherents of Jewish religion have por-

3:9

trayed themselves as the foremost victims of religious persecution, and they have certainly had their share, but they have also administered discriminatory persecution of others through the ages and are still doing so today.

There was a Jewish synagogue in Philadelphia, but the risen Lord Jesus calls it a "synagogue of Satan." This is similar to the time when Jesus told the Jewish leaders who were claiming that they were of their father, Abraham, "You are of your father, the devil" (John 8:44).

The Jewish religionists in Philadelphia claimed to be Jews, but Jesus declares that they were not Jews. Race, religion or heritage does not constitute a true Jew in the sight of God. The word "Jew" means "to the praise of God." The Israelite people of the Old Testament were selected to be the pictorial pre-figuring of the "people of God" who would function "to the praise of God." They did not function as such in faithfulness and thus did not serve as an adequate picture of the "people of God" in Christ Jesus, the Christian community. They forfeited their designation as "Jews," as "Israel," as the "People of God," the "chosen people." Racial and religious and nationalistic Jews who carry an Israeli passport are not real Jews in the sight of God any longer. Paul explains that "he is a Jew, who is one inwardly...by the circumcision of the heart, by the Spirit" (Rom. 2:29). The apostle goes on to explain that "they are not all Israel, who are descended from Israel" (Rom. 9:6), but that Christians now formulate the "Israel of God" (Gal. 6:16). Christians are now the real Jews in the sight of God, the spiritual "people of God" who are to function "to the praise of God" in Jesus Christ. Anyone who claims to be a Jew and is not a Christian is telling a lie. Jesus explained that those who went to the synagogue in Philadelphia and claimed to be Jews, were really not Jews, and were lying. Of course, Jesus had told the Jewish leaders on a previous occasion that they were identified with "their father, the devil...he is a liar, and the father of lies" (John 8:44).

Jesus went on to explain to the Philadelphian Christians that He would "***make them*** (the physical and religious Jews) ***to come and bow down at your*** (the Christian's) ***feet, and to know that I have loved you***" (3:9). This is consistent with the prophecy of Isaiah when he said, "the sons of those who afflicted you will come bowing to you *(the true Israel)*, and all those who despised you will bow themselves at the soles of your feet; and they will call you the city of the Lord, the Zion of the Holy One of Israel" (Isa. 60:14). Eventually all men will have to recognize that Christians are the "people of God," and "every knee shall bow and every tongue confess that Jesus Christ is Lord" (Phil. 2:10). Eventually all men will know that God has expressed His love for us in His Son Jesus Christ. "God so loved the world that He gave His only begotten Son" (John 3:16). When we receive Jesus Christ by faith we become Christians, the chosen "people of God," true Jews, the "Israel of God." "Who shall separate us from the love of Christ? Shall tribulations, distress, persecution?... Nothing shall be able to separate us from the love of God which is in Christ Jesus our Lord" (Rom. 8:35-39). The Christians of Philadelphia understood that sufficiency and security of God's love, recognizing that no one could shut the door on such, and that eventually it would be revealed for all to see who God's loved ones, God's people, really are Christians.

3:10

In the meantime, of course, religionists always claim to be "God's people." They are really gatherings of the adversary, the antagonist, for all religion is Satan's attempt to obscure and obstruct the church of Jesus Christ. Disguised "as an angel of light,...his servants disguise themselves as servants of righteousness" (II Cor. 11:14,15). Religion is a false profession of identification with God that formulates a parody of Christ's church.

3:10 Based on His observation of their situation in Philadelphia, Jesus assures them, "*Because you have kept the word of My perseverance, I also will keep you from the hour of testing, which is about to come upon the whole world, to test those who dwell upon the earth*" (3:10). What is Jesus telling the Philadelphian Christians, and all Christians of every age, in this verse? The key word, used twice in Jesus' sentence, is "*keep*." The Philadelphian Christians have "*kept*" Christ's word to "bear fruit with perseverance" (Luke 8:15). They have "*kept* His commandments" (John 14:15,23; 15:10; 17:6), "*kept* the faith" (II Tim. 4:7); "*kept* themselves in the love of God" (Jude 21). Jesus explains that He will "*keep* them from the hour of testing, which is about to come upon the whole world, to test those who dwell upon the earth." Although some interpret this to mean that Jesus was promising to keep the entire church out of the final tribulation by rapturing it in what was still the far-off future for the Christians of the first-century, it seems more consistent with the rest of Scripture to interpret Jesus' words in accord with how He previously used the verb *keep* when He asked the Father "to *keep* them (all Christians) from the evil one" (John 17:15). Jesus "*keeps* us from the evil one" (I John 5:18). We are "strengthen and protected" (II Thess. 3:3) by "the power of God" (I Peter 1:5), "rescued from temptation" (II Peter 2:9), for

"God will not allow us to be tempted beyond what we are able" (I Cor. 10:13). We are kept by the Spirit of Christ from "caving in" under the pressures and apostatizing. Jesus is not promising an escapist deliverance from the tribulations of life, but is promising the Christians of Philadelphia and the Christians of all time that He will provide what is necessary for their safekeeping in the midst of the many trials, hardships, and persecutions even unto death that will continually occur within this world.

Jesus seems to indicate that the "hour of testing" is to provide trials for "those who dwell upon the earth." These earth-dwellers are those who are "of this world" (John 17:14), identified with the "god of this world" (II Cor. 4:4), employing "earthly wisdom" (James 3:15). Both Christians and non-Christians have trials in life, but the purpose of trials in the life of a non-Christian are to reveal that he does "not have what it takes" to deal with them, whereas the Christian recognizes therein that he "has what it takes" to endure and persevere through the trials by the sufficiency of Jesus Christ. When Jesus warns that He is "*coming quickly*" (3:11), the most likely meaning is that He will soon be bringing some form of judgment upon those non-Christian "earth-dwellers" who were persecuting the Philadelphian Christians. Christians, on the other hand, are "heaven-dwellers" who are "seated in the heavenlies" (Eph. 2:6) and "citizens of heaven" (Phil. 3:20), and they recognize the spiritual provision of Jesus Christ that "keeps" them through all the providential situations of life.

Religionists are "earth-dwellers" who employ earthly and worldly ways, "which seem right to a man, but

3:11,12

the ends thereof are death" (Prov. 14:12). Often, in identification with the "god of this world" (II Cor. 4:4), they offer a false "easy way out" from the trials of life. Whenever religion offers an escapism from present problems and future tribulation, beware that they are not offering the "keeping power" that Jesus was extending to the Philadelphian Christians and Christians in every age.

3:11 The command of Jesus to the Philadelphians was to **"*hold fast what you have, in order that no one take your crown*"** (3:11). What did they "have" to which they were to "hold fast?" They had "all things" (I Cor. 3:21-23) in Christ, who is the "sum of all spiritual things" (Eph. 1:10). They were to "hold fast" to Christ in faith, to "hold fast their profession" (Heb. 4:14), and "hold fast His name" (Rev. 2:13). In so doing no one could take away that imperishable victory wreath (I Cor. 9:25), that "crown of righteousness that is laid up... for all who have loved His appearing" (II Tim. 4:8). Like the "crown of life" promised to the Christians at Smyrna, this is the crown of victory (*stephanos*), which Christians expect to receive at the ultimate victory celebration when Christ's victory is consummated for all time.

3:12 The promises of the risen Lord Jesus to the Philadelphian Christians are then expressed when Jesus says, **"*He who overcomes, I will make him a pillar in the temple of My God, and he will not go out from it any more; and I will write upon him the name of My God, and the name of the city of My God, the new Jerusalem, which comes down out of heaven from My God, and My new name*"** (3:12). To all who overcome the temptation to revert to religion by "holding fast" to the

Overcomer (John 16:33), Jesus promises that they will be made "a pillar in the temple of God."

Religion is so quick to pervert this, for they are most concerned with pillars and spires in physical buildings or temples, as evidenced by the temples that abounded in Philadelphia. They fail to understand that "God does not dwell in houses built by hands" (Acts 7:48; 17:24). In addition, religion encourages men to aspire to become "pillars" of leadership in the church (Gal. 2:9), often without any understanding of how Christ leads His church.

Jesus is telling Christians that by faithful receptivity of His life and ministry, they become an integral part of the church. The church is "the temple of the living God" (I Cor. 3:16; II Cor. 6:16), "fitted together, growing into a holy temple in the Lord" (Eph. 2:20-22). Christians are "living stones, being built up as a spiritual house for a holy priesthood" (I Peter 2:5). Functioning now as the collective "temple" in which God dwells and reigns, we look forward to the heavenly "temple" (Rev. 7:15; 21:22) and the perfect reign of God in Christ. Jesus goes on to explain that when we are a functioning part of the Church, the temple of God, in spiritual union with the Overcomer, Jesus Christ, we have an assurance that we have identified with the ultimate reality of the universe, and "will not go out from it any more" for we have found everything we need in Him. Some have speculated that Jesus may have been making a reference to the fact that the Philadelphians had "gone out" and fled the temples of their city many times when the unsettling earthquakes came, but since Christians are part of a spiritual temple, they never need to go out regardless of how unsettling the circumstances around them.

3:12

Furthermore Jesus promises Christians who overcome in Christ that He will write upon them the name of God, the name of the city of God, and His new name. Why all this emphasis on names? It might be an allusion to the Philadelphian tendency to keep changing the name of their city to identify with a Roman emperor, something they had already done twice in the century prior to Jesus' address here in the Revelation. This is indicative of religion to clamor after "names" of celebrities and important people. Jesus is promising Christians far more than a titular name. He is promising a permanent identification with the character of God. The prophet Isaiah indicated that God was going to provide "in My house and within My walls a memorial, ...I will give them an everlasting name which will not be cut off" (Isa. 56:5). Christians do receive a new everlasting name in Christ; we become "Christ-ones" in whom Christ lives forever.

In Christ we are identified as citizens of the "city of God, the New Jerusalem, the heavenly city." Religion has tried to engage in "city-building" ever since they tried to build the "tower of Babel" (Gen. 11:4-9). Again and again they have attempted to construct social community, but the city that religious man builds is but an evil Babylon that is nothing more than a parody of the City of God. But Christians who are faithfully functioning as overcomers participate in the New Jerusalem, the new spiritual "city of peace" "whose builder is God" (Heb. 11:10,16). We have "come to Mount Zion, to the city of the living God, the heavenly Jerusalem" (Heb. 12:22), and "the Jerusalem above is free" (Gal. 4:26). The genuine interpersonal relationships that the personal, triune God intended for man are to be found only in true Christian community in the Body of Christ, the church. Therein we are free to relate to one another in love and joy and peace and patience, expressing God's character one to another and functioning as God intended man to function, unto His glory.

In order to do so, we must continue to listen to God, to be discerning and obedient. *"He who has an ear, let him hear what the Spirit says to the churches"* (3:13). Apart from that constant spiritual communion with God we cannot experience all that God has for us in Jesus Christ.

Religion and the Church in Laodicea

Revelation 3:14-22

The original name of the city of Laodicea was Diospolis, meaning "city of Zeus." Antiochus II renamed the city in the middle of the third century B.C., naming it after his wife, Laodice. The name Laodicea is etymologically derived from two Greek words, *laos* meaning "people," and *dike* meaning "to judge" or "to decide." This name became particularly appropriate for the citizens of Laodicea, since they seem to have been quite interested in self-determination and self-rule and deciding for themselves. "We the people" will do as we please!"

The city was located on a plateau about 100 feet above the Lycus River valley. The Romans developed Laodicea into a major trade center, the hub of three major trade routes. Laodicea was part of a tri-city area (Col. 4:13) that included Hierapolis, six miles to the north, and Colossae, eleven miles to the east. Ephesus was about 100 miles to the west of Laodicea.

Being an important trade center, many in Laodicea became quite wealthy. Laodicea became the banking center of the region. The citizens were apparently so affluent and the city coffers so well-invested that when a major earthquake damaged the city in 60 A.D., they declined "imperial disaster aid." The historian Tacitus noted that they "recovered by their own resources."

3:14

One drawback to this well-settled city was the lack of a natural water supply. There were hot-springs in Hierapolis, six miles up the river valley, but by the time the water flowed down to Laodicea it was tepid and so full of minerals that it was distasteful. Jesus may have been alluding to this fact in the comments He makes to the church at Laodicea.

Religion was alive and well in Laodicea. Since the city had originally been Diospolis, "the city of Zeus," there was obviously a temple to Zeus, the foremost god in the Greek pantheon. There was a famous medical school in Laodicea apparently associated with Aesculapius, the Greek god of healing. This medical school had developed a "Phrygian powder" which was used as an eyesalve. Adding to the religious diversity of Laodicea were 7000 adult Jewish males who had been granted the right to preserve their religious customs in Laodicea.

The Church of Jesus Christ in Laodicea was probably established during Paul's extended stay in Ephesus (Acts 19:10; 20:31). Epaphrus may have been a native of the region who became a Christian under Paul's ministry in Ephesus, and later shared the gospel of Jesus Christ in the tri-city area (Col. 1:7; 4:12).

3:14 In beginning His message to the church at Laodicea, Jesus identifies Himself as "***The Amen, the faithful and true Witness, the Beginning of the creation of God***" (3:14). The self-sufficient Laodiceans needed to remember the source of all sufficiency. Jesus Christ, as God, is the creative source of all things. "All things came into being by Him, and apart from Him nothing came into being that has come into being" (John 1:3). That form of religion which seeks to deny the deity of

Jesus Christ, often interprets the statement that Jesus is "the Beginning of the creation of God" to mean that Jesus was the first thing God created. (They do the same with Col. 1:15). Not so! Jesus was "in the beginning with God, and was God" (John 1:1). As the eternal Word, Jesus is the "faithful and true Witness" who expresses and images God visibly within His creation. In His redemptive mission He faithfully exhibited the reality of deity within humanity even unto a martyr's death, wherefrom He was raised from the dead. Jesus is the "Amen," the essence and the validation of God. Religion in every age tends to think that man can create his own destiny, give witness to the veracity of his own conclusions, and affirm such with the punctuations of his own "amens."

As in all His addresses to the churches, Jesus begins His observations of the situation in the church at Laodicea by saying, "*I know your deeds...*" (3:15). In this case their deeds are not "wrought in God," and are therefore "dead works." **3:15**

Jesus continues His observations charging, "*You are neither cold nor hot; I would that you were cold or hot. So because you are lukewarm, and neither hot nor cold, I will spit you out of My mouth.*" The Christians in Laodicea were not "fervent in spirit" (Rom. 12:11), burning with zeal and excitement about the life of the Lord Jesus. Neither were they totally chilled to the point of apostatizing. Instead they were just lukewarm, tepid, apathetic and indifferent. Does this not picture the bland tepidity so often evident in religion? Attempting to cater to everyone at the same time, they take the "middle of the road" approach in order to appease the majority. Jesus is not content with such **3:16**

3:17

half-hearted neutrality. On an earlier occasion Jesus said, "He who is not with Me, is against Me" (Matt. 12:30). Jesus finds such dispassionate compromising to be nauseating and repulsive. He rejects such and would rather "spit you out of My mouth," that is, expel and repudiate such insipid and disinterested followers who do not appreciate what they have been given in Christ, and misrepresent such by their attitude and behavior. Vituperative antagonism is to be preferred over vacillating and vapid neutrality.

3:17 The Laodiceans had been lulled into misplaced security and misplaced sufficiency. They claimed that they were "*rich and wealthy, and had need of nothing*" (3:17). In the Old Testament the prophet Hosea lamented that some of God's people, and in particular Ephraim, said "Surely I have become rich, I have found wealth for myself" (Hosea 12:8), and the Lord was provoked to anger. Jesus had mentioned the rich man who said, "Soul, you have many goods...eat, drink and be merry," and God said, "You fool; this night your soul is required of you" (Luke 12:19).

Religion often fosters a false-security in physical wealth and riches. Time and time again religious "prosperity doctrines" have promised health and wealth to unsuspecting followers. Many religious groups cater only to the affluent and wealthy who can "dress for success." Perhaps the Laodiceans had been drawn in to such religious folly.

The Laodiceans were "banking" on their material riches, and were forgetting the prior command of Jesus when He said, "Lay not up for yourselves treasures upon earth, where moth and rust destroy, and where thieves break in and steal. But lay up for yourselves treasures in heaven, where neither moth nor rust destroys, and where thieves do not break in or steal: for where your treasure is, there will your heart be also" (Matt. 6:19-21).

In their self-sufficiency the Laodiceans claimed to have "need of nothing." It is the utmost of arrogant audacity for any man to claim that he is so self-sufficient that he has "need of nothing." Man is a derivative creature who is nothing, has nothing and can do nothing (John 15:5) in and of himself. We are needful creatures. We are in need of everything being provided for our identity, sustenance and activity. "Not that we are sufficient in ourselves, to consider anything as coming from ourselves, but our sufficiency is of God" (II Cor. 3:5). "My God shall supply all your needs according to His riches in glory in Christ Jesus" (Phil. 4:19).

Contrary to this need-awareness explained throughout the Scriptures, religion promotes humanistic self-sufficiency. The abundance of religious "self-help programs" being offered encourage people to assert, "I can do it; I don't need any help!" Joining the Laodiceans, they claim to have "need of nothing."

When a Christian recognizes that Jesus Christ is his sufficiency for all things, for his identity, his sustenance and his activity, then it can be affirmed that he is "lacking in nothing" (James 1:4). This is a recognition of spiritual sufficiency in Christ, rather that the false-sufficiency claimed by the Laodiceans based on their physical and material abundance.

3:18

Despite what the Laodicean Christians thought they had, Jesus explains to them that they are "*wretched and miserable and poor and blind and naked*" (3:17). They thought they had it all physically, but spiritually they were bankrupt. They were deceived, having no spiritual discernment. In their complacency they were not even aware of how miserable and wretched their condition really was. Thinking themselves to be rich, they were spiritually poor. Thinking themselves to be wise and to be able to "see things as they really are," they were spiritually blind. Thinking themselves to be clothed in moral cloaks of right behavior, they were spiritually naked. Were they not in the unenviable position of the emperor in the tale told by Hans Christian Anderson of *The Emperor's New Clothes*? Parading around in the pretense of having the best of everything, they only revealed their spiritual bankruptcy, blindness and nakedness.

3:18 Jesus advises the Laodicean Christians to make some faith responses whereby their spiritual lack can be supplied by Himself. In terms that the consumer-oriented Laodiceans could understand, Jesus urged them "*to buy from Me...*" (3:18). What Jesus has for us is not really "for sale" in any monetary market; it cannot be "bought." God's gracious provision can only be received by faith our receptivity of His activity. The prophet Isaiah foretold the availability of all things in Jesus Christ within the new covenant, saying, "You who have no money come, buy and eat...without money and without cost. ...Delight yourself in abundance" (Isa. 55:1,2). In fulfillment of this, Jesus makes available the solution to all the spiritual needs of the Laodicean Christians by advising them to "buy without cost," receive God's grace from Him.

The first investment the Laodiceans are encouraged to make is *"to buy from Jesus gold refined by fire, that they might become rich"* (3:18). The Laodiceans thought they were rich already (3:17), as do many religious organizations with accumulated assets and holdings totalling billions of dollars. Religion does not understand spiritual riches in Christ. Jesus indicates that we need to acquire that which is of spiritual value, which He calls "gold refined by fire." "Gold refined by fire" is best explained as the tested life of Jesus Christ, which was tested in the crucible of crucifixion. "In Christ are hidden all the treasures of wisdom and knowledge" (Col. 2:3), the "wealth that comes from a true knowledge of Christ" (Col. 2:2). When we receive Him by faith we have "the treasure in earthen vessels" (II Cor. 4:7), the "surpassing riches of His grace" (Eph. 1:7; 2:7), the "riches of the glory of His inheritance" (Eph. 1:18). Continuing to derive the fulfillment of all our needs by faith in Christ, we discover such "faith... more precious than gold which is perishable, even though tested by fire" (I Peter 1:7), for we might also experience the testing of the "gold" of Christ's life in the fires of personal adversity and suffering. His is the tested life more valuable than physical gold, which will persevere no matter how hot the fire gets.

Second, the Laodicean Christians and all Christians in every age are *"to buy...white garments, that they might clothe themselves, and the shame of their nakedness may not be revealed"* (3:18). Public nakedness was the ultimate shame and humiliation of the ancient world. Through the prophet Nahum the Lord says to Nineveh, "I will...show to the nations your nakedness, and to the kingdoms your disgrace" (Nahum 3:5). Christians are to clothe themselves in "white garments," representing the purity and holiness of the character of Christ. Later in the Revelation the bride, the church, is clothed in "fine linen, bright and clean...the righteous acts of the saints" (19:8), in preparation for the marriage of the Lamb. Religion seeks to substitute the ecclesiastical robes of hierarchy and the moral cloaks of social conformity, but the risen Lord Jesus requires that we "put on" the character of His righteousness in our behavior.

To solve the problem of spiritual blindness, Jesus advises Christians *"to buy...eyesalve to anoint your eyes, that you may see"* (3:18). Remember that the Laodicean medical school was renowned for its "Phrygian powder" that helped to relieve physical eye problems. After healing the man born blind Jesus said that those who "see may become blind," and "those who do not see may see" (John 9:39), because His priority was to address spiritual blindness so that people might see spiritual realities. The Psalmist requested, "Open my eyes that I may behold wonderful things from Thy Law" (Psalm 119:18), which revealed Jesus Christ. Paul prays for the Ephesians that the "eyes of their heart might be enlightened, that they might know the hope of His calling" (Eph. 1:17). Only by the presence of Jesus Christ in us do we "see" and "appraise spiritual things" (I Cor. 2:15) in order to see from God's perspective.

3:19   Having explained that spiritual riches, spiritual clothing and spiritual eyesight are found only in Himself, Jesus warns, *"Those whom I love, I reprove and discipline"* (3:19). Concerned that all men might be restored to the fullness of God's intent, Jesus is actively engaged in the disciplinary processes that keep Christians "on track." By the correcting and reproving work of His Spirit, He seeks to preserve us in His finishing work. "Whom the Lord loves He reproves" (Prov. 3:12). "Do not regard lightly the discipline of the Lord" (Heb. 12:5). "He disciplines us for our good, that we may share His holiness" (Heb. 12:10). Religion attempts to skirt around the reproof and disciplines of the Lord. Focusing on a syrupy and sentimental understanding of a loving God who always forgives and never censures, they by-pass God's active discipline and direction in Christian lives. What kind of a loving Father would forego the "tough love" that seeks the highest good of His children? Not the God who "is love" (I John 4:8,16).

The commands of Jesus to the Laodicean Christians, and to every Christian, are "***be zealous***" and "***repent***" (3:19). The word for "zealous" in the Greek text is from the same root as the word for "hot" in verses 15 and 16. This does not mean that we are to turn on the head of emotional excitement and excess, as happens in many religious environs. Rather, as the Christian allows the life of Jesus Christ to be operative in him, there we be a fervor, a passion, an enthusiasm about functioning as God intended. In order to do so, we must first "repent" of all the false religious methods of living the Christian life. We must "change our mind" so as to recognize our own inability, and "change our action" by allowing for the receptivity of His activity in our behavior by faith.

The ready availability of Jesus Christ to provide everything necessary in the Christian life is expressed in Jesus' words, "***Behold, I stand at the door and knock; if any one hears My voice and opens the door, I will come in to him, and will dine with him, and he with Me***" (3:20). Though religionists have long misused and abused this verse as an evangelistic appeal to unbelievers, it is the appeal of Jesus for intimate communion with Christians. Christians have already received the Spirit of Christ into their spirit or else they are not Christians (Rom. 8:9), but Jesus does not "force" His way into our behavioral expression. He makes His presence known by "knocking at the door," and those who are His "hear His voice and open the door." Jesus said earlier, "My own know Me...My sheep hear My voice" (John 10:14,16). "Everyone who is of the Truth, hears My voice" (John 18:37). Christians who are receptive to what Christ wants to do in their lives, open the door to participate in spiritual fellowship with the risen Lord Jesus, allowing Him to reside, abide and settle-in to the abode of their soul. Dining with Him now, partaking with and of Him, they look forward also to the "supper of the Lamb" (Rev. 19:9) when they will "eat and drink at His table in the kingdom" (Luke 22:30).

3:21 Thus Jesus promises to those Christians who overcome the solicitations to revert to religion by faithful receptivity from the One who has "overcome the world" (John 16:33), "*I will grant to him to sit down with Me on My throne, as I also overcame and sat down with My Father on His throne*" (3:21). Religion indicates that we "overcome" by conquering, battling or working diligently for "God's cause." Not so! We overcome by identifying with the Overcomer, the Lord Jesus Christ. In one sense we are already "seated with Him in the heavenly places" (Eph. 2:6), but there is a yet future consummation of Christ's victory when we "shall sit upon the throne, judging the tribes of Israel" (Matt. 19:28). Having endured, "we shall also reign with Him" (II Tim. 2:12). Christ overcame all temptations by the same faithful receptivity of the Father, and "sat down with His Father on His throne." Christ is "seated at the right hand of God in the heavenlies, far above all rule and authority and power and dominion" Eph. 1:20-22). "The High Priest has taken His seat at the right hand of the throne of the Majesty in the heavens" (Heb. 8:1).

Christians must have spiritual discernment *"to hear what the Spirit says to the churches"* (3:22). Only as we "listen under" the tutelage of the Spirit of Christ will we respond in obedience to be and do all that Jesus Christ wants to be and do in us. Thereby we can avoid the religious perversions that were creeping into the seven churches, and the similar satanic solicitations by which we are constantly tempted to misrepresent who we are in Christ.

Religion and the Seals

Revelation 4:1 – 8:1

As John begins to relate the second of the visions of the Revelation there is a movement from the *"historicals"* to the *"pictorials."* The seven churches of Asia were historical churches engaged in historical situations at the end of the first century. They provide the setting and the historical springboard from which the entirety of the Revelation is to be interpreted. Even though they are historically rooted at the end of the first century, they represent all congregations of Christians in every age, and the repetitive propensity of Christians to succumb to the temptation of substituting "religion" for the genuine dynamic of the life of Jesus Christ. In chapter four and following the style of the Revelation changes to pictorial imagery, but this style-change must not be used to divorce what follows from the preceding historical and textual context. Any legitimate interpretation of the Revelation must preserve a continuity with the setting and the subject introduced in chapters one through three. The unity of the Revelation must be preserved, otherwise it becomes a sequence of "revelations," as it is sometimes mistakenly referred to. There is no logical or chronological chasm between chapters three and four. There is no real change of theme or time, subject or setting, between the third and fourth chapters.

4:1 – 8:1

There is much diversity of interpretation among Christians at this point. (*See charts in Addendum E and F*). The *preterist* interpretation does not posit a change of theme or time between chapters three and four. The subject/theme of the preterist interpretation is fixed in the survival of first-century Christians under persecutive first-century conditions. The preterist interpretation lacks a transgenerational subject/theme that transcends all of time, and a translocational time/setting allowing the Revelation to apply to all Christian peoples in all ages.

The *historicist* interpretation embarks on a sequential chronological review of Western history. The subject/theme is progressively transgenerational, but the historicist interpretation does not have a translocational setting, for it is limited to Western history and an arbitrarily applied sequence thereof.

The *futurist* interpretation posits a great chronological gap between chapters three and four of the Revelation. Chapters two and three are interpreted as in the historical context of the first century, or sometimes figuratively applied to a progressive sequence of Western church history. Chapter four is then interpreted as applying to an alleged "tribulation period" of the yet future. This is a most radical exegetical leap of interpretative logic and chronology which creates an almost total severance of subject/theme and time/setting from the foregoing chapters. The interpretive necessity of historical and textual context is ignored. The futurist interpretation does not have a transgenerational subject/theme, nor does it have a translocational time/setting.

The *triumphalist/idealist* interpretation maintains the best contextual consistency of subject/theme and time/setting. This interpretation explains that there is a transgenerational theme throughout the Revelation whereby all Christians in every age are intended to understand the victory of Jesus Christ in the "enigma of the interim" between His physical comings. There is a translocational setting that is not limited to the past of the first century, nor to future events, but allows Christians in every century to find the Revelation personally applicable and to recognize the victory of Christ in the midst of their circumstances of life.

Employing the latter of the interpretive methods throughout this study, we can see the timeless Christocentric proclamation of "the revelation of *Jesus Christ*" (1:1). The Revelation was completely applicable to the Christians of the past centuries, is entirely applicable to Christians today, and will be fully applicable to the Christians of future times. The victory of Jesus Christ is recognized as being already realized, presently operative, and not yet fully consummated, therefore to be hoped for. This interpretive perspective provides a much-needed explanation of how Christians are to function in the present, enduring, persevering, and "abiding under" the pressures and problems of life by recognizing the sufficiency of God's grace in Jesus Christ. The way out is through! The much-needed distinguishing between Christianity and "religion" in every age is also to be noticed throughout the Revelation.

The contextual consistency of the triumphalist/idealist interpretation maintains the comprehensive and extensive import of the Revelation. The pictorial images of chapters four to seven become the second "frame" or "view" or "camera angle" of the images of the great visionary "movie in the round." They are the first "variation" in the eternal symphonic musical composition of God's Revelation.

So what is the time-frame of the action being pictured in chapters four and following? God is the great 'I AM" (Exod. 3:14) who is not proscribed by time and space. He is eternally present tense. In the eternity of God's realm and perspective, one does not have to ascribe a particular time/space parameter for His activities. The pictured action does not necessarily have to be chronologically sequential. It can be timelessly applicable.

Celebration of Victory

The scene for the pictures in chapters four and five is in the eternity of the heavenly realm. Having promised the Christians in the seven churches of Asia that overcomers would see the victory in Christ, the risen Lord Jesus goes on to give a picture of the victory celebration in the heavenlies. John was invited to view and describe the throne-room of God. From the heavenly "control-center," it is obvious that God has central authority in the sovereign transcendence of His majestic power. God has it all "under control." What is taking place on earth in the "enigma of the interim" is not taking God by surprise. Consistent with the obvious theme of conflict between God and Satan, between Christianity and "religion" throughout the Revelation, Caird[1] uses the illustration of a military headquarters with geographical maps on the wall. The commander is moving flags to different positions. This action of placing flags on a map is obviously symbolic, and may be descriptive of positions won, or may be determinative of positions they expect to occupy. In God's eternal foreknowledge the descriptive and the determinative may be one and the same, as might be the case in the Revelation.

In the scene that John describes throughout the Revelation there is an obvious celebration of victory. In each of the "camera angles" that John recorded with his literary camcorder, God in Christ is seen to be the victor and worthy of praise. Christ's "finished work" in the cross and resurrection is the basis of His victorious power (5:6,9; 7:14), for "He was declared the Son of God with power by the resurrection from the dead" (Rom. 1:4). The conflict that led to His suffering and death, though, is continued in those who are identified with Him and in whom Jesus Christ dwells. The life of Christ in Christians will elicit the same conflict with satanic religion that Jesus incurred while incarnated on earth, leading to continued personal suffering and physical death. This is what the Christians of the first century, and of every age thereafter, need to remember when their lives and the activities of the church do not appear to be very victorious. The Scriptures are abundantly clear about this identification with suffering and death, explaining that Christians will be hated (John 15:18), persecuted (Mark 10:30; John 15:20; II Cor. 4:9; II Tim. 3:12); afflicted (Col. 1:24); suffer (Acts 9:16; Rom. 8:17; II Cor. 1:5; Phil. 3:10; Col. 1:24; I Pet. 2:21; 4:13); experience tribulation (John 16:33; Acts 14:22;Rev. 1:9); and experience death (II Cor. 4:10,11; Phil. 3:10). Christians who understand this are the only ones who can "see" the victory in the midst of the ongoing conflict, and sing praises to God and Christ. Such Christians, along with John, already have a glimpse of the heavenly hymns of victory that are recorded particularly in chapters four and five of the Revelation.

4:1 – 8:1

Note the progressive extension of the choirs singing praise to God and Christ. First there is the hymn of the four living creatures (4:8), then the hymn of the twenty-four elders (4:11), then the hymn of the four living creatures and the twenty-four elders (5:9), then the hymn of the four living creatures, the twenty-four elders and myriads of angels (5:12), and then the hymn of every creature in heaven and on earth and under the earth and on the sea (5:13). Notice also the axiological emphasis of their praises. The word translated "worthy" in 4:11; 5:2,4,9,12 is the Greek word *haxios*, from which we get the English words "axiom" and "axiological." An axiom is a worthy, self-evident statement. "Axiological" has reference to a worthy determination of values and judgments. The ultimate "worth" of all things and peoples is in relation to Jesus Christ! Christians in the "enigma of the interim" when victory over world forces and religious pretenders does not seem apparent, are faced with axiological determinations of "worthiness," as to whether they regard Jesus Christ as the worthy investment of their lives, even unto death, banking on His victory. Is Jesus Christ the worthy axis of the universe to which all else must be related and around which all else turns; the One to whom all worthiness should be ascribed in praise?

The risen Lord Jesus is assuring the Christians at the end of the first-century and the Christians of every age through these pictorial images that His victory which He won on the cross when He said, "It is finished!" (John 19:30), is indeed the victory that can be counted on now by Christians in the midst of trial, and that the ultimate expression of that victory will be consummated in the heavenly glory with eternal hymns of praise. The intent of the Christic Story-teller is the same as His intent in all of His story-telling including the parables and analogies recorded in the gospel accounts. He is emphasizing the radical character of what God has made available in the new covenant, the restoration of God's intent for man, the kingdom which operates by divine grace, the judgment upon those who reject such, particularly the "religionists" who oppose and counteract God's work in His Son, Jesus Christ, and the expectant hope that Christians can have for participation in the eternal victory celebration in heaven.

John begins this segment of His visionary record by noting the chronological sequence of his viewing. "*After these things,*" after the things viewed in chapters one through three, he saw "*a door open in heaven*" (4:1). A door must be opened for man to see heavenly realities and look into the presence of God. Perhaps this is the door that was opened by Christ, making the way to heaven open by His crucifixion and resurrection. John heard "*the first voice which...was like a trumpet,*" the same voice he records having heard in 1:10, inviting him to "*Come and see what must take place after these things*" (4:1). After the historical situation of the seven churches at the end of the first-century, we are granted a panoramic picture of the activity that takes place in the "enigma of the interim." There is nothing in these words that would indicate a chronological gap that jumps thousands of years to the time of the so-called "Tribulation Period." The transgenerational subject/theme and the translocational time/setting allow for reference to events throughout Christian history.

4:1

Controlled by the Holy Spirit, i.e. "*in the spirit,*" John sees "*One sitting on a throne*" (4:2). Jesus had just promised the Christians of Laodicea that they

4:2

4:3-5

might "sit with Him and the Father on His throne" (3:21). The throne signifies one who is in control, ruling and victorious.

4:3 Similar to the vision of Ezekiel (Ezek. 1:26-28), there was a brilliant and dazzling luminance which describes the presence of God (4:3), an "unapproachable light" (I Tim. 6:16) in which God is cloaked (Ps. 104:2), and the appearance of a *"rainbow around the throne"* which was a symbol of God's covenant (Gen. 9:16) of His faithfulness, mercy and sovereignty. As a purposeful counterfeit, the anti-Christian New Age religion uses the symbol of the rainbow today.

4:4 Around the throne of God, John saw *"twenty-four elders sitting on thrones"* (4:4). The number "twelve" seems to be the number illustrative of God's People, as there were twelve patriarchs in the old covenant and twelve apostles in the new covenant (21:12-14). The twenty-four elders represent the full complement of God's People from both old and new covenant periods, this being the predominantly accepted interpretation since the earliest centuries of church history. These twenty-four elders were "clothed in white garments" of Christ's righteousness and had golden victory-wreath "crowns on their heads," in identification with Christ's victory.

4:5 John saw and heard *"flashes of lightning and sounds and peals of thunder"* (4:5), representing God's presence, majesty and power. Moses saw and heard such when He came into the presence of God on Sinai (Exod. 19:16); Elihu describes God's presence as such (Job. 37:1-5); the Psalmist describes God's activity in such language (Ps. 77:18). The fullness of the work of the Holy Spirit was also evident to John as represented by the "*seven lamps of fire which are the seven Spirits of God*" (4:5). God appears to have been separated from the rest of creation, distanced by a "*sea of glass like crystal*" (4:6).

4:6

In and around the throne of God, John saw "*four living creatures*" (4:6), like unto *a lion, a calf, a man and an eagle* (4:7). This is similar to Ezekiel's vision recorded in Ezek. 1:5-28 where he saw "four living beings." The imagery is also similar to that seen by Isaiah where he saw angelic seraphim calling out "Holy, Holy, Holy is the Lord of hosts" (Isa. 6:3). The "four living creatures" may represent the complete order of angelic beings, or they may represent the whole order of animate creation. Whoever they are, they have penetrating insight "*full of eyes in front and behind*" (4:7,8), and they recognize and praise the holiness of the "*Lord God, the Almighty, who was and who is and who is to come*" (4:8), in the eternality of His divine activity.

4:7

4:8

Seeing the "*glory and honor and thanks*" expressed to God by the "four living creatures" (4:9), the "twenty-four elders cast their derived victory crowns before the throne" and worship God also (4:10). They express the worthiness of God *to receive glory and honor and power* based on His creative work (4:11), in like manner as David explained that "the heavens declare the glory of God" (Psalm 19:1).

4:9

4:10

4:11

John then explains the primary props around which this second section of the revelatory vision is cast. In God's hand was a scroll with writing on both sides of the papyrus (5:1), similar to the scroll Ezekiel saw (Ezek. 2:9,10). Perhaps the two-sided writing indi-

5:1

5:2-5

5:2 cates the extensive and comprehensive content of the scroll. The scroll was "sealed with seven seals" (5:1), again bearing similarity to the vision of Isaiah about a "sealed scroll" (Isa. 29:11,12). John saw and heard a "strong angel" (cf. 10:1; 18:21) ask *"Who is worthy to break the seals and open the scroll?"* (5:2). No one

5:3 *"in heaven, on the earth, or under the earth"* was able to do so (5:3), perhaps suggesting the unworthiness of all creation because of sin, or perhaps just the inability of any part of the created order to perceive from God's perspective and to understand the full extent of His sovereignty.

5:4 John, the tender, loving apostle, admits that he wept when *no one was found worthy* to open the scroll (5:4). These do not seem to be the tears of a thwarted selfish desire to "see the future," but the honest tears of disappointment in the postponement of seeing the ultimate consummation of Christ's victory over all satanic forces. "You would cry too if it happened to you," and if you thought the purpose of God might be thwarted and you could not see Christian faith vindicated at last.

5:5 One of the twenty-four elders told John to *"Stop crying,"* and to look to Jesus (5:5). Is it not true that our whining and weeping ceases when we look away from the unworthiness of the created order to the worthiness of Jesus Christ? The elder said to John, *"Behold, the Lion that is from the tribe of Judah, the Root of David, has overcome so as to open the scroll and its seven seals"* (5:5). These are obvious references to Jesus Christ. The Messianic prophecy of Jacob to his sons referred to a "lion" from the tribe of Judah, from which the scepter of power shall not depart (Gen. 49:9,10), and in fulfillment of such Jesus "was descended from Judah" (Luke 3:33; Heb. 7:14). Likewise Jesus is from the "root of David," as God first explained to David that his "descendant would establish his kingdom" (II Sam. 7:12,16; Ps. 89:4,29,35,36) and the prophets later spoke of the "root" and "branch" of David (Isa. 53:2; Jere. 23:5) who would reign as King. In the first sermon of the church at Pentecost, Peter refers to "God's oath to David to seat one of his descendants upon His throne" (Acts 2:30), and the risen Lord Jesus affirms conclusively "I am the root and the offspring of David" (Rev. 22:16). Jesus has indeed "overcome" the world (John 16:33), having "disarmed the rulers and authorities and triumphed over them" (Col. 2:14,15) in His "finished work" of death, resurrection and Pentecostal restoration.

John saw that the "*Lamb slain*" (5:6,9) was indeed able to break the seals and open the scroll. Such is the redemptive basis of His victory! Isaiah had indicated that the Messiah would be "like a lamb" (Isa. 53:7). John the Baptist introduced Him as "the Lamb of God who takes away the sin of the world" (John 1:29). Peter refers to Jesus as "a lamb unblemished and spotless" (I Peter 1:18), and Paul identifies Christ as the "Passover lamb who has been sacrificed" (I Cor. 5:7). Jesus died as the lamb sacrificed for the sins of mankind, and John sees Him "*standing*" by the throne (5:6), "alive forevermore" (1:18), having risen victorious from His death by crucifixion. As such the "*seven horns*" that John speaks of (5:6) refer to His omnipotent authority, the "*seven eyes*" (5:6) to His omniscient understanding as He functions in the complete activity of the Holy Spirit omnipresently "*sent out into all the earth*" (5:6).

Exercising the authority that is rightfully His by His equality with the Father and by His resurrection from the dead (Matt. 28:18), the risen Lord Jesus took the

5:7 scroll from the authoritative right hand of the Father God (5:7). The four living creatures and the twenty-four
5:8 elders responded in worship. They *"fell down before the Lamb"* (5:8). They each had a harp, which has long been identified as a melodic instrument of praise toward God (Psalm 33:2). Many strange conjectures have been proffered of how Christians will sit around heaven playing harps for eternity, based primarily on this verse and on Revelation 14:2. The four living creatures and the twenty-four elders also had *"golden bowls of incense, which were the prayers of the saints"* (5:8). The aroma of incense has been identified as a sensory metaphor of sweet-smelling prayers of praise unto God. David asked that his "prayer be counted as incense before God" (Psalm 141:2).

5:9 Along with their praise and prayers, John explains that he heard the four living creatures and the twenty-four elders *"sing a new song"* (5:9). Some have identified the "old song" as the song of Moses and Israel recorded in Exodus 15. The Psalmist refers to a "new song of praise" (Ps. 40:3; 98:1). Isaiah prophesies that God will "declare new things" causing His people to "sing to the Lord a new song" (Isa. 42:9,10). The "new things" have been made available in Jesus Christ (Eph. 4:24; Heb. 8:8: 10:20), in response to which we can all sing the "new song." The "new song" expresses the axiological "worthiness" of Jesus Christ to break the seals of the scroll based on His death and resurrection. Murdered by crucifixion, the death of Jesus was the redemptive ransom whereby He "purchased with His blood" the just price that God had declared must be the consequence of sin (Gen. 2:17). The universality of the benefit of Christ's death for all mankind is expressed in its being efficacious for *"every tribe and* *tongue and people and nation"* (5:9). By His historical resurrection and the reception of His life by faith, all Christian persons become *"a kingdom and priests to God"* (5:10), in fulfillment of God's intent that His people should be "a kingdom of priests and a holy nation" (Exod. 19:6). Peter explains that Christians are "a royal priesthood, a holy nation" (I Peter 2:5,9). John referred to our being "a kingdom, priests to God" at the beginning of the Revelation (1:6), and will later refer to our being "priests of God and of Christ, and reigning with Him for a thousand years" (20:6). Christians are indeed "kings and priests," and we "reign in life through Christ Jesus" (Rom. 5:17) "upon the earth" (5:10), anticipating our future reign "over the nations" (2:26) and even "over the angels" (I Cor. 6:3).

5:10

The praise continues as the choirs get larger. Added to the voices of the four living creatures and the twenty-four elders are now the voices of myriads of angels (5:11). Again they express the worthiness of Jesus Christ to be praised and worshipped on the basis of His redemptive sacrifice, and that He is qualified thereby to receive *"power and riches and wisdom and might and honor and glory and blessing"* (5:12). Jesus was "declared the Son of God with power by the resurrection from the dead" (Rom. 1:4), and is "the power of God" (I Cor. 1:24). The riches of God are ours in Him (Eph. 1:7,18; 2:7). He is the "wisdom of God" (I Cor. 24,30). We are "strong in His strength" (Eph. 6:10). By His death He was crowned with "glory and honor" (Heb. 2:9). We are "blessed with every spiritual blessing in heavenly places in Christ Jesus" (Eph. 1:3).

5:11

5:12

The choir eventually swells to include *"every created thing which is in heaven and on the earth and un-*

5:13

der the earth and on the sea, and all things in them" (5:13). They continue to sing praises and to worship the risen Lord Jesus as God, declaring His "***dominion forever***" (5:13) reminiscent of Daniel's vision (Dan. 7:13,14). Later the voices of the martyrs will be added to those singing heavenly hymns of praise (7:10,12).

After this glimpse into the heavenly throne-room of God and His Son, Jesus Christ, and the victory songs of all the created order, John focuses our attention on the seals of the scroll which Jesus breaks (6:1-17; 8:1). Why is it important to go back and consider the breaking of the seals which were introduced earlier (5:1-3)?

Jesus is always realistic about our present condition on earth. We may be able to look to the future and see in a vision the victory celebration of Jesus Christ (chapters four and five), but we are still "in the world" (John 17:11,18) and experiencing the hindrances of that one who is the "god of this world" (II Cor. 4:4), who still has "the power of death" (Heb. 2:14). Faithful Christians continue to be brutalized and killed (Rom. 8:36; 12:1; I Cor. 15:31; II Cor. 4:10,11; Phil. 3:10). Christians are mocked, ostracized, and treated with injustice. Life is not fair in this world! The Christians at the end of the first century were aware of this, as well as Christians in every age since then. The risen Lord Jesus is also aware of what is going on in the world, and by the pictorial representation of the breaking of the seals explains the on-going worldly and religious phenomena over which He is victorious. The victory has been won by His "finished work" (John 19:30) in the past, and we can look forward with hope and assurance to the heavenly consummation of the victory in the future, but the present circumstances seem to loom so large on the horizon of human perspective. We concur with Paul that we are "more than conquerors through Christ" (Rom. 8:37), but the diabolical effects of "the ruler of this world" (John 12:31; 14:30; 16:11) seem to be winning the day, especially that most subtle satanic subterfuge of religion. The conflict between Christ and Satan, between Christianity and religion, continues to rage in every age. Jesus wants to assure Christians in every age that He will be victorious over every diabolic expression of religion which might arise throughout church history.

Revealing Himself to be the only One qualified to break the sequence of the seals, Jesus is encouraging Christians throughout the "enigma of the interim" to remain firm in their identification with Him, the Overcomer. Only by faithful receptivity of His character and activity will Christians participate in His victory. The arena of testing is right now. We live on the battlefield in the midst of spiritual warfare between God and Satan, between Christianity and religion. Day by day, moment by moment, we make the decisions of faith as to whether we will trust Jesus Christ, even unto death and martyrdom. Jesus instructed His followers previously, "Blessed are those who are persecuted for the sake of righteousness. Blessed are you when men revile you, and persecute you, and say all kinds of evil against you falsely, on account of Me" (Matt. 5:10,11). He who "loses his life for My sake, shall find it" (Matt. 10:39).

Some basic questions must be asked in order to arrive at some interpretive meaning to this next sector of the vision in chapter six. Without positing some presuppositions, the subsequent interpretations scatter in diverse directions.

6:1

What does the scroll represent? The scroll was first mentioned in 5:1-5, but it is the seals of that same scroll that are being opened in chapter six, with the seventh seal broken in 8:1. Only by positing some meaning to the contents of the scroll can we explain some significance to its being opened by the seals being broken. Numerous explanations have been proffered. Some have conjectured that the scroll represents the Bible and its contents which only Jesus can open and explain. Some would limit the contents to the Old Testament, while others suppose that the contents of the scroll is the New Testament, God's new covenantal agreement, His "last will and testament" through His Son, Jesus Christ. The "book of life" containing the names of the redeemed has also been suggested since it is mentioned elsewhere in the Revelation (3:5; 13:8; 17:8; 20:12,15; 21:27). Other explanations of the content of the scroll include the "gospel message," God's Plan for the Ages, God's redemptive plan, God's plan for His kingdom, God's foreknowledge of future events, etc. In that the Christians of the first century and every century thereafter have desired to know how all things are going to "turn out," and John was so keen to understand the contents of the scroll that he wept when he thought it might not be opened (5:4), a reasonable explanation of the contents of the scroll might be that it contained God's knowledge and awareness of the spiritual conflict in the "enigma of the interim" between His comings, and how His determined consummation of Christ's victory would be worked out in the future.

Who is responsible for the sealing of the scroll? We know that Jesus Christ is the only One able to break the seals (5:5), but who put them on the scroll in the first place? The two alternative answers to this question would seem to be either God or Satan. Did God put the seals on the scroll, or did Satan put the seals on the scroll? Those who attribute the sealing of the scroll to God are quick to point out that the seven-fold number of the seals represents God's perfect purpose, but could Satan be counterfeiting God's activity? Those who attribute the sealing of the scroll to Satan point out the destructive elements of the sealed activities.

What is the purpose of the scroll being sealed? Obviously God's purpose will be different from Satan's purpose. If God sealed the scroll then the purpose of its being sealed may indicate the sovereign divine control of all things which are "sealed" from the finite understanding of man. The sequential removal of the seals might then represent the progressive disclosure and "revelation" of God's ultimate victory in Jesus Christ despite the apparent victories of religion. If Satan sealed the scroll, then perhaps his purpose was to place his "mark of ownership" on the church, to falsely assert his authority, and to thereby "seal up" the gospel message and God's activity within His church, which Jesus then "breaks" in order to reveal His victory.

What do the seals signify? In Biblical times seals were used for a variety of purposes. They were used as a mark of ownership, as a seal of authority, to certify approval or genuineness. They were used for closure of an object that was to be secret or hidden in order to assure safekeeping and protection against tampering. If God did the sealing of the scroll, then the seals might represent how the infinite panorama of God's sovereign control of all things is "sealed" from man's finite understanding. If Satan sealed the scroll it might represent his desire to close, cover and hide the content of what

6:1

God is doing in His Son, Jesus Christ, in order to keep such unrevealed. The opening of the seals by Jesus Christ might then be the "revelation" of the reality of Jesus Christ and His victorious sufficiency despite the diabolic religious efforts of Satan to misrepresent what God is doing, the very theme we have seen within the Revelation.

Perhaps we have a situation, illustrated by the sealing of the scroll, where both the purposes of God and Satan are served simultaneously. This would not be the first time that the devil was used to serve God's purposes. It would be similar to the occasion when God asked Satan, "Have you considered My servant Job?" (Job 1:8), or when Paul explained that God favored him with a thorn in the flesh, "a messenger from Satan" (II Cor. 12:7). Though God is the essential cause of all things, He is not the culpable and blameworthy cause of evil contrary to His character. The destructive element of the seals as intended by Satan may be allowed and used by God to work out His purpose within His people until the fullness of time when Jesus returns to consummate His victory.

6:1 The first four of the seven seals have similar settings, for when Jesus, *"the Lamb,"* breaks the seals on the scroll, the "four living creatures" respectively invite John to observe what is happening. In each case a different colored horse carries a rider with a particular assignment. These "four horsemen of the Apocalypse" are widely recognized symbols of the Revelation. Though Zechariah saw four chariots drawn by different colored horses (Zech. 6:1-8), there is not any direct evidence for equating the images.

What do the four horsemen of the Revelation represent? Interpretations of their meaning have varied widely, sometimes with explanations that are opposite and antithetical one to the other. Take for example the suggested implications of the *"white horse"* and its conquering rider.

Some have identified the rider of the white horse revealed in the **first seal** as Jesus Christ. Their rationale is that the only other reference to a rider of a white horse in the Revelation (19:11-16) is an obvious reference to Jesus who is "Faithful and True" (19:11), the "Word of God" (19:13, the "King of Kings and Lord of Lords" (19:16). In addition they will explain that Jesus goes forth to conquer (6:2) or overcome by the triumphant progress of the gospel.

In direct contradiction to such an interpretation there are others who identify the rider of the white horse as the "Antichrist." They explain that the *"bow"* (6:2) was a militaristic instrument of destruction, and that the Antichrist is identified with the Destroyer. Likewise they explain that Jesus does not need to go out to *"conquer"* for He has already "overcome the world" (John 16:33), but the Antichrist seeks to conquer mankind in order to thwart Christ's activity.

Aligned in principle with the latter interpretation, it seems more consistent to see all four of the horsemen as destructive phenomena. Though often ingeniously identified as catastrophic events such as famines, world wars or natural disasters in the past, present or future, it seems more viable to identify the action of the four horsemen as the continuing activities of diabolic religionists throughout the history of the church. Religious

6:2

interpreters do not want to address their own devious and devilish motivations, so it is convenient for them to point to historical events as fulfillment of these images rather than to the satanic tendencies of their own religion.

6:2 The rider of the *"white horse"* is masquerading as a pure and righteous victor. The victorious commanders of the marauding armies of old would return to their country or city riding a white stallion/steed as the symbol of self-justified victory. Jesus purposefully did just the opposite. Riding to victory in the "triumphal entry" into Jerusalem, Jesus rode on a donkey to show that His power and victory was not like that of the physical world, explaining "My kingdom is not of this world" (John 18:36). Religionists, on the other hand, disguise themselves as "servants of righteousness" (II Cor. 11:15) as they are led by Satan who "disguises himself as an angel of light" (II Cor. 11:14). The history of religion is replete with their carrying weapons of military violence and their constant clamoring after crowns (as evidenced by the papal crown in Roman Catholicism). Religion goes forth *"to conquer"* (6:2). The Greek word used of the "conquering" activity of the rider of the white horse is *nike*. This is the same root word that was employed in reference to the Nicolaitans (2:6,15), describing religionists who "conquer the people." Religion seeks to conquer the people by whatever means possible in order to build their own "kingdom" and "empire." Constantine is perhaps the prime example of this religious tendency, allegedly having seen a "cross" in the sky and heard a voice saying, "By this sign conquer!" By the self-justified reasoning of "conquering by the cross," religion has conducted militaristic crusades and violent inquisitions throughout history. Religion is deaf to the words, "Not by might nor by power, but by My Spirit, says the Lord of hosts" (Zech. 4:6).

The breaking of the **second seal** reveals a "*red horse*" with a rider whose mission it is to "*take peace from the earth*" (6:4). This horseman has a "*great sword,*" and by his impetus men "*slay one another*" (6:4). Jesus said earlier, "Do not think that I came to bring peace on the earth; I did not come to bring peace, but a sword" (Matt. 10:34). Later He said, "Peace I leave with you; My peace I give to you; not as the world gives" (John 14:27). The world seems to define "peace" as "the absence of conflict," and Jesus knew that His coming would not orchestrate "the absence of conflict." Rather His coming would inflame the conflict of God and Satan, Christianity and religion. Christians are not immune from this spiritual conflict and the physical manifestations of such. The red horse may signify the "bloody" results of hostility, violence, strife and rebellion that have been instigated by religion. Most of the wars of world history have some relation to religious conflict. Religion creates conflicting ideologies which become the *cause celebre* of fundamentalists who will fight to their death to defend their idolatrous ideology. Religion is the banner under which much of the murder, mayhem and slaughter throughout the world has taken place. Only Jesus Christ can expose such and overcome such. 6:4

When Jesus breaks the **third seal** of the scroll He reveals a "*black horse*" with a rider who has "*a pair of scales in his hand*" (6:5). This horse and rider seems to represent the "darkness of injustice." He offers a "*quart of wheat*" or "*three quarts of barley*" for an entire day's wage (6:6). God is "a God of faithfulness, without 6:5

6:6

6:6

injustice" (Deut. 32:4), but religion has administered some of the grossest examples of inequity and injustice among men. Religion uses and abuses people. The expedient "good" of the religious organization and its leaders is foremost. Economic discrimination is rampant in religion as greedy leaders stockpile riches for themselves. They are not "prophets," but are merely engaged for "profit." *"Do not harm the oil and the wine"* (6:6), they cry, for the religionists want to preserve such commodities of luxury for their own self-indulgence. Jesus promised His followers that they would have to renounce all possessions and endure injustice, which often comes at the hand of religion which claims to be God's agent.

6:8

The removal of the **fourth seal** reveals an *"ashen,"* pale-green horse. The Greek word for the horse's color is *chloros*, from which we get the words "chlorine" and "chlorophyll." Perhaps it was a sickly, deathly green; the color of a corpse! The rider of this horse is identified with the name *"Death,"* and he was being followed by *"Hades"* (6:8). We know that "the one having the power of death is the devil" (Heb. 2:14). Hades is to be defined as "the place of the dead." We have already noted that religion fosters physical death as *"men slay one another"* (6:4) over ideological, geographical and political issues. There is no life in religion! There are religious ways that seem right to man, "but the ends thereof are death" (Prov. 14:12). That the pale-green horse and its Death-rider are given *"authority over a fourth of the earth"* (6:8) may not represent merely a geographical limitation but a qualitative limitation of Satan's murderous activity, evidencing that God is still sovereignly in charge and limiting the devil's destruction. Meanwhile religion does *"kill with the sword and* *with famine and with pestilence and by the wild beasts of the earth"* (6:8), representing varied forms of death (Jere. 15:2; 24:10). It is tempting to identify the "wild beasts" as the religionists themselves who know no civility in their attempts to rule with the threat of death and hades, but that might be questionable exegesis. Based on the substitutionary death of Jesus Christ and His resurrection, Paul could taunt the one having the power of death, saying, "O death, where is your victory?" (I Cor. 15:55). Christians are still called upon to follow Jesus "even unto physical death" (2:10), but the "sting of death" has been removed (I Cor. 15:55,56) by the eternal life that we have in Jesus Christ, and we can give "thanks to God, who gives us the victory through our Lord Jesus Christ" (I Cor. 15:57).

The breaking of the **fifth seal** connects with the reality of death by martyrdom that was alluded to within the messages to the seven churches as the Christians there bore the deadly brunt of religious persecution (2:10,13). Christian martyrs through the centuries have suffered from the violence, injustice and death caused by religion. When the fifth seal is removed Jesus reveals *"the souls of those who had been slain because of the word of God, and because of the testimony which that had maintained"* (6:9). These souls are said to be *"underneath the altar"* which would seem to allude to a temple-like scene in heaven, but we know that there is no temple there (Rev. 21:22), so it may indicate that they are "near to the heart of God." Those who have inflicted death upon these Christian martyrs are **"those who dwell on the earth"** (6:10). In contrast to Christians who are "citizens of heaven" (Phil. 3:20), religionists are "earth-dwellers" and "world-agents" of the "god of this world" (II Cor. 4:4). The primary "front" for Satan's

6:11

earth-bound "world-system" is religion. Christians have often failed to recognize that the chief earthly enemy of the Christian faith is religion. Christianity is not be identified with or aligned with religion. Religion is Satan's organized counterfeit and subterfuge to deceive mankind and undermine the work of Christ. It is always antagonistic to Christians. Religion is responsible for more deaths by martyrdom among Christians that any other agent. Many Christians have been murdered in the midst of religious "heresy-hunting" and inquisitions as documented in *Foxe's Book of Martyrs*. Religion then turns around and plays off of the martyrs to create an incentive for their adherents to "measure up" to the sacrifice of the martyrs. It uses martyrs as incentive for vengeance against alleged enemies. It even beatifies martyrs into elevated "saints" to be revered and worshipped instead of Jesus Christ. No wonder the martyrs cry out to God to judge the earth-dwelling religionists and avenge their blood (6:10)! Their cry is not an uncharacteristic cry for retaliatory vengeance, but expresses their desire to see Christianity vindicated against the injustice of religion which has promulgated such murderous martyrdom of faithful Christians.

6:11   The martyrs are given "***white robes***" (6:11) representing the pure and righteous character of Christ, and are told that they "***should rest for a while longer***" (6:11) in the rest of perfection they enjoy in Christ. This mention of "rest" cannot be legitimately used for religious concepts of "soul rest" or "soul sleep" after death, as some have attempted to do. The martyrs are to rest in Christ "***until their fellow servants and their brethren who were to be killed even as they had been, should be completed also***" (6:11). The full measure of those identified with Christ's suffering and the completion of Christian martyrdom will come when Christ returns.

At the breaking of the **sixth seal** by Jesus Christ, John sees a destructive scenario that he can only describe in terms of a complete cosmological upheaval. The images he uses are those of a *"great earthquake,"* the *"sun became black...,"* the *"whole moon became like blood,"* *"the stars of the sky fell to the earth,"* *"the sky was split apart...,"* and *"every mountain and island were moved out of their places"* (6:12-14). If this were referring to an actual cosmological catastrophe then the persons mentioned in verse 15 would have had no place to hide themselves. In the language of hyperbole John uses the figurative metaphors of judgment and destruction (cf. Isa 13::6-11; 34:2-4; Haggai 2:6; Zeph. 1:14,15, etc.). Peter used similar images when he spoke on Pentecost and indicated that the prophecy of Joel 2:28-32 was being fulfilled that day with "wonders in the sky, ...blood, and vapor and smoke, the sun turned into darkness, and the moon into blood" (Acts 2:18-20). When the Spirit of Christ was made available to indwell mankind spiritually there at Pentecost, there was an obvious divine judgment upon Satan's world system described in terms of destruction, dissolution and disintegration. Satan's hold on mankind was being shaken loose, especially the tyranny that he exercises over men in religion. Religion seeks to construct a false security in a social system wherein there is no spiritual enlightenment, no reflection of divine Light, and the guidance of heaven is forsaken. God's judgment will most certainly come to destroy and dissolve the religious world. It will be shaken in violent upheaval and everything will fall apart in disintegration. (Despite such, religion continues to create fear-based reactions

6:12-14

to natural cosmological events and eventual catastrophes to scare people into accepting their bondage, crying, "Earthquakes are a sign that the end is near!")

6:15 When God's judgment comes against religion, men will scurry to *"hide themselves in the caves and among the rocks of the mountains"* (6:15), fearing the day

6:16 of reckoning (Isa. 2:12-17). They will plead that the mountains and rocks fall on them (cf. Hosea 10:1-8), for they fear *"the presence of Him who sits on the throne, and the wrath of the Lamb"* (6:16). Jesus is not just a Lamb "meek and mild," for His wrath will be displayed toward all sin and the religion which fosters

6:17 such. God hates religion! *"Who is able to stand"* in the day of God's wrath (6:17)? Only those who "stand in Christ."

Between the opening of the sixth seal and the seventh seal there is an interval (chapter seven) that serves to add suspense concerning how Christ's victory over religion will be consummated. A somewhat parenthetical interlude is used to explain the continuity and discontinuity that exist between Israel and the Church. This is a much needed explanation, for the primary religious theologies of our day, be they Covenant, Dispensational or otherwise, fail to preserve a Christocentric understanding that recognizes how the promises of God to Israel are fulfilled in Christ and His Body, the Church.[2]

7:1 Explaining the chronological sequence of his viewing, John notes that *"after"* he saw the breaking of the first six seals he saw *"four angels standing at the four corners of the earth, holding back the four winds of the earth"* (7:1). Though the religion of past centuries used the "four angels at the four corners of the earth" as a literalistic proof-text to denounce Copernicus and

Galileo and their observations of the earth being round, what John seems to be describing is that the four angels seem to have the authority to allow the "ill-winds" of religion to sweep in upon the peoples of the earth. The destruction wrought by the "four horsemen" has been enough, and God disallows and prevents any further destructive influence of religion as illustrated by the "four winds."

Another angel ascends from *"the rising of the sun,"* from where Light originates, i.e. from God, *"having the seal of the living God"* (7:2). This angel declares that God's bondservants, i.e. Christians, need to have the seal of God's ownership and possession as protection and safekeeping against further destructive "winds" of religion.

7:2

The number who were thus sealed was *"one hundred and forty-four thousand from every tribe of the sons of Israel"* (7:4). Many varied interpretations have been suggested for the meaning and identity of the "one hundred and forty-four thousand" who were sealed. Some identify these persons as Jews and attempt to use these verses as proof that the twelve tribes of Israel still exist unto the present time. Jehovah Witnesses identify the "one hundred and forty-four thousand" as their own faithful ones. Some identify them as Christian martyrs throughout the history of the church, while others would identify them as Christian "virgins" (14:4). If twelve be accepted as the number representing God's people (see comments on 4:4), then twelve (representing the twelve patriarchs of the old covenant) times twelve (representing the twelve apostles of the new covenant) times one thousand (representing the full complement and magnitude of God's activity) equals

7:4

"one hundred and forty-four thousand." The number is used to refer to the completeness, the full complement of God's People in the new Israel of Christ's Church (cf. Matt. 19:28; Rom. 2:29; 9:6; Gal. 3:29; 6:16).

7:9 Then John, again noting the chronological sequence of his viewing, writes that *"after these things"* he saw *"a great multitude, which no one could count, from every nation and tribe and peoples and tongue, standing before the throne and before the Lamb, clothed in white robes, and palm branches in their hands"* (7:9). Who were the persons in the great multitude? They represent all Christians in every age. Whereas the number "one hundred and forty-four thousand" was used previously to indicate figuratively the full complement of the redeemed, the "multitude which no one could count" is now mentioned to show that God's people are innumerable. Such is a further fulfillment of God's promises to Abraham when He indicated that his spiritual descendants would be more numerous "than the stars" (Gen. 15:5; 22:17; 26:4) and the "sand on the seashore" (Gen. 22:17; 32:12), i.e. innumerable. Those in the multitude are from "every nation, tribe, people and tongue," evidencing the universality of the benefit of the gospel of Jesus Christ for all men. They are "standing before the throne," which gives answer to the question of those identified with religion who asked, "Who is able to stand?" (6:17). All Christians who "stand in Christ Jesus" are thus qualified to stand before God's throne and recognize His authority. In the imagery that John saw, the multitude of Christians was clothed in the "white robes" of Christ's righteousness, having "palm branches in their hands" signifying victory and triumph just as the palm branches represented when they were waved at the triumphal entry of Jesus into Jerusalem on that Sunday morning one week prior to His resurrection.

The Christian multitude expresses a heavenly hymn of praise directed to the "great God and Savior, Christ Jesus" (Titus 2:13), saying *"Salvation to our God who sits on the throne, and to the Lamb"* (7:10). All of creation then joins the multitude in worship of God (7:11,12).

7:10

7:11,12

One of the elders asks John if he knows who these people in the multitude are and from whence they have come (7:13). John defers the answer, saying, *"My lord, you know,"* so the elder proceeds to identify them. *"These are the ones who come out of the great tribulation, and they have washed their robes and made them white in the blood of the Lamb"* (7:14). The "great tribulation" is not necessarily a designated title for a particular seven year period which some expect to take place in the future. Christians in every age have suffered from the "great tribulation" of living "in the world," facing the hostility of Satan's "world-system" and its religious "front," and the constant tribulations of life. The "anomaly of Christianity" in the "enigma of the interim" is indeed tribulational. Jesus told His followers, "In the world you have tribulation" (John 16:33). Paul explained, "Through many tribulations we must enter the kingdom of God" (Acts 14:22). John had already indicated that he was a "fellow-partaker in the tribulation" (1:9). The multitude is comprised of all Christians who have "washed their robes" in the "washing of regeneration" (Titus 3:5), and they have been "made white in the blood of the Lamb," that is, cleansed from sin by the substitutionary death of Jesus Christ. Thus reconciled to God, they can stand *"before*

7:13

7:14

7:15 *the throne of God"* (7:15). As Isaiah had promised, Christians "will not hunger or thirst, neither will the scorching heat or sun strike them down; for God... guides them to springs of water" (Isa. 49:10) in the Spirit of Christ (John 4:14; 7:38,39). "Blessed are those who hunger and thirst for righteousness, for they shall be satisfied" (Matt. 5:6). Jesus Christ, the Lamb, is also the Shepherd of all Christians (John 10:11,14), leading them to the *"water of life"* in Himself. Though there are tears from the eyes of Christians throughout the tribulational period here on earth, "Blessed are those who mourn, for they shall be comforted" (Matt. 5:4). Even Jesus wept at the tribulation of Lazarus' death (John 11:35). The "God of all comfort" (II Cor. 1:3,4) does wipe the tears from our eyes in the midst of our present adversities, and has promised that eventually at the consummation of Christ's victory there will be no more death and no more tears (Isa. 25:8; Rev. 21:4).

What John was seeing was intended to offer the confident expectancy of hope to the Christians at the end of the first century and in every century thereafter. Yes, there is tribulation and trial as Satan's religious efforts make war against Jesus Christ within His people in every age, but the victory won on the cross will be consummated, and Christians will join in heavenly hymns of praise around the throne of God and the Lamb.

8:1 With that message of hope clearly portrayed by the preceding imagery, the seventh seal is broken by Jesus Christ (8:1). All religious attempts to "seal" the reality of the gospel of Jesus Christ are broken. The time wherein God desires to demonstrate that the life of Jesus Christ in man "really works no matter how hard the going gets" is now fulfilled. The consummated victory of Jesus Christ is now revealed! The reaction of the entire created order to this unadulterated and unhindered presence of God in Christ can only be to "be still and know that He is God" (Psalm 46:10). John writes, "*there was silence in heaven for about half an hour*" (8:1). Was the "half an hour" the approximate time that John experienced still silence in the midst of his vision, or does it represent a period of time when Christ's victory is consummated? We do not know. Some have interpreted this period of time as a delay before judgment is pronounced by the imagery of the trumpets, like the suspenseful delay before the verdict is read in the courtroom, or the "calm before the storm." When God's victory is culminated and His judgment on diabolic religion is pronounced, creation can only react in silence. "The Lord is in His holy temple. Let all the earth be silent before Him" (Hab. 2:20; Zech. 2:13).

The question must be asked, "What is the risen Lord Jesus attempting to tell Christians in this portion of His Revelation? What is the transgenerational and translocational message to all Christians?" Jesus is encouraging Christians in every century to remember that His "finished work" in the cross and resurrection is the basis of His victory over Satan and his diabolic endeavors of death, sin and religion. The spiritual conflict continues to rage between God and Satan, between Christianity and religion. Christians will be called upon to endure tribulation and persecution, and to experience identification with Christ's suffering and death. To whatever extent we have lapsed into religious blindness and self-centeredness we need to repent. The overview of religious endeavors portrayed in the "seals" of this passage, the breaking of that religious activity by the Lord Jesus Christ, and the glimpses into the heavenly throne-room where glorified Christians are singing heavenly hymns of praise, all serve to give Christians hope of the ultimate consummated victory. Thus we are assured of the sufficiency of Christ within us presently whatever the circumstances of our physical lives might entail.

Religious interpreters will always overlook or purposefully whitewash any suggestion that their own religious methods and effects are being revealed as Jesus breaks the seals. They will inevitably identify the images as events of history or as future events, thus destroying the intent of Christ's Revelation to inspire hope in His victorious "finished work." Paul S. Minear correctly explains that

> "the stock-in-trade of false prophets is to exploit for their own purposes the authentic visions of prophets like John."[3]

Religionists develop their own eschatological grids and place them over God's revelation, and say, "See how it fits. See what you can expect in the future. Follow us because we understand what God is doing!" Thereby they continue to "conquer the people" and encourage genuine Christians to take their focus off of the sufficiency of Jesus Christ in their lives right now. Only as Christians continue to look to Christ can they "see" the victory of Christ in the midst of the conflict and sing praises to God and Christ in preparation for their participation in the heavenly hymns.

ENDNOTES

1. Caird, G.B., *A Commentary on the Revelation of St. John the Divine*. London: Adam and Charles Black. 1966. pgs. 60,61.
2. Fowler, James A., *Covenant Theology, Dispensational Theology, or Christocentric Theology*. Fallbrook: C.I.Y. Publishing. 1993.
3. Minear, Paul S., *New Testament Apocalyptic*. Nashville: Abingdon Press. 1981. pg. 77.

8:2 – 11:19

Religion and the Trumpets

Revelation 8:2 – 11:19

The risen Lord Jesus reveals to John the third vignette of His divine perspective. The first "frame" or "camera angle" was what we called "religion and the churches" (2:13:22). The second "view" was what we called "religion and the seals" (4:18:1). The third way of looking at the situation we shall call "religion and the trumpets" (8:2–11:19). These visions are not in chronological sequence, one following after the other as later events in history or in the projected future, but rather are synchronous, giving another viewpoint of the same period of time. They are parallel images so that Christians can see what God is doing from another viewpoint, or through another filter of the Divine intent.

Jesus' intent in the Revelation is to reveal Himself as the victor over Satan, evil and religion. That victory was accomplished when Jesus died on the cross and exclaimed, "It is finished!" (John 19:30). In the "enigma of the interim" between His first coming and His second coming there is continued spiritual conflict and warfare as the diabolic Evil One operates as "the god of this world" (II Cor. 4:4) and disguises himself in the activities of religion (II Cor. 11:13-15). Jesus wants to assure His followers that despite the present turmoil and tribulation wherein they may have to suffer or even die, He is still victorious and in control of the universe, and they can have the confident expectation of the hope of His ultimate consummation of victory when He returns. Such a transgenerational and translocational message of hope and assurance is the revelation by which Jesus seeks to encourage Christians in every age and every place throughout Christian history.

The primary imagery that Jesus employs in this third revealing "view" is that of seven angels blowing seven trumpets which introduce a particular revelation of God's activity. What is the significance of the trumpets? Throughout the Scripture record trumpets have been employed for various purposes. While the Israelites were still in the wilderness God instructed Moses to make some trumpets which were to be used for summoning the people together (Numb. 10:3), to sound a warning alarm (Numb. 10:6; Jere. 6:1; Ezek. 33:3), to be used in battle (Numb. 10:9; Jere. 4:5; 51:24-30; Ezek. 7:14), and to be used in the celebration of feasts (Numb. 10:10; Joel 2:15). The trumpet sound is also used to announce the coming "day of the Lord, the day of wrath, destruction, darkness, gloom and clouds" (Zeph. 1:14-16; Matt. 24:31; I Thess. 4:16). The trumpet blasts pictured here in chapters eight through eleven of the Revelation signify an alarm that God is about to engage in battle and there will be horrible effects of destruction and death when God begins to act against the enemies of His people, Christ's church.

God's objective in having the angels sound the trumpets before He begins His acts of judgment is that the religious "dwellers of the earth" (8:13;11:10) might hear the warning and repent. God is not a blood-thirsty God who delights in vengeance and death. God "has no pleasure in the death of the wicked, rather that he should turn from his ways and live" (Ezek. 18:23). The Lord does not "wish that any should perish, but for all to come to repentance" (II Peter 3:9), that "all men everywhere should repent" (Acts 17:30). Only when men obstinately refuse to repent and submit to the One who created them, rejecting the reconciling mediator and Messiah, Jesus Christ, does God act in judgment, and especially on those who choose counterfeit religion instead of Christ.

The judgment images that God displays toward religionists when the trumpets are sounded have some obvious correlations with the plagues that came upon Egypt preceding the exodus in the Old Testament. God, acting through Moses, was engaged in the preserving of His people in the old covenant era. He was demonstrating His divine power to prevail over satanically energized human authorities and institutions. He was bringing judgment on those who would oppress His people and enslave His people in bondage. In like manner, the trumpets portrayed in this part of the revelatory vision reveal that God is preserving His Christian people in the victory that Christ won on the cross. God is demonstrating that He is in control and will prevail over the satanically energized authorities and institutions of religion. He will bring judgments upon those who enslave people in the oppressive bondage of religion. What an encouragement this should be to Christians in every age between the two advents of Jesus Christ. Remember that the etymological meaning of "religion" is to "bind up," in contrast to being "set free" in Jesus Christ to be all that God intends man to be (John 8:32,36; Gal. 5:1,13).

8:2-4

8:2 This third visionary sector begins with seven angels being given seven trumpets (8:2). Although Jewish tradition indicated that there were seven archangels there is no evidence here to identify these seven angels as archangels. Neither do we know whether these seven angels are the same seven angels referred to later (15:1,6-8; 16:1; 17:1; 21:9). They may simply represent the perfection of angelic activity.

Each of the angels is given a trumpet. Seven trumpets were also employed when seven priests blowing seven trumpets marched around Jericho for seven days, as recorded in Joshua 6:4-16. They too were announcing God's coming judgment and destruction. Some interesting similarities are apparent, though not suggested by the text. Just as the city of Jericho had to fall so that the Israelites could carry the ark of the covenant to Jerusalem, so the religious city of Babylon must fall so that the ark of new covenant blessings (11:19) can be experienced without hindrance by Christians in the New Jerusalem.

8:3 John saw another angel standing at the altar of the heavenly temple-scene (8:3). This angel had a golden censer with incense which represented the prayers of Christians going up before God. This imagery of incense in connection with the prayers of Christians has been used previously (5:8), and the concept of our prayers being a sweet and fragrant aroma before God can be seen in the Psalmist's request, "May my prayer be counted as incense before Thee" (Ps. 141:2). The import of these introductory verses (8:3-5) may be to stress the importance of prayer among Christians throughout that period between Christ's comings. Prayer expresses a willingness to see the situation from

God's perspective, to accept God's action and allow such to be fulfilled. Indeed, "the effectual prayers of righteous men, availeth much" (James 5:16). By our prayers we "listen under" God unto obedience, and seek God's activity in the situation at hand. Many have been the prayers throughout Christian history that God might vindicate His righteousness and bring judgment upon the powers of evil religion.

The angel in John's vision *"took the censer, filled it with fire from the heavenly altar and threw it to the earth"* (8:5). The fire of God's judgment is hurled to the earth. An answer to prayer, no doubt! It is accompanied by *"thunder, lightning and an earthquake,"* representing the awesome presence of God's power. At one point in His earthly ministry in the midst of confronting the religionists, Jesus said, "I have come to cast fire upon the earth; and how I wish it were already kindled" (Luke 12:49). The coming of the perfect life of Jesus Christ necessitates the flipside of the judgment of Satan, sin, evil and religion. The "No" that is the other side of God's "Yes."

8:5

As with the seven seals, the first four of the trumpet blasts are packaged together, the fifth and sixth receive more protracted explanation, and then there is an interval between the sixth and the seventh. In all of the trumpet announcements God is bringing His providential judgment upon those who have identified with Satan and his religious efforts.

At the sound of the first trumpet *"hail and fire, mixed with blood"* are thrown to the earth (8:7). These effects are similar to the judgment plagues sent upon Egypt (Exod. 9:18,23), evidencing God's power to those who

8:7

8:8,9

were oppressing God's people. Likewise the hostile religious oppressors of Christian peoples are being warned by the first trumpet and its announced display of divine power that God will not tolerate religious assaults forever. Religion is going to get "pounded" and "burned," and the fact that the effects are "mixed with blood" probably signifies death.

John explains that he saw *"one third of the earth and the tree and the grass being burnt up"* (8:7). In each of the judgment effects following the first four trumpets, the symbolic picture-language refers to "a third" of a particular object being affected. Such a reference to "one third" evidences the restricted scope of God's judgments throughout the interim of Christian history. God's historical judgments in the interim of the church age are partial, but not complete. A significant portion of mankind are affected, but not all. God is still seeking the repentance of religionists. Complete destruction will come later when God "destroys the destroyers" (11:18).

8:8 The second trumpet announces and warns of *"a great mountain burning with fire thrown into the sea"* (8:8). Some have thought that this refers to volcanic activity, but the imagery goes far beyond natural phenomena. Only the omnipotent power of God can heave the mountain of religion into the deep-blue sea! Jeremiah used similar pictorial language when he prophesied for God saying, "I will make you (Babylon) a burnt out mountain" (Jere. 51:25), and "the sea has come up over Babylon" (Jere. 51:42).

8:9 John observed that *"a third of the sea became blood, a third of the creatures in the sea died, and a third of the ships were destroyed"* (8:8,9). Religion has certainly polluted many waters with the blood of its death-deeds. Again we have the similarity with the Egyptian plagues when the waters were turned to blood (Exod. 7:20).

Upon the sounding of the third trumpet, *"a great star fell from heaven, burning like a torch"* (8:10). Although some would again point to the natural phenomena of a meteorite falling through the atmosphere with a fiery trail like a torch, it is more likely that the picture is symbolic. Religion may appear to be so lofty as a luminary of the heavenlies, but it is a "falling star" which will burn like a torch. The imagery is similar to that expressed by Isaiah when he said, "You (Babylon) have fallen from heaven, O star of the morning, ...you have been cut down to the earth" (Isa. 14:12).

8:10

This particular star is identified with the symbolic name of *"Wormwood"* (8:11). Wormwood was a plant that grew in the region of Palestine which produced a bitter oil from its leaves. The mention of "wormwood" became equivalent to the concept of bitterness. "The lips of an adulteress drip honey..., but in the end she is bitter as wormwood" (Prov. 5:3,4). Through the prophet Jeremiah, God says to the Israelites who had turned to false religion, "I will feed them with wormwood" (Jere. 9:15; 23:15). The activities of religion have created much bitterness. They have polluted many river and waters (8:10,11) with their "galling" poison, and brought death to many men (8:11).

8:11

When the fourth trumpet was sounded *"a third of the sun, moon and stars were smitten, so that they were darkened and ceased to shine"* (8:12). Again we see a similarity with the ninth plague when there was "dark-

8:12

ness over the land of Egypt" (Exod. 10:21). Religion is identified with the "world forces of darkness" (Eph. 6:12), in Satan's (Acts 26:18) "domain of darkness" (Col. 1:13). Speaking to religious Nicodemus, Jesus said, "This is the judgment, that light is come into the world, and men loved the darkness rather than the light, for their deeds were evil" (John 3:19). Jesus also indicated that "sons of the (religious Jewish) kingdom would be cast out into the outer darkness..." (Matt. 8:12). God can bring a darkness upon religion, which not even they can tolerate. The prophet Joel cried, "Blow a trumpet in Zion, for the day of darkness is coming; a day of darkness and gloom" (Joel 2:2).

8:13 Between the fourth and fifth angelic trumpet blasts John saw "an eagle flying in midheaven, saying with a loud voice, *'Woe, woe, woe, to those who dwell on the earth, because of the remaining blasts of the trumpet which are about to sound"* (8:13). The eagle is sometimes portrayed as a symbol of strength that flies above all others and is powerful to destroy. "Like an eagle the enemy comes against the house of the Lord" (Hosea 8:1). The "eagle swoops down to devour" (Hab. 1:8). The Greek word *aetos* can also be translated "vulture." Jesus said, "wherever a corpse is, vultures will gather" (Matt. 24:28; Luke 17:37). The bird of prey is announcing that the results revealed by the remaining three trumpet blasts will be worse than the first four. The first four consequences might be called the "four trumpet warnings," whereas the last three consequences of God's actions might be called the "three trumpet woes."

The woes of divine judgment are directed toward "those who dwell on the earth" (8:13). This is a prominent designation throughout the Revelation for the religionists who are part of Satan's world-system (cf. 3:10; 6:10; 11:10). In contrast to religious "earth-dwellers," Christians are "citizens of heaven" (Phil. 3:20), "seated in the heavenlies" (Eph. 2:6).

At the sound of the fifth angel blowing the fifth trumpet, John *"saw a star from heaven which had fallen to earth; and the key to the bottomless pit was given to him"* (9:1). Though the imagery is similar to that which was revealed after the third trumpet (8:10), an entirely different scenario unfolds. This star is personified. When the king of Babylon is represented as a star fallen from heaven (Isa. 14:12), this has often been given a secondary interpretation as the fall of Lucifer from heaven in order to become the diabolic Evil One. Later in the Revelation it is revealed that "the great dragon, the serpent of old who is called the devil and Satan, was thrown down to the earth from heaven, and his angels were thrown down with him" (Rev. 12:9). Jesus explained that the seventy witnesses were effective for He saw "Satan fall from heaven like lightning," and He goes on to indicate that He gave them "authority to tread upon serpents and scorpions, and over all the power of the enemy" (Luke 10:18,19). The fallen one that John observed was given "the key of the bottomless pit" (9:1), so as to have authority over the underworld and the "abyss" which even the demons want to avoid (Luke 8:31).

From the bottomless pit issued forth *"smoke like that of a great furnace"* (9:2). "Where there is smoke there is fire," goes the saying, and this smoke may have come from the "unquenchable fire of hell" (Mark 9:43). Smoke can represent the deception and delusion of "the prince of the power of the air" (Eph. 2:2).

9:3   *"Out of the smoke came forth locusts"* (9:3), which are often a symbol of destruction and judgment as they were in the eighth plague of locusts upon Egypt (Exod. 10:12). These locusts can attack like scorpions to inject their poisonous venom. Religion arises straight from the pit of hell with the full authority of Satan behind it, shrouded in the smoke of deception and delusion, and injects its poisonous error like a scorpion.

Notice, though, that the sovereign God is still in control! He permits (9:5) only a limited tormenting of
9:4   non-Christians who do not have the seal (9:4) of God's Holy Spirit in their lives. The limitation is expressed by
9:5   the time-period of *"five months"* (9:5,10), which some have noted is approximately the life-cycle and infestation-span of a locust, but which probably represents simply the limitation of time.

9:6   The sting of a scorpion can bring such a painful torment that a person can wish they were dead (9:6). Many of the more thoughtful unregenerate people throughout history have indicated that they thought dying would be preferable to living in the destructive world in which we live, with its religious corruption, brutalization and senseless activity. The only remedy, of course, is to know the life of Jesus Christ which transcends all worldly chaos and religious corruption.

9:7-10   The symbolism of the locusts is further expanded (9:7-10) to include some of the most grotesque and revolting images of diabolic forces of "the spiritual hosts of wickedness" (Eph. 6:12). The locusts are likened to horses equipped for battle, just as the prophet Joel also likened locusts to "war horses" (Joel 2:4). The word for "locust" in several languages is identified with horses, as can be seen in the German word *heupferd* meaning "hay-horse," and the Italian word *cavalletta* meaning "little horse." Many have noted a physical resemblance between horses and locusts, but the imagery that John observes goes far beyond such physical similarities into horrifying pictorializations of lionized femininity, metallic weaponry and stinging power all evident within religion.

These diabolic religious forces which make war and *"hurt men"* (9:10), *"have a king over them"* (9:11), who is probably the same one who is the personified fallen star (9:1). He is "the angel of the abyss; his name in Hebrew is **Abaddon**, and in Greek he has the name *"Apollyon"* (9:11). Both the Hebrew and Greek words mean "destroyer," which is the activity of the devil, and his destruction is evidenced in religious activity. **9:10,11**

The sixth trumpet sound reveals a voice coming from the golden altar which is before God, which tells the sixth angel to, *"Release the four angels who are bound at the great river Euphrates"* (9:14). God is still in control for He controls the releasing of these four evil angels. They come from the region of the Euphrates river where the Assyrians (Isa. 8:7) and the Parthian barbarians, some of the most feared enemies of God's people came. This is an army straight from hell, prepared for this destruction (9:15). They number *"two myriads of myriads"* or two times ten thousand times ten thousand, which is two hundred million; an army that is incalculably immense. The breastplates on the riders of the horsemen in this army are emblazoned in red, blue and yellow (9:17) to match the *"fire, smoke and brimstone"* which issues forth from the mouths of the horses (9:18). These lion-headed (9:17), fire-breath- **9:14**

9:15

9:17

9:18

9:19 ing mounts with serpentine tails (9:19) do much harm upon a third of mankind. The "old serpent" (12:9) is indeed the authority that directs the cavalry charge of this immense army of religion that does such harm to so much of mankind.

God's purpose in allowing such is that mankind might see the destruction, repent of their evil and religious ways, and receive the sole Savior of mankind, His Son, Jesus Christ. Modern men often have a difficult time understanding how God can permit such widespread devastation and death. In large part this is due to our having developed an idolatrous view that physical life is infinitely precious and to be preserved at all cost, while physical death is the ultimate tragedy. This is not so! That which is eternally valuable is the spiritual and divine life of Jesus Christ. "It is appointed unto all men that we should die physically and face judgment" (Heb. 9:27). The certainty of such physical death is established; the only question is the timing of our death. We must remember the transient insecurity of this life, and not be deceived by the religious ideology that idolizes physical life. In His sovereignty God can and does use the physical death of mankind, even in large numbers, as an object lesson to the rest of mankind to encourage them to choose the life which is eternal in Jesus Christ.

9:20 Sad to say, even when God does allow "the one having the power of death" (Heb. 2:14) to cause devastating destruction and death through his religious efforts, the *"rest of mankind"* (9:20) often do not respond in repentance toward God. Why? They remain recalcitrant in their allegiance and worship of the gods of their own making, the idolatrous images which they make with their own hands (Ps. 115:4; 135:15), whether they be of gold, silver, bronze, iron, wood, stone (Daniel 5:23) or the hardened concrete of inflexible thinking. These impotent idols cannot see, hear, eat, smell or walk (9:20; Deut. 4:28; Ps. 115:5-8; Dan. 5:23), but they adhere to them anyway, for they are really worshipping themselves, "the creature rather than the Creator" (Rom. 1:26), and at a deeper level they are worshipping demons (9:20; Acts 17:22; I Cor. 10:20). All religion is demonically inspired! All religion is idolatry! God has repeatedly explained to mankind, "I have no pleasure in the death of anyone who dies. Therefore, repent and live" (Ezek. 18:32); "Repent and turn from your idols" (Ezek. 14:6). But the vast majority of mankind obstinately refuse to change their minds about what they falsely perceive to be their own self-generative capabilities, and thus fail to change their action so as to derive and receive all from God in faith in order to function as God intended.

Throughout that merciful period between Christ's comings when God seeks the repentance of all mankind and tests His own people, the majority of mankind *"do not repent of their murders nor of their sorceries nor of their immorality nor of their thefts"* (9:21). These behaviors contrary to the character of God are rampant in society today and are often tolerated or encouraged in religious practices, including the drugs of sorcery (Greek: *pharmaceutikos*). The conclusion of the Revelation indicates that "sorcerers, immoral persons and idolaters" will be outside of the heavenly gate (22:15).

Between trumpets six and seven we have an apparent interlude (10:1 – 11:13), similar to what was observed between the breaking of the sixth and seventh seals (7:1-17). Perhaps this is to highlight how the "enigma

10:1,2

of the interim" serves God's purposes. The parenthetical delay may expose God's continued desire for the repentance of all men, giving them more time. Within that time the full complement of God's martyred witnesses also accumulates as they are "faithful unto death" (2:10). The interval also provides a sense of suspense of what is yet to come in the climax of that which is revealed by the seventh trumpet.

10:1 John observes *"another strong angel"* (10:1), other than the one referred to in 5:2, who was *"clothed with the cloud"* of God's invisible presence, had a *"rainbow on his head"* representing God's faithfulness, whose *"face was like the sun"* radiating the Light of God, and whose *"feet were like pillars of fire"* symbolic of God's presence and undergirding (Exod. 13:21). Some have speculated that this angel was Gabriel, while others have identified him as Jesus Christ, but he must remain an unidentified angel. Whoever he was, he was of colossal
10:2 size and awesome power for *"he placed his right foot on the sea and his left on the land"* (10:2), perhaps indicating that God is bigger than anything religion can muster.

The angel had *"a little scroll which was open"* in his hand (10:2). What was inscribed in this scroll and what does it represent? Many have conjectured that it is the Bible or "God's Plan for the ages," but perhaps it contained the same basic message as the sealed scroll in chapters five, six and seven of the Revelation, which we have suggested was the written record of God's foreknown awareness of what was to happen in that time between Christ's comings, including the trials and deaths of Christians.

When the strong angel *"cried out with a loud voice, the seven peals of thunder uttered their voices"* (10:3), perhaps declaring the judgments of God, but we do not know for a *"voice from heaven"* (10:4) told John to *"seal up"* what had been uttered and *"do not write them,"* perhaps only postponing such until they could be further illustrated later in the Revelation. The angel then *"lifted his right hand"* (10:5) and took an oath *"that there should be delay no longer, but in the days of the seventh angel and the seventh trumpet, then the mystery of God is finished, as he preached to His servants the prophets"* (10:7). The martyrs had asked, "How long?" (6:10), and now the angel indicates that a time will come when God will delay *"no longer."* The divine delay for the purpose of men's repentance (II Peter 3:9) will come to an end, and God's determinative judgment will be set in motion. This is all tied to the action of the seventh angel and his seventh trumpet which is referred to in 11:15-19. At this time the "mystery of God," once concealed but now revealed, will be brought to completion. The opportunity to receive Jesus Christ, the mystery of God (Col. 2:2) will be concluded, as God made known through "His servants the prophets" (Joel 3:7) in both old and new covenants.	10:3 10:4 10:5 10:7
John was told to take the little scroll from the big angel (10:8), and when he did so the angel said, *"Take it, and eat it; and it will make your stomach bitter, but in your mouth it will be sweet as honey"* (10:9). The Psalmist had declared that the words of God were "sweeter than honey to his mouth" (Ps. 119:103), and Ezekiel used the same imagery of eating a scroll which was sweet as honey (Ezek. 2:9; 3:3). Jeremiah explained that God's words were a "joy and delight to his heart" (Jere. 15:16), but on the other hand they "re-	10:8 10:9

10:11 sulted in reproach and derision all the day long" (Jere. 20:8). God's witnesses will find that the gospel is sweet, but there are bitter consequences of identifying with and partaking of Jesus Christ. There is both joy and sorrow for Christians until Christ comes again. The way of victory is the way of pain, even unto the bitterness of physical death. Recognizing such, John is commissioned to *"prophesy again"* (10:11), to proclaim Jesus Christ among *"many peoples and nations and tongues and kings"* while time still remains.

11:1 Another interactive scenario begins when John is given *"a measuring rod like a staff"* and told to *"measure the temple of God, and the altar, and those who worship in it, but leave out the outer court"* (11:1). The act of measuring signifies the recognition and distinguishing which leads to a measured understanding of God's purposes and what God is doing by His Son, Jesus Christ prior to His return. The true worship of God in the temple of Christ's church (I Cor. 3:16; II Cor. 6:16; Eph. 2:21; I Peter 2:5), conducted by all Christians as priests (I Peter 2:5,9; Rev. 1:6; 5:10), can never be quashed or snuffed out. The prayers of Christians emanating from the altar like incense from the inner temple

11:2 sanctum will be heard. But in the outer court of that same temple, representing the Church of Jesus Christ, the "holy community" of Christian peoples will be *"tread under foot by the nations"* (11:2) until "the time of the Gentiles be fulfilled" (Luke 17:24). The church will not be overcome, for "the gates of hades shall not overpower it" (Matt. 16:18), but in the outer court of their physical lives Christians are vulnerable and exposed to the trampling effects of religious persecution, suffering and the death of martyrdom. As the "city of God," the *"holy city"* prepared and build by God

(Heb. 11:10,16), the "heavenly Jerusalem above" (Heb. 12:22; Gal. 4:25), Christians are subject to religious hostility and will be "hated on account of His name" (Luke 21:17). The duration of this suffering is divinely limited, though, as expressed by the time periods of ***"forty-two months"*** (11:2), which is ***"twelve hundred and sixty days"*** (11:3) by Jewish calendar calculation, which is "three and a half years." "Three and a half" is half of the complete and perfect number, seven, indicating that the time of destruction will be limited and incomplete. God continues to protect His own!

During this divinely limited period of time when the church will be persecuted, God will grant the authority of Jesus Christ (Matt. 28:18) to His ***"two witnesses, who will prophesy, though clothed in sackcloth"*** (11:3). God's has always demanded that testimony be validated by "two witnesses" (Deut. 17:6; 19:15; Numb. 35:30; Matt. 18:16; John 8:17; II Cor. 13:1; Heb. 10:28). Jesus sent out the seventy witnesses "two by two" (Luke 10:1-24). All Christians in the church of Jesus Christ are called to be His witnesses (Acts 1:8), so the "two witnesses" are best understood to be the necessary complement of Christian witnesses who are willing to invest their lives for Jesus Christ, even unto martyrdom, for the Greek word translated "witness" is *martur*. Jesus identified Himself as the "faithful witness" (1:5). John considered himself a "witness" (1:2). All Christians comprise the necessary "two witnesses." Speculations have run rampant as interpreters have attempted to identify the "two witnesses" as Moses and Elijah, Peter and Paul, James and John, Luther and Calvin, or as non-personal entities such as Old Testament and New Testament, or as law and gospel. Such specific identifications are trivial diversions which do not serve

11:4-6

to encourage all Christians to be witnesses who proclaim Jesus Christ, even in the context of humiliation and hardship (illustrated by the garb of "sackcloth") unto death until Christ returns.

11:4 The "two witnesses" are further identified as *"the two olive trees and the two lampstands that stand before the Lord of the earth"* (11:4). The two olive trees may represent the oil of the Holy Spirit which is necessary for the light to be expressed in the lampstands, which were earlier identified as churches (1:20). Christians are called to be "the light of the world" (Matt. 5:14), but can be such witnesses only by the power of the Holy Spirit. "Not by might nor by power, but by My Spirit," says the Lord of hosts (Zech. 4:6)in the Old Testament passage which employs the same imagery of olive trees and lampstands (Zech. 4:2-14). There the two olive trees and lampstands seem to be representative of Zerubbabel, the king, and Joshua, the priest. All Christians are anointed to represent God as kings and priests (I Peter 2:5,9; Rev. 1:6; 5:10), which serves to verify the "two witnesses" as all Christians.

As Christian witnesses are empowered by the Holy Spirit, the fire of divine judgmental action in Jesus Christ proceeds from their mouths. God told Jeremiah that He was making His words in his mouth to be fire in order to consume the religionists (Jere. 5:14). The

11:6 Christian witnesses have supernatural power to *"shut up the sky"* (11:6) like Elijah (I Kings 17,18) and to bring forth plagues (11:6) like Moses (Exod. 7-12), for Jesus promised that "greater works than I have done, you shall do" (John 14:12). God's powerful works through Christians are unlimited as we remain available to His supernatural ability.

When the witnesses *"have finished their testimony"* (11:7) and the delay is over (10:6), the beast of religion *"that comes out of the abyss will make war with them, and overcome them and kill them"* (11:7). The physical lives of many of God's Christian witnesses will be given up in martyrdom, "faithful unto death" (2:10). The corpses of Christians will be strewn throughout the streets of the *"great city"* (11:8) of religion, later to be identified as Babylon (14:8; 16:19; 18:10), which is historically linked to the religious efforts at Babel (Gen. 11:9). That this is not a literal city on earth is evident from the words of John which explain that this city is also "mystically" or "spiritually" called Sodom and Egypt and Jerusalem (11:8). Sodom is the symbol of God's judgment on rebellious perversity (Gen. 19:23; Lk. 10:12; 17:29). Egypt represents the captivity from which God delivered His people (Jude 1:5). The earthly city of Jerusalem *"where the Lord was crucified"* (11:8) stands for the center of enslaving Jewish religion (Gal. 4:25) and the persecution of God's Christian people (Luke 13:33-35). This religious community of Babylon, a.k.a. Sodom, Egypt, Jerusalem, is comprised of *"peoples and tribes and tongues and nations"* (11:9) who will observe the corpses of the martyred Christians for a divinely limited time represented by the period of "three and a half days." The "earth-dwelling" religionists (3:10; 6:10; 8:13; 11:10) gloat over the indignity of disallowing the bodies to be buried (11:9), rejoicing with glee and merriment over the death of the Christian witnesses which they perceive to have tormented them (11:10), and over which they now think they have been victorious. Little do they realize what God is yet to do to express the victory that has been accomplished in Christ Jesus, the victory over all religion!

11:11 After the limited time of indignity, pictured as *"three and a half days,"* the Christians are resurrected. The *"breath of life from God comes into them"* similar to the imagery employed in Ezekiel's vision of life restored in the valley of dry bones (Ezek. 37:10). "A loud voice" of divine origin "from heaven" invites the resur-

11:12 rected Christians to, *"Come up here"* (11:12); to leave the ignominy of the religious city and dwell forevermore in the "heavenly Jerusalem" (Heb. 12:22) which is "above" (Gal. 4:26), the "new Jerusalem" (Rev. 3:12; 21:2,10). They are translated into the heavenly realm via the *"cloud"* (11:12) of God's presence (Matt. 17:5; Acts 1:9). This is no "secret rapture," as some suggest, for the religious *"enemies beheld them"* (11:11,12) and were fearful.

11:13 The religious world is once again *"shaken"* by an earthquake-judgment of God with divinely limited effects which encompass only *"a tenth of the city"* and the death of *"seven thousand people"* (11:13). *"The rest were terrified and gave glory to the God of heaven"* (11:13). Do they really repent, or are they just responding in order to attempt to save their own skins? Sometimes the similar phraseology of the Revelation seems to indicate genuine repentance (14:7; 15:4; 16:9), but other scenarios cause us to question whether they will repent (6:15-17; 9:20,21; 13:3,4).

11:15 Finally we come to the seventh trumpet sounded by the seventh angel (11:15). It reveals loud voices from heaven declaring, *"The kingdom of the world has become that of our Lord, and of His Christ; and He will reign forever and ever"* (11:15). When the "god of this world" (II Cor. 4:4) is totally overcome and the reign of religion is terminated, then in "the new heaven and the new earth" (Isa. 65:17; II Pet. 3:13; Rev. 21:1) Christians will experience the unhindered reign of Christ as "King of Kings and Lord of Lords" (17:14; 19:16) for eternity. Based on His victory at the cross and resurrection Jesus reigns already in the life of a Christian (Rom. 5:17,21), for we "have been transferred into the kingdom of Christ" (Col. 1:13), but the Lord Jesus Christ will reign in unhindered supremacy forever and ever in the heavenly realm. Along with the twenty-four elders we will worship the Almighty God and the Son, Jesus Christ (11:17). God's bondservants, the prophets, along with the saints and all those who fear the name of Jehovah will receive their eternal reward (11:18).

11:17

11:18

On the other hand, the final and complete judgment of God will come upon the religionists and those who do not receive Christ as their eternal life. The just wrath of God will be poured out, and the nations without God will be enraged as they face judgment (11:18). God will *"destroy those who destroy the earth."* All of those identified with the "destroyer," the devil, as all men are who are not identified with Jesus Christ (Eph. 2:2), and who by their religious endeavors have been destructive to mankind and the earth that God created as the dwelling place of man will be finally destroyed. They will face "eternal destruction, away from the presence of the Lord" (II Thess. 1:9).

The final image in this vision reveals *"the ark of His covenant appearing in the heavenly temple"* (11:19). This would appear to represent the unhindered access that Christians have to all the new covenant blessings of God in Jesus Christ, "every spiritual blessing in heavenly places" (Eph. 1:3) including the "law of God written on our hearts" (Heb. 8:10; 10:16). The opposite of His

11:19

blessings are the cursings of His judgment, and these, too, are illustrated by lightning, thunder, earthquake and hailstorm which are brought to bear upon those who refuse to receive Jesus Christ.

What is the ever-applicable message that the risen Lord Jesus has for Christians in every age within this panoramic vision of the trumpets? It might be that the prayers of Christians are indeed efficacious in calling for the release of the fires of God's judgment to vindicate His righteousness and the victory of Jesus Christ. God's providential judgments will most certainly be enacted against religion throughout the interim between Christ's advents, and religion is essentially impotent to counteract that which God does. The pre-set limitations of God's mercy will eventually come to an end. The sufferings of the saints will not last forever. In the meantime, God gives every opportunity for those involved in religion to repent and to rely solely on the dynamic of the life of Jesus Christ. "Unless you repent, you will all likewise perish" (Luke 13:5).

Religion and the Beasts

Revelation 12:1 – 15:4

The apostle John records a fourth perspective of the panoramic picture of God's reign throughout the "enigma of the interim." It is another "overlay" that provides a different "filter" on God's activities during that period between the two physical advents of Jesus Christ. This fourth "camera-angle" illustrates more clearly the conflict that continues to take place between God and Satan, between Christianity and religion.

The Christians at the end of the first century, and Christians in every period prior to Christ's return, find it necessary to recognize the spiritual conflict that is transpiring in the universe and upon the earth. In this fourth vision John records for us an expanding and escalating hostility. First there is the conflict between a woman and the dragon (12:1-6), followed by conflict between the angel, Michael, and the dragon (12:7-16), and between the woman's children and the dragon (12:17). Then the woman's children are engaged in battle with the sea-beast (13:1-10) and with the earth-beast (13:11-18). Inherent within these symbols is the message that the forces of evil will continue to come against Christian peoples. This is in fulfillment of what Jesus said, "If they persecuted Me, they will persecute you" (John 15:20).

12:1

It was the evil forces of Satan acting through religion that persecuted Jesus, and likewise it is primarily through the "front" of religion that the Evil One continues to harass and do battle against Christians. Will Christians endure and persevere in their faithful reliance upon the victory that Jesus Christ won at the cross, or will they revert to religious practices that effectively deny Jesus Christ? This is the issue being addressed throughout the Revelation, and even more particularly in these chapters.

The Dragon

12:1 John begins by indicating that he saw a *"great sign appear in heaven"* (12:1). A "sign" signifies something of spiritual significance, and a "great sign" is something of special significance. It is important to note that the setting is "in heaven," so as not to interpret earthly events as directly equivalent to that which is being pictured, though such events may correlate as counterparts to the activity in the heavenly realm.

In the heavenlies John saw *"a woman clothed with the sun, and the moon under her feet, and on her head a crown of twelve stars"* (12:1). The identity of this woman has long been debated. Since she bore a male child (12:5) who is apparently the Messiah, Mary the physical mother of Jesus has often been the earthly identification given to the woman. This is particularly true in Roman Catholic interpretation with their undue emphasis on Mary. Others have identified the woman as Eve who was promised that she would have "enmity with the serpent" and her "seed would bruise the snake" (Gen. 3:14,15). Eve thought that she had borne "the manchild of Jehovah" (Gen. 4:1) when she gave birth to her first son, Cain. Others have identified the "woman" as the physical nation and race of Israel, since Jesus was born into their ethnic group as a Jew. Another opinion is that which identifies the "woman" as the Christian church. One variation of this latter view is the liberal idea that the birth and life of Jesus is but a "myth" that was spawned by the early religious community of Christians. Another variation is that which explains that it is through the activity of the church that the life of Jesus is given birth regeneratively in Christian people. All of these interpretations, seem to be earth-based explanations which relate the symbol to events on earth, rather than "in heaven." Some more abstract interpretations identify the "woman" as God's creative activity which gives birth to the Messiah, or as God's perfect intent for man which gives birth to the need for a reconciling mediator. Although precise identification of the "woman" is not necessary to understand the picture-show being presented, it might be beneficial to consider the contrast of this "woman" and the "mystery of the woman" who is "Babylon the great, the mother of harlots" (17:4), the "woman who is the great city, which reigns over the kings of the earth" (17:18). If the "woman" who is the mother of religion is identified as a city, perhaps the heavenly Messianic maternity is also to be identified in a city or a community. What some have called the "Mother Zion" concept, might be what Paul was expressing when he wrote, "the Jerusalem above is our mother" (Gal. 4:26). The heavenly community, identified as the City of Peace, Jerusalem, can be understood to provide the spiritual maternity of the Messiah.

If we accept this latter interpretation of the "woman" as "Jerusalem above" in heaven, then it is easy to understand that she is *"clothed with the sun"* (12:1), in the garment of God's light. The "Jerusalem above" is a spiritual reality that is above physical phenomena, and therefore the *"moon is under her feet"* (12:1). Since the number twelve is representative of God's people, the woman is symbolized as having *"a crown of twelve stars"* (12:1), for the "Jerusalem above" is comprised of the totality of God's people.

12:2 The heavenly *"woman"* was pregnant *"with child"* (12:2). Isaiah uses similar imagery of physical Israel being pregnant, but they could not give birth to a deliverer, only "to wind" (Isa. 26:17,18). The "Jerusalem above" provides heavenly maternity for the Messiah, and does *"give birth to a son"* (12:5). "Zion travailed and brought forth a boy" (Isa. 66:7-9).

Many varied attempts have been made to link the birth of the male child (12:5) to physical and historical phenomena. The most obvious is the incarnation of Jesus Christ when "in the fullness of time God sent forth His Son, born of a woman" (Gal. 4:4); the "virgin bore a son" (Isa. 7:14); the Son of God "was made in the likeness of men" (Phil. 2:7). The resurrection of Jesus Christ is also referred to as a "birth" for by "life out of death" Jesus provides the availability of the "birth of life" for all mankind. Quoting the Messianic psalm (Ps. 2:7-9), Paul explained that by the resurrection God had "begotten His Son" (Acts 13:30-35). As the "first-born from the dead" (Col. 1:15; Rev. 1:5), Jesus allows for the regenerative birth of His life in Christians, "first-born among many brethren" (Rom. 8:29), "born again to a living hope through the resurrection of Jesus Christ from the dead" (I Peter 1:3). Paul also referred to his travailing "in labor until the life of Christ was formed in" the Galatian Christians (Gal. 4:19). Perhaps no historical event is being indicated by "the birth of the male child," but merely the general presentation of the life of Jesus Christ to the world by the heavenly community of the "Jerusalem above." On the other hand, perhaps all of the above explanations can serve as a comprehensive earthly counterpart to the woman giving birth.

In the meantime, John saw *"another sign"* signifying something of spiritual significance. He saw a *"great red dragon"* (12:3), who is later specifically identified as *"the serpent of old who is called the devil and Satan"* (12:9). Monster-dragons were often employed in prophetic picture-language. Isaiah refers to Nebuchadnezzar, king of Babylon, as being "like a monster" (Isa. 51:34), and Ezekiel refers to Pharaoh, king of Egypt, as "the great monster" (Ezek. 29:3). Evil is often portrayed as personified in dragon-form (Ps. 74:13,14). The Satanic dragon is pictured as having *"seven heads and ten horns,"* for he masquerades and disguises himself as representing the perfection of thought and full complement of authority. *"On his heads were seven diadems"* or royal crowns, for the devil misrepresents himself as the perfection of royal power as he tries to parody and usurp the "King of Kings and Lord of Lords" (19:12,16). Despite his rebellion against God, he has only a limited effect as illustrated by *"his tail sweeping away a third of the stars of heaven"* (12:4).

The diabolic dragon stands by the woman who is about to give birth so that he might devour her child (12:4). If the birth of the child had its counterpart in the incarnation we might think of Satan's effort through King Herod to kill the baby Jesus (Matt. 2:13-16). If the resurrection of Jesus is the counterpart then we might consider Satan's activity in the temptations of Jesus as

12:5,6

well as his murderous efforts leading to the crucifixion and subsequent resurrection. Perhaps the birth pictured in the vision comprehends both counterparts in its signification of the heavenly presentation of the life of the Son of God, which Satan always seeks to deter, abort and devour.

12:5 In the imagery that John describes, the woman gives birth to a son *"who is to rule all the nations with a rod of iron"* (12:5). The obvious reference to Jesus Christ as the "son" is apparent by the allusion from the Messianic psalm wherein God says, "I have installed My King upon Zion, My holy mountain. Thou art My Son. I will give the nations as Thine inheritance. Thou shalt break them with a rod of iron" (Ps. 2:6-9). Isaiah prophesied that "a child will be born, a son will be given, and the government shall rest on His shoulders" (Isa. 9:6). Later in the Revelation Jesus is explicitly identified as the One who "rules with a rod of iron" (19:15).

Immediately after the birth of the son in the vision that John saw, *"her child was caught up to God and to His throne"* (12:5). This is difficult to "square" with a particularized identification with the incarnational birth of Jesus. If the "birth" unto life in resurrection is accepted as the interpretation, then the subsequent ascension of the Lord Jesus when He was "lifted up" (Acts 1:9) into heaven seems to apply more easily. Then again, from the heavenly perspective of eternity the presenting of the life of Jesus unto the world of mankind was soon followed by the return of the physical Jesus into the heavenly presence.

12:6 John then records that *"the woman fled into the wilderness where she had a place prepared by God,* *so that she might be nourished for one thousand two hundred and sixty days"* (12:6). Viewed from the historical counterpart of Jesus' incarnational birth, some have suggested that this corresponds with Joseph and Mary fleeing to Egypt, but this interpretation lacks an allegorical alignment for the child of the woman being "caught up to God and His throne" (12:5). If the heavenly "Jerusalem above" is the spiritual mother of the Messiah, then the "wilderness" may represent the place of divine protection, safety and sustenance. The "wilderness" served as such for the Israelites in the Old Testament. The "wilderness" to which the woman flees may symbolize the place of spiritual refuge outside of the predominant religious community, where she remains until the "New Jerusalem" is fully consummated as the unhindered "City of God" in the heavenly realm. The fact that the "woman" remains there for one thousand two hundred and sixty days, which is forty-two months or three and a half years (cf. 11:2; 13:5), indicates that this is an abbreviated time which is divinely restricted. It does not last forever!

The combatants in the spiritual conflict within the heavenlies then changes from the woman versus the dragon to *"Michael and his angels waging war with the dragon"* (12:7). This is similar to Daniel's vision of Michael guarding the people of God in the "time of distress" (Dan. 12:1). Many of the ideas utilized in interpreting these verses are based on concepts of heavenly warfare between good angels and Luciferian angels which are derived from Milton's *Paradise Lost*, rather than from the Scriptures. We must beware of imposing an unbiblical grid upon our interpretation.

12:8-10

12:8,9 Within the heavenly realm John records the picture of a conflict between "Michael and his angels" and "the dragon and his angels" (12:1). Perhaps the battle was over the work of Jesus Christ and what He would accomplish in His redemptive mission on earth. The dragon and his angels *"were not strong enough"* (12:8) and were *"thrown down"* (12:9). They were defeated and knocked out! This is certainly true when it comes to the soteriological work of Jesus Christ, for the victory cry is issued when Jesus exclaims, "It is finished" (John 19:30) from the cross. The Satanic forces lost the spiritual battle as it was acted out on earth. The "works of the devil were destroyed" (I John 3:8) and the "devil was rendered powerless" (Heb. 2:14) when Jesus "disarmed the rulers and authorities, triumphing over them" (Col. 2:15). It was the beginning of the end for the dragon who is identified as the "serpent of old" (12:9) linking him with the "serpent" in the garden (Gen. 3:1,14,15), and also identified as "the devil" meaning "slanderer" and as "Satan" meaning "adversary." He is also the deceiver who "deceives the whole world," having done so ever since he deceived the whole world of mankind through Adam and Eve, and he continues to lie (John 8:44) and deceive through false religious workers (II Cor. 11:13-15). The important thing for Christians to remember is that Satan has been "thrown down" and defeated by the victory of Jesus Christ.

12:10 That is the reason for the victory announcement being exclaimed by a *"loud voice in heaven, saying, 'Now the salvation, and the power and the kingdom of our God and the authority of His Christ have come'"* (12:10). By the death and resurrection of Jesus Christ salvation has come to mankind. "Now is the day of salvation" (II Cor. 6:2). We are "made safe" from the misuse and abuse of our humanity by Satan, in order to be restored to functional humanity by the indwelling life of the risen Lord Jesus. By the resurrection Jesus became the "Son of God with power" (Rom. 1:4), the spiritual power (Acts 1:8) that works within every Christian (II Cor. 12:9; Eph. 3:20; Col. 1:29). By the acceptance of His vicarious death and the reception of His resurrection life, Christians are "transferred to His kingdom" (Col. 1:13), and "made to be a kingdom" (Rev. 1:6) over which Christ reigns. *"The authority of Christ has come"* (12:10), "all authority in heaven and on earth" (Matt. 28:18), for "God has made Him both Lord and Christ" (Acts 2:36).

The diabolic slanderer, *"the accuser of Christian brethren"* (12:10) has been overcome. The one who seduced man to sin in the first place (Gen. 3:1-6), then began to accuse mankind of their sin to induce shame and increased religious performance. But "there is now no condemnation for those who are in Christ Jesus" (Rom. 8:1). By "the blood of the Lamb" (12:11), the death of Jesus Christ, Satan's endeavors to control mankind were overcome. When Jesus was "lifted up" on the cross, judgment came upon the world-system, and "the ruler of the world was cast out" (John 12:31,32).

It is true that Satan continues to *"come down"* (12:12) to us in temptation. He still seeks to counterfeit and undermine the life of Jesus Christ in Christians (II Cor. 11:13-15). As the "god of this world" (II Cor. 4:4), he is still the deceitful destroyer, the "adversary who prowls about like a roaring lion, seeking someone to devour" (I Peter 5:8). Despite his *"great wrath"* at having been defeated by Christ, he *"knows he has a short time"*

12:13,14

(12:12) to engage in his destructive activities, for the time of the end has been determined by God (Acts 1:7).

In the meantime, as Christians identify with Christ, the Overcomer (John 16:33), they continue to overcome (2:7,11,17,26) Satanic activity, united with Christ in the *"word of witness"* (2:11), "the word of the cross" (I Cor. 1:18). They recognize that the spiritual life which is in Jesus Christ is of ultimate value, and are willing to lose their physical lives, *"even to death"* (12:11), in order to proclaim the victory of Jesus Christ over sin, death and evil. Jesus said, "He who loves his life loses it; and he who hates his life in this world shall keep it to eternal life" (John 12:25). Paul could thus write, "I do not consider my life as dear to myself" (Acts 20:24), for Christians are not engaged in self-preservation of their physical lives but in witness to the eternal life of Jesus Christ, "faithful unto death" (2:10). In confidence we can *"rejoice as heaven-dwellers"* (12:12), "citizens of heaven" (Phil. 3:20), because we know the victory of Christ over Satan and his "earth-dwellers" who specialize in religion.

12:13 John continues to relate the heavenly picture-show, explaining that *"when the dragon saw he was thrown down"* and defeated by the victory of Christ on the cross, *"he pursued the woman who gave birth to the male child"* (12:13). Unable to attack the "Jerusalem above", he attacks the earthly counterpart and representation of such in the Christian community. With a *"river"* of lies and a *"flood"* of hatred and violence,

12:14 the devil pours forth his rage. In that divinely limited period of crisis and suffering which will not last forever, symbolized by *"a time and times and half a time"* (12:14), three and a half years, Satan does his work, but

God's people are protected. Just as the Israelites were portrayed as having been "borne on eagles wings" by divine protection from the Egyptians (Exod. 19:4; Deut. 32:10,11), the *"two wings of the great eagle were given to the woman"* (12:14), to the people of God in the "Jerusalem above," indicating God's protection. This does not mean, though, that Christians are protected from or exempted from Satan's destructive activity. ***"The dragon went off to make war with the rest of the woman's offspring, who keep the commandments of God and hold to the testimony of Jesus"*** (12:17). These "offspring" of the "Jerusalem above" are obviously Christians who in the "enigma of the interim" suffer the effects of conflict with Satan and his agents. The church of Jesus Christ will not be destroyed (Matt. 16:18), but Christians do experience much pain and suffering as the devil in his death-throes seeks to thwart the finished work of Christ. Meanwhile Christians "keep the commandments of God" (John 14:15,21; 15:10), recognizing that God is always the dynamic of His own demands, and they "hold to the witness of Jesus" even unto death.

12:17

The Beasts

The ongoing conflict of the dragon and the Christian offspring of the woman is illustrated when John sees the devil standing on *"the sand of the seashore,"* and *"a beast coming up out of the sea"* (13:1). The sea is often represented as a great reservoir of evil from which monsters arise in symbolic imagery. Satan recognizes that he is going to have to take a different approach and employ a different ploy in the spiritual battle against God. He attempts to establish a beach-head by employing the technique of "religion." There is no greater

13:1

13:2,3

"beast" than religion! It is a real monster! Previously referred to as killing the Christian "witnesses" (11:7), the beast from the reservoir of evil is now represented as *"having ten horns,"* a parody of complete power or authority, *"and seven heads,"* a presumption of perfect wisdom. *"On his horns were ten diadems,"* a pretense of full royal regency and a parody of Jesus who is "King of Kings" (19:16). Religion has certainly engaged in the presumption of royal power and perfect knowledge. On the heads of the beast were *"blasphemous names"* whereby it misrepresented itself as God. Religion loves to put "titles" on all its "heads," calling them "Holy Father," "Righteous One," "Most Honorable," and "Reverend," among others.

13:2 The beast is described with characteristics of different animals (13:2), similar to the "four beasts" who are likened to animals in Daniel 7:2-7. One must beware of the deceiving leopard spots of religion, the strong and surly bearishness, and the lion-like mouth that would kill and devour. John has already referred to the religious tendency of Balaam (2:14) which "devours man." It is further explained that *"the dragon has given to the beast his power and his throne and great authority"* (13:2). The beast of religion drives its authority and empowering from Satan, "the ruler of this world" (John 12:31; 14:20; 16:11), "the god of this world" (II Cor. 4:4), who had the audacity to offer Jesus some of his authority when he tempted Him in the wilderness (Luke 4:6).

13:3 On one of the heads of the beast was a *"fatal wound, as if it had been slain and was healed"* (13:3). Religion constantly portrays itself as a "victim" of unfair persecution. They develop a "martyr-complex" which complains that "everybody is out to get us." In this case it appears that the beast of religion is attempting to parody the death and resurrection of Jesus. The phrase used to describe the beast "as if slain" is the same Greek verb construction used to describe the Lamb in 5:6. The preterist interpreters who seek to find a counterpart in the first century point to the suicide of Nero on June 9, A.D. 68, and the subsequent myth of his resurrection, which is known as the *Nero redivivus* legend, but it is not necessary to find a particular historical event to fulfill the symbol since this diminishes the transgenerational and translocational application of the Revelation.

13:4 *"The whole earth was amazed and followed after the beast"* (13:4). "The whole world lies in the Evil One" (I John 5:19). Religion is man's natural propensity. In their devotion to man-made religion, mankind is really "worshipping the dragon." In parody of God's people exclaiming, "Who is like Thee, O Lord?" (Exod. 15:11), sinful men extol satanic religion, saying, *"Who is like the beast, and who is able to wage war with him?"* (13:4). Natural men are awed by and convinced of the invincible power of religion, and are willing to worship such, taking no account of its evil character.

13:5,6 The beast of religion *"speaks arrogant words and blasphemies against God"* (13:5,6). Paul explained that the "man of lawlessness, the son of destruction, opposes and exalts himself above every so-called god or object or worship, displaying himself as being God" (II Thess. 2:3,4). Religion continues to arrogantly proclaim that it speaks for God, making moral pronouncements and political directives that are contrary to the ways of God. The religious beast *"blasphemes God's name and His tabernacle, and those who dwell in heaven"* (13:6). Religion cannot tolerate the character of God nor the

13:7-9

tabernacling of the presence of God within Christian people in like manner as God tabernacled in Jesus when "the Word became flesh" (John 1:14). This is why religion constantly misrepresents and berates the indwelling presence of Jesus in Christians.

13:7 Genuine Christianity, the life of Jesus Christ functioning in Christians, is always in conflict with religion, which *"makes war with the saints to overcome them"* (13:7). "Saints" are Christians, "holy ones" in whom the Holy One, Jesus Christ, lives. Religion always seeks to "overcome" Christians, to "conquer" them. The Greek word used in this verse is *nike*, which we have noted previously in reference to the Nicolaitans (2:6,15) and the rider of the white horse who "went out conquering and to conquer" (6:2).

13:8 As "the whole world lies in the Evil One" (I John 5:19), they will all worship the beast (13:8) of religion, except for the Christians *"whose names have been written from the foundation of the world in the book of life of the Lamb who has been slain"* (13:8). By the foreknowledge of God the names of Christians have been entered in the heavenly register of those who have eternal life in Jesus Christ. Presently these Christians

13:9 must be discerning and faithful. *"If any one has an ear, let him hear"* (13:9), just as the risen Lord Jesus told the seven churches, representing all Christians. Part of Christian discernment is the realization that the demonic warfare and the deception is but for a limited duration. The beast of religion has "authority to act for only forty-two months" (13:5), a divinely limited time which will not last forever. This prompts the *"perseverance and faith of the saints"* (13:10) in order to "abide under" the painful present circumstances by being receptive to the divine indwelling activity of the Savior.

13:10 On the other hand, those *"gathered together for captivity, to captivity they will go, and those who kill with the sword, with the sword they must be killed"* (13:10). This is similar to the language of God threatening His judgment on Israel and Egypt through His prophet Jeremiah (Jere. 15:2; 43:11). Religion "gathers people together" for captivity. In fact, religion is the greatest of captivities as it captivates men's thinking and behavior and "binds them up" in rules, regulations and rituals. The etymological root of the word "religion" is the Latin word *religo* meaning "to bind up." The risen Lord Jesus declares that religionists who captivate others will be captives forever in hell. During His earthly ministry Jesus said that those who "live by the sword, will be killed by the sword" (Matt. 26:52). Religion has certainly been marked by militaristic warfare, "living by the sword" as they fight for their *cause celebre* of moral or doctrinal correctness. They will be killed in like manner as they have killed.

13:11 Sensing his ineffectiveness in seducing Christians by the general "beast of religion," Satan sees the need to become even more deceptive by presenting another form of the beast. *"From the earth,"* out of his world-system, Satan brings forth *"another beast"* (13:11) who is in the form of a counterfeit lamb. Some have attempted to link the two beasts with the ancient legend of the two beasts, Leviathan from the sea and Behemoth from the earth. Others have suggested a diabolic trinity of evil in the dragon, the sea-beast and the earth-beast, representing the devil, the world and the flesh. Tri-unity is to be reserved as an attribute of God

13:11,12

alone; never to be attributed to evil. These suggestions are questionable and without much merit. The symbols seem to point to another form of the beast of religion, who will later be identified with "the false prophet" of religion in 16:13; 19:20 and 20:10.

This second form of the beast is described as having **"two horns like a lamb"** (13:11). This is an obvious attempt to portray itself as Christ-like. It is a satanic subterfuge to parody the Lamb, Jesus Christ. Religion often seeks to project itself as Christ or His representative. Jesus said, "Beware of the false prophets who come to you in sheep's clothing" (Matt. 7:15), while Paul mentioned those religionists who "disguise themselves as apostles of Christ or servants of righteousness" (II Cor. 11:13-15).

As this second form of the beast of religion is somewhat re-formed to better deceive Christians, some might want to identify the first beast as Roman Catholic religion and the second beast as Protestant religion from the Reformation. In this case some will identify the "two horns" of authority either as Luther and Calvin, or perhaps as Calvin and Arminius. It is best, however, to avoid such attempts at precise historical and personal identification, and to simply recognize the deceitful attempts of religion to parody the reality of Jesus.

13:12 Disguised as a lamb, this second beast of religion belies his disguise, for **"he spoke as a dragon"** (13:11). His voice is that of the one who activates all religion, the devil. This is a "dragon in sheep's clothing." The authority of this second beast (13:12) is also derived from Satan (13:4) with the intent of causing men to worship Satan through religion.

13:13 The second beast *"performs great signs and deceives people by those signs"* (13:13,14). It is indicative of religion to attempt to justify its power by manifestations of miraculous "signs and wonders." Moses explained to Israel that "if a prophet or dreamer arises giving you a sign or wonder, saying, 'Let us go after other gods,' do not listen to the words of that prophet, for the Lord your God is testing you." (Deut. 13:1-3). Throughout the earthly ministry of Jesus the religionists were constantly asking Jesus to "show them a sign" (Matt. 16:1), and Jesus explained that they should seek Him "not because they saw signs" (John 4:48; 6:26). In like manner as this second beast, Paul refers to "the lawless one whose coming is in accord with the activity of Satan, with all power and signs and false wonders" (II Thess. 2:9). Religion employs the deception of the diabolic deceiver by deceiving men with alleged "supernatural signs" supposedly attributable to God, but really derived from the power of Satan. Many have been duped into believing in religion because having seen a supernatural manifestation of the miraculous, they concluded it was God at work, when it was actually the devil. The beast of religion *"even makes fire come down out of heaven to the earth in the presence of men"* (13:13). This is a parody of Pentecost. Religion will try to counterfeit every supernatural expression of Christianity with false Pentecostal "signs" and pseudo-charismatic gifts.

13:14 The idolatrous intent of religion is evidenced as the second beast tells people *"to make an image to the beast"* (13:14). The Greek word for "image" is *eikon* from which we get the English word "icon." Religion specializes in making external and idolatrous "graven images." Unable to accept that "Christ is the image of God" (Col. 1:15; II Cor. 4:4), and that God desires

13:15-17

that His divine character be visibly expressed in the behavior of man, religion instead seeks to construct an external visible expression. These may take the form of tangible likenesses of creatures or men as well as religious buildings, or they may be intangible constructs of belief-systems and morality, or the ecclesiastical organizations of institutional religion. Idols all the same!

13:15 Religion proceeds to attempt *"to give breath to the image of the beast"* (13:15), to make it *"come alive,"* and invest it with spiritual life and activity, while also making it *"speak"* (13:15) with pompous pronouncements of piety. Those who *"do not worship the image of the beast are killed"* (13:15). Religion will tolerate no refusal to conform to its tenets. The intolerance of religion is well documented in its destruction and death of nonconformists.

13:16 This second beastly form of religion *"causes all to be given a mark on their right hand, or on their forehead"* (13:16). Conformity of outward identification is important to religion. Religious adherents must be identified by what they do with their "hands" in moral activity and by what they think with their "heads" in an epistemological belief-system. Religion "brands" people so that the whole of society will be "stamped" by their religious adherence and it will "mark" everything
13:17 they do. This includes the right to economic exchange, for *"no one should be able to buy or to sell, except the one who has the mark, of the name of the beast or the number of his name"* (13:17). Religion creates an in-bred favoritism for conformists who bear the "mark" of the "name" of the beast, perhaps by expressing the diabolic character of the one who energizes religion, for "name" often represents character. The "number of his name" also represents the character of the devil in

"self-effort." Those who do not share the "mark" are stigmatized for economic ostracism and boycott. History adequately records these repressive economic actions of religion, and such can still be seen today in the exclusivistic economic practices of evangelicals with their "sign of the fish" on business cards and advertising.

13:18 Christians constantly need the wisdom of Christ (I Cor. 1:24,30) to discern Satan's activity from Christ's activity, to distinguish between religion and genuine Christianity. *"Here is wisdom,"* declares the risen Lord Jesus. *"Let him who has understanding calculate the number of the beast, for the number is that of man; and his number is six hundred and sixty-six"* (13:18). Throughout the Revelation numbers have symbolic significance. Seven is the number of divine perfection, and if the number seven were triplicated as seven hundred and seventy-seven it would represent the triune perfection of the Godhead. The number six falls short of that which is of God. Man certainly falls short of that which is of God and brings glory to God (Rom. 3:23). Six hundred and sixty-six is a number that comes short of perfection. It is a parody on the divine trinity of perfection represented by seven hundred and seventy-seven. It is a number that represents the beast of religion, which though inspired and energized by the self-oriented, rebellious activity of Satan, is evidenced by man's self-effort to appease and please God apart from Jesus Christ. Religion is man's best efforts to construct moral systems and theological formulations and institutional structures. It is the best that man can do as he tries to reach God, just as he did at Babel (Gen. 11:1-9).

The "number of the beast" is explicitly identified as "the number of man" (13:18). Many translations and

13:18

interpretations of this text supply an indefinite article which indicates that the number of the beast is "a man." The original Greek language of the Revelation has no indefinite article, and proper hermeneutic principles allow us to supply such in English translation only if the context demands such for clarity of expression. Such is not the case in this instance. When the indefinite article is supplied it gives the impression that the second beast is to be identified as a singular and particular individual man. This has led to much religious obsession with decoding the cryptographic number of "six hundred and sixty-six" in order to identify a particular person. Speculations have included Nero, Caligula, other Roman emperors, Mohammed, various Roman Catholic popes, Martin Luther, John Calvin, Napoleon, Mussolini, Hitler, various United States presidents, leaders of Russia, etc. The numbers can arbitrarily and subjectively be twisted in order to apply to anyone! When such a procedure is employed the primary emphasis of the vision is missed. There is no need to identify this number as a particular historical individual. When the indefinite article is not supplied, a consistent contextual meaning is evident as the "number of the beast" is explained to be the "number of man" or the "number of mankind" as he engages in religious endeavors. Those who would demand a translation and interpretation that supplies the indefinite article identifying the number of the beast as "a man," must also allow the Jehovah's Witnesses to do the same in their translation of John 1:1, wherein they indicate that the Word was "a god." Few Christian religionists would want to allow such, but equity of translation technique would demand such.

Christian Victors

In this fourth vignette of the vision, like the others of the Revelation, Jesus encourages Christians in every age of the assured victory for those who persevere and do not succumb to religion. The conflict with religion will be intense and the present experience may be painful unto death, but the participation in victory will be even more pleasant than can be imagined.

John looked and saw Jesus Christ, *"the Lamb, standing on Mount Zion"* (14:1). Jesus was standing as Victor on top of the mountain. This was not physical Mount Zion in Palestine, but the "heavenly Jerusalem" (Heb. 12:22), the "Jerusalem above" (Gal. 4:26). The prophet Micah foretold that "the house of the Lord (Jesus) would be established in the top of the mountains,... where He would judge many people, ...and the Lord shall reign over the people of God in mount Zion forever" (Micah 4:1-7). Likewise, the Psalmist expresses that God "has set His king upon the holy hill of Zion" (Ps. 2:6). John sees the fulfillment of these Messianic prophecies in Jesus Christ.

Accompanying Jesus on the victory hill is the full complement of God's people from both old and new covenant periods, the *"one hundred and forty-four thousand, who have the name of Jesus and the name of the Father written on their foreheads"* (14:1). These are Christians who have identified in thought and behavior with the character of God. They have the "mind of Christ" (I Cor. 2:16) in order that the character of God might be exemplified in their behavior unto God's glory. This is in contrast to the identification of unbelieving religionists (13:1,6,8,17).

14:2-4

14:2 John hears a combined *"voice from heaven"* that conveyed the divine presence in *"the sound of many waters like the sound of loud thunder"* (14:2). At the same time it was the voice of melodic praise *"like harpists playing on their harps,"* as noted in 5:8. The

14:3 people of God were singing *"a new song"* (14:3; 5:9) which only the people of God, represented by the number of full complement, "one hundred and forty-four thousand," could learn, *"who had been purchased from the earth"* (14:3). Only Christians who "have been bought with a price" (Acts 20:28; I Cor. 6:20; 7:23) by the redemption of Jesus Christ, and received the Spirit of God so as to "appraise spiritual things" (I Cor. 2:12-16), can understand and appreciate the agony and the ecstasy of this "new song" of praise to God for the eternal blessings in Jesus Christ (Eph. 1:3).

14:4 These people of God are further identified as those *"who have not been defiled with women, for they have kept themselves chaste"* (14:4). This does not mean that the full complement of God's people in heaven are males, nor that they are celibate males or "virgins," nor that they have never sinned (Rom. 3:23), especially sexually (I Cor. 6:11). What it does imply is that Christians have been made pure in heart by the presence of the purity of Jesus Christ and are to allow the purity of His character to be expressed in their behavior in order to be presented to the Bridegroom "as a pure virgin" (II Cor. 11:2), "holy and blameless" (Eph. 5:27).

They are *"the ones who follow the Lamb wherever He goes"* (14:4). Christians are disciples who are to follow Christ's direction wherever He leads as Lord. Denying themselves and taking up their cross, they follow Jesus (Matt. 10:38; Mk. 8:34), "following in His steps" (I Pt. 2:21), even unto death (John 13:36).

They *"have been purchased from among men as first fruits to God and to the Lamb"* (14:4). Christians are redeemed so as to be dedicated to God as His rightful portion in the first-fruits of the harvest (James 1:18).

The heavenly people of God are further identified as having *"no lie found in their mouth"* (14:5). They are not as those who "have exchanged the truth of God for the lie" (Rom. 1:25), and have the indwelling spiritual "liar" operating in them (John 8:44). These who "love and practice lying" will be outside of the heavenly city (Rev. 22:15). Rather, Christians have received the Spirit of Christ who is the Truth (John 14:6), and are to represent His truth in all they say and do (Eph. 4:25; John 3:21). This does not mean that they have never spoken a verbal falsehood, but that the One who is Truth is expressed through them.

These victorious people of God singing a new song in heaven are finally described as *"blameless"* (14:5). All Christians have been made "holy and blameless" in Christ (Eph. 1:4; Col. 1:22). "If the root (Jesus) be holy, so are the branches" (Rom. 11:16).

John then begins to describe a sequence of angelic activities which serve to encourage Christians in every age of the eternal victory that is in Jesus Christ in contrast to the judgment that befalls those who are not identified with Jesus Christ and are involved in religion.

The first angel *"has an eternal gospel to preach to those who live on the earth"* (14:6). During the difficult

14:7,8

trials that Christians experience during the "enigma of the interim," many may wonder whether the gospel is really "good news" since it brings with it "bad news" of suffering, persecution and pain. This angel declares that the gospel is truly the "good news" for all mankind of the vital indwelling dynamic of the life of the risen Lord Jesus restoring mankind to function as God intended, of which we should not be ashamed (Rom. 1:16).

14:7 The angel also admonishes all to *"fear God, give Him glory, and worship the Creator"* (14:7), because His hour of judgment has come by the sending of His Son into the world (John 3:19).

14:8 The second angel declares that *"Babylon the great has fallen"* (14:8). This was historically pre-figured in the Old Testament as the prophets indicated that "Babylon has fallen" (Isa. 21:9; Jere. 58:8,9). On the spiritual plane, Babylon, the city of religion, the religious community, has fallen by the victory of Jesus Christ over all of Satan's activities (I John 3:8). The angel further explains that the femininely personified city of religion *"has made all the nations drink of the wine of the passion of her immorality"* (14:8). This will be repeated in a subsequent vision (17:2; 18:3), of which this angelic statement seems to be a precursor. The city of religion will be identified as "the mother of harlots" (17:5). The entire practice of religion is immoral and contrary to the character of God. Religion fosters and encourages intoxication with unfaithfulness, self-indulgence, self-gratification, sensual passions, and with false loyalties and liaisons. The "deeds of the flesh" which include "immorality, impurity, sensuality, drunkenness and carousing" (Gal. 5:19-21) are indicative of religious behavior.

The third angel exclaims that *"if anyone worships the* **14:9,10**
religious beast and the visible expression thereof, and
identifies with religion in thought or action, marked
on forehead or hand, they will partake of the full
undiluted strength of the wine of the wrath of God"
(14:9,10). The Psalmist used similar judgment terminology, referring to "a cup in the hand of the Lord, and
the wine is well mixed, and the wicked must drain and
drink down its dregs" (Ps. 75:8). The prophets used the
same imagery, even in reference to Babylon (Isa. 51:17;
Jere. 25:15-17). This third angel amplifies the imagery **14:11**
of judgment by declaring that religionists *"who worship*
the beast and his image and receive the mark of his
name, will be tormented with fire and brimstone forev-
er and ever, with no rest day and night" (14:10,11).

The purpose for this trilogy of angelic announcements **14:12**
is to provide an incentive for Christians to persevere
and remain faithful. *"Herein is revealed the necessity*
for the perseverance of the saints," says John (14:12).
We must *"keep the commandments of God"* by recognizing that God is the dynamic of His own demands,
and continue to have *"faith in Jesus"* which is the
response of our receptivity of God's activity.

A loud voice then tells John to write down what is the **14:13**
second of the beatitudes in the Revelation. *"Blessed are*
the dead who die in the Lord" (14:13). All Christians
who are "faithful unto death" (2:10) are "blessed" of
God rather than cursed with the wrath and judgment
of God. The *"from now on"* phrase can be attached to
several of the verbs in this verse. It can mean "*blessed*
from now on," "*die* from now on," or "*rest* from now
on." The Spirit of God concurs with the unidentified
voice, indicating that Christian martyrs who die because

of their identification with Jesus Christ, *"will rest from their labors"* and from the difficulties of living in this hostile world.

14:14 The next scenario that John sees is a *"white cloud"* representing the presence of God, with *"one like a son of man"* sitting on the cloud (14:14). The identification is similar to that described by Daniel of "one like a son of man" whose kingdom would not be destroyed (Dan. 7:13,14). In both passages the reference seems to be to Jesus Christ, though some have interpreted the personage here in the Revelation who is *"sitting on the cloud"* as but another angel. The *"golden victory crown"* (14:14) on His head, though, would better signify Jesus and His "everlasting dominion" (Dan. 7:14).

The fact that the person pictured also wields a *"sharp sickle in His hand"* also seems to illustrate the divine action of harvest imagery, which becomes the primary theme of the remaining verses of this chapter. The interpretive question is whether this is the harvest of judgment or the harvest of the ingathering of God's people. Both symbols are used throughout the Scriptures. The harvest of judgment is referred to as "a threshing floor" (Jere. 51:33), and as the "wine press of God's wrath" (Isa. 63:2-6) upon wickedness (Hosea 6:11; Joel 3:11). On the other hand, the idea of harvest is used more particularly in the New Testament to refer to the gathering of people into God's fold, as Jesus explained that "the fields were white unto harvest, but the workers are few" (John 4:35-38; Matt. 9:37; Lk. 10:2), but we are to "put in the sickle, because the harvest has come" (Mk. 4:29).

Those who would interpret the imagery of 14:15-20 as that of judgment point out the similarity of terminology with the Old Testament statements of harvest judgment. They also note that *"the hour having come to reap"* is similar to the previous mention in this same chapter of *"the hour of His judgment having come"* (14:7), that **"the power over fire"** (14:18) is often associated with judgment (Matt. 18:8; II Thess. 1:7), and that the wine press is that of *"the wrath of God"* (14:19).

Those who interpret the action of these verses as the ingathering of God's harvest of souls will note the previous reference in this same chapter of Scripture to the imagery of Christians being the "first-fruits" of the harvest (14:4). They will point out the similarity of the *"harvest being ripe"* (14:15,18) to the statements of Jesus (John 4:35).

Perhaps the imagery is broad enough to encompass both concepts of harvest as is seen in Jesus' parable of the wheat and the tares (Matt. 13:36-43). The wheat is gathered along with the tares, but the tares are "burned with fire." The predominant emphasis of this passage (14:15-20) here in Revelation still seems to be that of judgment, especially when we note that the action of the wine press takes place *"outside the city"* (14:20), meaning outside of the New Jerusalem where God's people dwell. The extensive blood-bath that results from the wine press outside the city seems more representative of God's judgment upon non-Christians and religionists than the blood-bath of martyrs, though that has been quite extensive as well.

15:1

15:1 John then saw *"another sign in heaven"* (15:1) with *"seven angels who had seven plagues"* representing the perfection and completion of God's judgment of wrath. This might also indicate that the foregoing harvest imagery what that of judgment.

15:2 Then John saw the contrast of those who were *"victorious over the* (religious) *beast"* (15:2), those who are "conquerors through Christ" (Rom. 8:37), who had not identified with the visible expression of religious ecclesiasticism and that numerical equivalent of human effort energized by Satan. The people of God were *"standing on the sea of glass, holding harps of God,"* the tranquil setting of melodic worship before God's throne. They
15:3 sing *"the song of Moses"* (15:3), for the song that the Israelites sang in their pre-figurative deliverance from Egypt (Exodus 15:1-18) is like unto *"the song of the Lamb"* (15:3) celebrating Christian deliverance over
15:4 sin, death, Satan and religion. God's *"righteous acts"* and His victory in Jesus Christ have indeed *"been revealed."*

What is the purpose of this perspective of the Revelation? Christians in every age must understand that the spiritual source of earthly conflict against them is to be traced back to Satan, the devil, the serpent, the dragon (chapter 12). The "beasts" through which Satan acts to administer his evil is in varied forms of religion (chapter 13). But we must ever be reminded that "the victory is ours in Christ Jesus," and that there are dire consequences of judgment for those who succumb to temptation and religion (14:1 – 15:4).

Interspersed throughout each of these chapters is a call for Christians to respond with faithful perseverance. "Rejoice, you who dwell in the heavenlies, for the devil only has a short time" (12:12). "Be discerning (13:9) and understanding (13:18) about the activity of religion." "Recognize the necessity and incentive for perseverance in keeping God's commandments and responding in faith to Jesus Christ" (14:12). Can you sing the song of those who have "come off victorious from the beast of religion" (15:2)? Every day is decision-time for Christians to decide if they will remain faithful to Christ. Whenever we might lapse into religion, we need to repent of our sin and turn again to the receptivity of the activity of Jesus Christ.

Religion and Babylon

Revelation 15:5 – 19:10

The risen Lord Jesus has exposed religion in the churches, revealed the working of religion by the imagery of the breaking of the seals, warned religionists by the trumpet blasts, identified the diabolic connection of the religious beast with the satanic dragon, and He now shows the destruction of the religious community represented as Babylon. It must be remembered that these are synchronous panoramas of what happens in "the enigma of the interval" between Christ's comings, rather than chronologically sequential segments of past history, present experience or future events.

Jesus Christ is preparing Christians in every age for the difficult trials they will encounter prior to His returning to earth again. His victory has been accomplished by His "finished work" (John 19:30) in death, resurrection and Pentecostal outpouring. Satan's work has been "rendered powerless" (Heb. 2:14) and "destroyed" (I John 3:8). Nevertheless the conflict continues so that the choice of faith among mankind may continue to be operative, and Christians might recognize the necessity of continuing their receptivity of divine activity in their lives, even if it means being "faithful unto death" (Rev. 2:10). Satan's substitute for "salvation through sanctification" (II Thess. 2:13) is self-righteousness through religion. The static activities of religion are the antithesis to the dynamic life of Jesus Christ being lived out through Christians. Satan will do all he can to quench the expression of Christ's life in Christians which serves to glorify God. But religion will not win the day. God will judge those who chose religion instead of Jesus Christ.

The scenario that unfolds in this perspective of the Revelation reveals God's judgment upon those in the religious community. The third vision of the seven trumpets indicated God's warning of judgments upon religion, and there was an interval before the seventh trumpet to intensify the call for repentance. The seven bowls of judgment in this "clip" of the big picture proceed uninterrupted with little or no expectation of repentance (16:9,11). The religionists seem to have become incorrigibly "fixed" in their attachment to the false god of religion, with "hardened hearts" toward all that God has for them in Jesus Christ.

As with the trumpet-judgments, these bowl-judgments have an obvious correlation with the plague-judgments that came upon Egypt prior to the exodus (Exod. 7-11). God's judgment came upon Egypt, the oppressors of God's people, in a series of natural phenomena which serve as a pre-figuring of God's judgment action against religion. The images of natural disaster employed in this vision symbolize the invisible and spiritual realities of God's judgment. The natural order of the physical universe is not be destroyed in these judgment scenes, for that will be presented later in 21:1.

Seven Bowls

John again describes the image of a temple in heaven (15:5), representing the presence of God. In the old covenant the "tablets of testimony" (Exod. 32:15) were the tablets of the decalogue, the ten commandments, which were in the Holy of Holies of the tabernacle. Stephen declared that "our fathers had the tabernacle of testimony in the wilderness" (Acts 7:44; Numb. 1:50; 17:7; 18:2)), but after Christ has come "the Most High does not dwell in houses made by human hands" (Acts 7:48). The *"tabernacle of testimony"* was only a pre-figuring, "a shadow of heavenly things" (Heb. 8:5). "The temple of the tabernacle of testimony in heaven" is an expression of the dwelling-place of the witnesses of God in His presence.

15:5

Seven angels came out of the heavenly temple with seven plagues (15:6), representing God's judgment. They were *"clothed in linen, clean and bright, and girded with golden vests"* (15:6). These represent priestly garb (Exod. 28:36-39).

15:6

One of the four living creatures John saw earlier (4:6,8; 5:6) gave the seven angels *"seven golden bowls full of the wrath of God"* (15:7). Bowls or basins were vessels used as containers for the blood of sacrificed animals in the religious function of the old covenant temple (Exod. 24:6; 27:3). Jeremiah reports that the Babylonians carried off all the temple basins to Babylon (Jere. 52:18), indicating the destruction of Jewish religion. But those stolen bowls will come back to haunt the figurative Babylon as the bowls from the heavenly temple are "full of the wrath of God," and religionists "will drink of the undiluted wine of the wrath of God"

15:7

15:8 (14:10). That the golden bowls of heavenly temple service were previously filled with the fragrance incense of the prayers of the saints (5:8) serves to illustrate that God's wrath is not incompatible with His compassion.

John also observes that *"the temple was filled with smoke from the glory of God and from His power"* (15:8). Smoke sometimes represents the fire of divine judgment or the darkness of hell-fire (9:1,2), but it would appear that it here represents the concealing of the invisible presence of God as was noted by Moses (Exod. 19:18) and Isaiah (Isa. 6:4) in the Old Testament. The completion of God's judgment activity against all that is contrary to His character is deemed so necessary that *"no one was able to enter the temple until the seven plagues of the seven angels were finished"* (15:8).

16:1 A loud voice emanating from God's presence in the heavenly temple commanded the seven angels to *"Go and pour out the seven bowls of the wrath of God into the earth"* (16:1). The psalmist and the prophets spoke of God's wrath and indignation being "poured out upon the nations which do not call upon God's name" (Ps. 79:6; Jere. 10:25; Zeph. 3:8). The angels are instructed to "pour out the seven bowls of God wrath into the earth," or into the world-system of Satan in which religion functions.

16:2 When the first angel poured out his bowl of God's wrath into the earth, *"it became a loathsome and malignant sore upon those who had the mark of the beast and who worshiped his image"* (16:2). The plague of boils (Exod 9:9,10) may have pre-figured this judgmental consequence. A disgusting and ugly cancer is inflicted upon religionists. The previous discussion of the beast and those identified with him (13:16-18; 14:9,11; 15:2) explained that religion is "marked" and "stamped" with the character of Satan, and engages in the idolatrous worship of external expressions of ecclesiasticism, morality, doctrine, etc. God judges such diabolic identification and idolatrous worship of religion.

16:3 The bowl of the second angel is poured out into the sea, whereupon the sea becomes the *"blood of a dead man, and every living thing in the sea dies"* (16:3). This judgment may have been pre-figured by the plague of turning the water into blood (Exod. 7:17-21). As the sea is often portrayed as the reservoir of evil (13:1), this bowl seems to represent the judgment of death that will come upon those operating in the cesspool of religion.

16:4 *"The third angel poured out his bowl into the rivers and springs of waters, and they became blood"* (16:4). This too may have been pre-figured by the plague wherein God judged Egypt by "turning their rivers to blood, and from their streams they could not drink" (Ps. 78:44). The *"rivers and springs of water"* are the sources for the quenching of thirst. Religion offers a false fulfillment of man's God-given need of spiritual thirst, and God will judge those engaged in such fraudulent activity.

16:5 After this third picture of judgment John records the spontaneous shout of praise from *"the angel of the waters"* (16:5). Angels were often regarded as having specific guardianship over natural phenomena such as fire (14:18) or wind (7:1). The angel declares, along with the psalmist (Ps. 119:137), that God is righteous and holy in His judgment of the religionists and their

16:6 activities. The rationale for such is that it was these very religionists that *"poured out the blood of saints and prophets"* (16:6; 17:6; 18:24), and now they in turn must drink blood. The punishment fits the crime! The "oppressors become drunk with their own blood" (Isa. 49:26). *"They deserve it,"* declares the angel. This is justice! *"Yes,"* says a voice from the heavenly altar, which may be the collective voice of the "souls under

16:7 the altar" (6:9), *"true and righteous are Thy judgments, O Lord God, the Almighty"* (16:7). Note that the KJV translates "they deserve it," as "they are worthy," transferring the pronoun to indicate that Christian martyrs are worthy of God's judgment on religionists because their blood has been shed. The context does not seem to support the translation of the KJV.

16:8 The fourth angel then appears, pouring out his bowl upon the sun (16:8). God's judgment of fire scorches the religionists with fierce heat. Religion which has burned godly men at the stake, shall suffer the fire and the heat themselves. By contrast, for those faithful ones in the presence of God, the "sun does not beat on them, nor any heat" (7:16).

16:9 Do the religionists repent? No! Religion is recalcitrant in its rebellion (2:21; 9:20,21; 16:11). Instead, *"they blasphemed the name of God who has the power over these plagues"* (16:9,21), just as they are represented as doing in the figure of the beast (13:1,5,6; 17:3).

16:10 It is *"the throne of the beast"* (16:10) upon which the fifth angel pours out his bowl of God's wrath. The headquarters of religion, where they assume kingly authority on a "throne given to them by the devil" (13:2) as a parody of the authority of God on His throne, will be judged. Pre-figured perhaps by the judgment plague of darkness, the kingdom of religion will become darkened with "a darkness which can be felt" (Exod. 10:21). As they try to function without light, *"they gnaw their tongues because of pain."* This is contrasted, of course, with the absence of pain in the heavenly realm (21:4). Still, they do not repent, and continue to blaspheme God (16:11).   **16:11**

Then the sixth angel *"poured out his bowl upon the great river, the Euphrates; and its water was dried up, that the way might be prepared for the kings of the east"* (16:12). As with the judgment pictured in the sixth trumpet, the Euphrates river was the easternmost boundary of the territory given to God's people, beyond which lived the Assyrians and the Parthian barbarians who were used of God to invade and plunder God's people when they were unfaithful and turned to false religion. These occasions seem to have pre-figured the judgment of God in allowing the invasion of hostile and powerful forces upon adulterous religion. When the waters of the Euphrates are dried up, this allows easy access for the "kings of the east" to launch their assault. There is no reason to attempt to identify the "kings of the east" as particular world leaders in any given period of time, for it is merely a symbol of hostile and barbarian forces that attack the peoples of religion.   **16:12**

Following the description of the sixth bowl of judgment John saw a trio of images that represent those on whom these bowls of judgment are being poured. The dragon is the satanic source of evil (chapter 12). The beast is Satan's religious agency of evil (chapter 13). The false prophet is the religious method of evil, which Jesus said "would arise and show signs and wonders, in

16:13,14

order, if possible, to lead the elect astray" (Mark 13:22). This trio are subjected to God's judgments, and will eventually be destroyed (20:10).

16:13 Out of the mouths of these three figures come *"three unclean spirits like frogs"* (16:13). This may have been pre-figured by the plague of frogs (Exod. 8:1-7),
16:14 but John identifies these frog-like spirits as *"spirits of demons"* (16:14). Inherent within all idolatrous religion is demonic activity, as Paul explained to the Athenians (Acts 17:22) and the Corinthians (I Cor. 10:19-21). Recognizing that "we wrestle not against flesh and blood, but against principalities and powers" (Eph. 6:12), Paul was concerned that Christians would not "fall away from the faith, paying attention to deceitful spirits and doctrines of demons" (I Tim. 4:1). Demonic propaganda proceeds from the mouths of this threesome of religion.

Demonic activity also deceives men by *"performing signs"* (16:14) which are taken to be derived from God, but are actually the activity of Satan. Paul warned the Thessalonians of "the lawless one... whose coming is in accord with the activity of Satan, with all power and signs and false wonders" (II Thess. 2:9). Religion attempts to parody the supernatural activity of God, as explained in the previous vision of the beast who "deceives those who dwell on the earth because of the signs which it was given him to perform" (13:14).

The demonically inspired religious agencies *"go out to the kings of the whole world, to gather them together for the war of the great day of God, the Almighty"* (16:14). By their propaganda and demonstrations of power religion tries to influence governmental leaders and mobilize them to serve its purposes. Governments often cater to the power of religion and enter into alliances with religious leaders. The Messianic psalm indicates that "the kings of the earth take their stand against the Lord and against His Anointed, ...but God has installed His King upon Zion, the holy mountain" (Ps. 2:2,5). The conflict between God and the religious/governmental alliances has taken place in the past, continues to take place, and will take place until the ultimate showdown and war between Christ and the confederacy of evil. John sees them *"gathered together at the place which in Hebrew is call Har-Magedon"* (16:16). The Hebrew word *Har* means "mountain," and the word *Magedon* has often been connected with the site of Megiddo in the plain of Esdraelon at the foot of Mount Carmel. Megiddo was the site of much warfare throughout Biblical history (cf. Judges 4,5; II Chron. 35:20-27). In fact, the background of the name Megiddo seems to mean "attack, raid, maraud, plunder or pillage." Religion, like Megiddo, is a natural battleground, and engages in plundering attacks on those around them, desiring to the very end to be "king of the mountain." The physical site of Megiddo in Palestine symbolizes by its name and its history what religion does. This does not mean that Megiddo will be the physical site of what has been called "the final battle of Armageddon." The emphasis is not on the geographical location, but on the figurative significance of a mountain of destruction in the conclusive battle between Satan and Christ. In the pre-figuring of the physical Babylon as the opponent of God's people, they were identified as a "destroying mountain" (Jere. 51:25) which seems to coincide with the meaning of "Har-Magedon."

16:15-18

Apparently parenthetically, the risen Lord Jesus reminds Christians of His impending return which will be unannounced and unexpected, a sudden surprise *"like a thief"* (16:15). Jesus used the same metaphor with the church at Sardis (3:3), and Paul explained that "the day of the Lord will come just like a thief in the night" (I Thess. 5:2). A sense of urgency is intended, encouraging God's servants to be alert (Luke 12:37), watchful and discerning. Employing the third beatitude of the Revelation, Jesus says, *"Blessed is the one who stays awake and keeps his garments, lest he walk about naked and men see his shame"* (16:15). Christians are to be clothed with the character of Christ's righteousness and holiness, keeping their eyes open to the spiritual significance of what is happening.

16:17 When the seventh angel poured out the final bowl *"upon the air, a loud voice came out of the temple from the throne, saying, 'It is done.'"* (16:17). Remembering that Satan is "the prince of the power of the air" (Eph. 2:2), this scene depicts the completion of God's judgment upon religion. The victory of Christ over Satan was accomplished on the cross from which Jesus exclaimed, "It is finished!" (John 19:30), but the consummating completion of that which was set in motion on Golgotha is being portrayed here in the Revelation. God's judgment on religion will be "done," and the entirety of His restoration of the perfect order will be "done" (21:6).

16:18 Illustrating this final bowl of judgment were *"flashes of lightning and sounds of peals of thunder"* (16:18) representing God's powerful presence (4:5), as well as *"a great earthquake"* like none ever experienced previously. Religion is truly shaken up, but God's people are participating in "a kingdom which cannot be shaken" (Heb. 12:28).

Religion is wrenched apart in the scene where John sees *"the great city split into three parts"* (16:19). The "great city" is identified as *"Babylon the great."* The designation of Babylon was apparently derived from the religious effort at Babel (Gen. 11:1-9) which became a situation of confusion and a symbol of futility. The Babylon of ancient history is repeatedly referred to throughout the Old Testament as a feared opponent of God's people (Isa. 47,48; Jere 25,50,51; Ezek. 26-28; Dan. 2,7), which served as a pre-figuring of the satanically inspired evil of the spiritual city of Babylon, the religious community, and its barbarous adversarial assaults on the community of saints, the holy city of the new Jerusalem (21:10). Previously in the Revelation "the great city" is linked "mystically" or spiritually with the designation of Sodom and Egypt and Jewish Jerusalem (11:8), all of which represent communities of false religion, and could conceivably be connected with the "three part" split of Babylon.

In His omniscience God remembers the atrocities of Babylon, and gives to the collective religious community *"the cup of the wine of His fierce wrath"* (16:19). The "bowls" of judgment become the "cup" of judgment which religion must drink. The religious community will drink the cup like Jim Jones' community in Guyana, and be burned up (17:16) like David Koresh's community in Waco, Texas!

In this final divine judgment *"the cities of the nations fell"* (16:19) with all the social structures that are held together by religion. *"Every island fled away"* (16:20);

16:21 all the religious refuges and hiding places are removed. *"The mountains were not found"* (16:20); the religious high-places where they encourage "mountain-top experiences," build their idolatrous temples, and continue to pile up mountains of traditions will vanish. Religion gets *"pounded"* with *"huge hailstones"* (16:21), which may have been pre-figured by the plague-judgment of hail upon Egypt (Exod. 9:22) and the punishment of the Amorites (Josh. 10:11). Despite the *"plague of hail which is extremely severe"* (16:21) the religionists refuse to repent, and with hardened hearts they *"blaspheme God."*

Babylon the Great

The seventeenth and eighteenth chapters of the Revelation provide an expanded and detailed explanation of the judgment of the seventh bowl against Babylon. The action of God against the religious community and the consequences of such judgment are more specifically illustrated.

17:1 John reports that *"one of the seven angels who had the seven bowls came"* and invited him to come and see *"the judgment of the great harlot who sits on many waters"* (17:1). The "great city" (16:19) of Babylon is the "great harlot," as identified in 17:5. Whereas the Judaic city of Jerusalem was pictured as a harlot (Isa. 1:21) by its unfaithful participation in religion, the figurative city of Babylon, the community of religion, has prostituted itself with mankind, both figuratively and literally, in defiance of God. The "waters" on which this harlot sits are later identified as "peoples and multitudes and nations and tongues" (17:15), evidencing the universality of religion among men.

17:2 The religious prostitute has *"committed immorality with the kings of the earth, and those who dwell on the earth were made drunk with the wine of her immorality"* (17:2). There has always been an intimate intercourse between religion and the politicos of government as they meet each other's needs. Many have been intoxicated with the immorality of religion, with the self-indulgence and self-gratification of sensual passions and illicit liaisons. Just as judgment came upon Nineveh "because of the many harlotries of the harlot, the charming one, the mistress of sorceries, who sells nations by her harlotries," and God said, "'I am against you, and I will lift up your skirts over your face, and show to the nations your nakedness and to the kingdoms your disgrace" (Nahum 3:4), so God will judge the harlotry of religion.

17:3 Under the influence of the Holy Spirit, *"in the Spirit,"* John was carried away into a wilderness where he saw *"a woman sitting on a scarlet beast, full of blasphemous names, having seven heads and ten horns"* (17:3). The woman is the harlot of the religious community who is riding on the beast of religion (chapter 13) which has "seven heads," representing the religious pretense of perfect knowledge, and "ten horns," representing the religious parody of absolute power, with "blasphemous names" by which religion disparages God (13:1,5,6) expressed by the heads.

17:4 *"The woman was clothed in purple and scarlet, and adorned with gold and precious stones and pearls"* (17:4). Purple and scarlet clothing provides a parody of the eminence and importance of royalty, for she will later declare herself a "queen" (18:7). Her excessive adornment reveals her to be but a gaudy tramp, just

17:4,5

as religion is enamored with the external trappings of wealth and splendor. The harlot is to be contrasted, of course, with the "woman" who gives birth to the Messiah (12:1,6,14) which, if this represents the "Jerusalem above" (Gal. 4:26), can also be identified with "the bride" (19:7,8), who is clothed with the "bright and clean" garments of the purity of Christ's character.

If you have ever seen a drunk prostitute, you can envision God's portrayal of the religious community. She is *"drunk with the blood of the saints"* (17:6) and *"has in her hand a gold cup full of abominations and the unclean things of her immorality"* (17:4), whereupon she invites all to "drink to her success!" Such a drunken slut is a disgusting sight, and yet they think they are so beautiful and entertaining. The cup of the religious harlot is filled with all that is abominable to God and with the filth of spiritual fornication which is contrary to the character of God. The harlot is "high" on the blood of the saints, for it is religion that is guilty of most of the deaths by martyrdom of God's people, as Jesus explained to the religious scribes and Pharisees their guilt of "all the righteous blood shed on earth" (Matt. 23:35).

17:5 Upon the forehead of this "scarlet woman" on the "scarlet beast" was written a title of identification, *"Babylon the great, the mother of harlots, and of the abominations of the earth"* (17:5). The religious community is the womb for, gives birth to, and is the nurturer of the prostitution of God's created humanity. Religion is the mother of infidelity and every abominable misrepresentation of God's character. This diabolic character of religion is "written" upon all the depraved thinking that it generates.

The label by which the woman was identified was a *"mystery"* to John. He *"wondered"* at its meaning (17:6,7), but the angel volunteered to explain the mystery so that it would become a mystery "once concealed, but now revealed." The wisdom (17:9) to understand such, though, is only found in Christ, who is our wisdom (I Cor. 1:24,30). All those who are not Christians, whose names are *"not written in the book of life from the foundation of the world"* (17:8), the registry of heavenly citizenship known by the foreknowledge of God, they will continue to wonder at the mystery of the imagery of the woman and the beast. Indeed they still do as they continue to proffer increasingly absurd speculations about the meaning of the symbols contained in the Revelation. The world of mankind apart from Jesus Christ is constantly amazed at religion and how it works. Religion "keeps popping up!" You cannot keep it down. When the superstition and ignorance of religion are exposed and religion regresses, this is inevitably followed by the resurgence of religion in another form. Religion will continue to survive with "ups and downs" so long as man and the satanic world-system exist. It is *"the beast that was and is not and will come"* (17:8).

17:6,7

17:8

The angel thus explained the religious beast to John as that which *"was and is not, and is about to come up out of the abyss and to go to destruction"* (17:8). This may be a reference to the Judaic form of religion which was operative for centuries in the past, but at the time when John saw the vision of the Revelation it was no longer functioning since it was destroyed along with Jerusalem in 70 A.D. That did not mean, though, that the Judaic form of religion and many others as well would

17:9-16

not "come up out of the abyss" (17:8) from the source of Satan, and be doomed to destruction.

17:9 Continuing to detail the meaning of the religious beast, the angel explains that *"the seven heads are seven mountains on which the woman sits"* (17:9). The heads of religion are engaged in the "high places" of religious hierarchy and academic "higher learning." They can also be illustrated as *"seven kings"* in their pretense of the fullness of authority and power. The
17:10 form of religion that *"has not yet come"* (17:10) but *"will come"* (17:8) and *"is about to come"* (17:10) may be the institutionalized misnomer of the "Christian religion" which was created when Constantine tried to merge Christianity with the Roman empire in the fourth century. The beast of so-called "Christian religion" is still with us today, *"remaining a little while"* (17:10) which is obviously relative to the context of God's eternity.

It appears that the angel is telling John that there will be an alignment of religion with the complete authority
17:12 of world government, symbolized by *"ten horns which are ten kings"* (17:12). That alliance of government and religion will be brief, *"for one hour"* (17:12), where-
17:13 upon the government leaders will abdicate their *"power and authority to the beast"* (17:13), to the religious
17:16 leaders. Together they will then *"hate the harlot and will make her desolate and naked, and will eat her flesh and will burn her with fire"* (17:16). Does this mean that the marriage of religion and government will betray and double-cross the religious community? This would be consistent with the love/hate relationship of religion and Satan, as well as the self-destructive tendency fostered by the destroyer of men. Like the sisters,

Oholah and Oholibah which symbolize the religious harlotry of Samaria and Jerusalem in Ezekiel 23, the harlot of the religious community will be made *"desolate and naked"* (17:16). It will suffer the indignity of having its flesh eaten, as did another symbol of religion, Jezebel (II Kings 9:36; 2:20), and will be *"burned up with fire"* (17:16). The angel explains that God in His sovereignty has put it into the hearts of the world leaders to give up their kingdoms to the religious beast, in order *"to execute God's purpose by having a common purpose, until the words of God should be fulfilled"* (17:17). God can use Satan, religion and human government for His purposes, for ultimately everything serves the supreme purposes of God.

The imagery of chapter seventeen is summed up when the angel explains to John that *"the woman whom you saw is the great city, which reigns over the kings of the earth"* (17:18). The "great city," Babylon, is equated with the harlot-woman, as labeled in 17:5, forming the religious community which rides on the back of the religious beast (17:3). Religion and the religious community *"reign over the kings of the earth"* (17:18) and manipulate human government in one way or another. Together they *"wage war against the Lamb"* (17:14), for the alliance of religion and human government is in conflict with Jesus Christ and those identified with Him, *"those who are the called and chosen and faithful"* (17:14), i.e. genuine Christians. The outcome of this war has already been determined, for *"the Lamb will overcome them, because He is Lord of lords and King of kings"* (17:14). Jesus Christ has won the victory over all satanic efforts (I John 3:8: Heb. 2:14). His conquest was established by His death on the cross (John 19:30), whereby He overcame the world (John 16:33), and "sat

18:1,2

down on the throne of His Father" (Rev. 3:21) as "the ruler of the kings of the earth" (Rev. 1:5). He is the divine "God of gods" (Deut. 10:17), "Lord of lords and King of kings" (I Tim. 6:15; Rev. 19:16).

18:1 The eighteenth chapter of the Revelation provides another "window" on God's judgment of Babylon, the city of harlotry, representing the religious community. Several of the images employed are similar to the pictorialization employed in the prophecy of Jeremiah as he told of the fall of physical Babylon, which served as a pre-figuring of the fall of the diabolically spiritual Babylon which is being referred to here in the Revelation.

John sees *"another angel coming down from heaven, bearing God's authority"* (18:1), and illuminating earth with the reflection of God's glory, which can only be described as "unapproachable light" (I Tim. 6:16).
18:2 The angel declares, *"Fallen, fallen is Babylon the great!"* (18:2), in like manner as the announcement of the pre-figuring of the fall of the Babylon of old (Isa. 21:9). The religious community will ultimately and finally be destroyed.

Rightfully so, for the religious community *"has become a dwelling place of demons and a prison for every unclean spirit, and a prison of every unclean and hateful bird"* (18:2). Religion is always a habitation of demons. It is by definition idolatrous and demonic activity. When Paul saw the idols in Athens, he explained that they were very "religious," with great respect for demons (Acts 17:22), and went on to tell Timothy that "in later times some will fall away from the faith, paying attention to deceitful spirits and doctrines of demons" (I Tim. 4:1). "Every unclean spirit" is operative in religion, contrasted with "nothing unclean" in the New Jerusalem (21:27). "Every unclean and hateful bird" is present in religious activity, meaning that the scavenger birds which prey upon others, such as hawks, kites, ravens and vultures (cf. Isa. 34:11,15) illustrate religious activity as they prey upon others.

18:3

The angel reiterates that *"the nations have drunk of the wine of the passion of her immorality, and the kings of the earth have committed immorality with her, and the merchants of the earth have become rich by the wealth of her sensuality"* (18:3). The peoples of the world have definitely been intoxicated with the religious passion for self-indulgence, self-gratification and self-fulfillment. Religion traffics in sensual experiences (Gal. 5:19), and promotes intimate and illicit associations. World leaders have been seduced by religion and have entered into mutually self-gratifying alliances with religion. The merchants of the earth have become rich, since much of the economy of the world is greatly influenced or controlled by religion. The justice of God demands that He judge religion!

18:6

A voice from heaven (18:4) urges that God should *"pay back"* religion *"even as she has paid"* (18:6), according to her deeds. The principle of just retribution is ordained by God. Paul wrote, "Do not be deceived, God is not mocked; for whatever a man sows, this he will also reap" (Gal. 6:7). In the pre-figuring of God's judgment on physical Babylon, she was to be "repaid according to her work" (Jere. 50:29), "for all the evil they have done" (Jere. 51:24). The punishment should fit the crime. In like manner as religion has destroyed, she shall be destroyed. Religion must drink the deadly brew which she has mixed and distributed. It might

18:7-10

appear that God is being urged to repay *"double"* with *"twice as much"* (18:6) judgment consequence, but the word can also mean "to duplicate with equivalence."

18:7 This would coincide with the next statement, *"To the degree that she glorified herself and lived sensuously, to the same degree give her torment and mourning"* (18:7). Religion has certainly engaged in proud self-glorification, saying "Look at us; at our buildings and our statistical successes!" She has "lived sensuously," as can be seen in what she calls "worship," which is often but sensuous stroking of personal pleasuring. Religion pompously declares herself a *"queen, who will never see the mourning of widowhood,"* just as Babylon of old declared (Isa. 47:7,8). She may indeed be the "queen of the house of prostitution," married to Satan until they are both destroyed in the end.

Jesus said, "Everyone who exalts himself shall be humbled" (Luke 14:11), so the hubris and pride of religion will result in the humbling and pain of *"torment and mourning"* (18:7). Her preening pride will lead to **18:8** *"plagues of judgment, pestilence and mourning and famine, and she will be burned up with fire"* (18:8).

18:9,10 The *"kings of the earth"* for whom religion served as paramour and mistress, will stand at a distance for their own self-preservation, and *"will weep and lament over her burning"* (18:9), crying *"Woe, woe, the great city, Babylon, the strong city!"* (18:10), for they will see that she was "damned" and "cursed" of God. They will be surprised at the suddenness of the judgment on religion and how rapidly she is destroyed, in "one day" (18:8), even *"one hour"* (18:10,17,19).

18:11 Likewise, *"the merchants of the earth will weep and mourn over the destruction of religion, because no one buys their cargoes any more"* (18:11). Religion not only purchases a vast amount of goods to invest on itself, but has fostered an attitude of physical materialism among men, and often directly or indirectly controlled the corrupt flow of commerce. In particular, religion has trafficked in commodities which are expensive and luxurious, extravagant and ostentatious, non-essential items which project glamour and prosperity and wealth, which they have used for their own self-indulgence and personal pleasure. The inventory listed in 18:12-14 even includes *"slaves and human lives,"* as religion has indeed fostered such and profited from such. The merchants lament the destruction of religion (18:15-19), for she was their ticket to prosperity.

18:21 To cap off the picture of the final destruction of the religious community, John sees *"a strong angel take up a stone like a great millstone and throw it in the sea, saying, 'Thus will Babylon, the great city, be thrown down with violence, and will not be found any longer.'"* (18:21). This imagery was also pre-figured in the conclusion of the prophecy of Jeremiah when he indicated that "a stone should be tied to the scroll and it should be thrown into the middle of the Euphrates, saying, 'Just so shall Babylon sink down and not rise again.'" (Jere. 51:63,64).

18:22 Some of the social consequences of the departure of religion are noted by the strong angel, which are similar to those noted by Jeremiah when he warned the people of Judah (Jere. 25:10). *"The sound of harpists and musicians and flute-players and trumpeters will not be heard in you any longer"* (18:22). Religion has long utilized and employed musicians to entertain people and play upon their emotions. God's judgment will silence "the noise of the sound of their songs" (Isa. 24:8; Ezek. 26:13), which is not pleasing to Him. *"No craftsman of any craft will be found"* in the religious community any longer (18:22). The best of the world's craftsmen have often been employed by religion for the construction of idolatrous buildings, furniture and other items. *"The sound of a mill will not be heard"* in the context of religion any longer (18:22), for religion has engaged in industry deriving great profits from business.

18:23 The late-night fellowships will cease as *"the light of the lamp will not shine any longer"* (18:23) in the religious community. The gladness and merriment of weddings which have long been a specialty of religion, and a source of great profit, will be silenced (cf. Jere. 7:34; 16:9; 25:10; Lk. 17:27); *"the voice of the bridegroom and bride will not be heard in you any longer"* (18:23). The religious merchandising by which the peoples of the earth have been deceived and bewitched will

18:24 cease (18:23). It is religion that is responsible for most of *"the blood of prophets and of saints and all who have been slain on the earth"* (18:24), as noted previously (16:6; 17:6), and as explained by Jesus (Matt. 23;35; Lk. 11:50).

The voice from heaven had encouraged Christians to avoid, escape and disassociate from religious involvement. "Come out of her, my people, that you may not participate in her sins and may not receive of her plagues; for her sins have piled up as high as heaven, and God has remembered her iniquities" (18:4,5). Just as at Babel when religion tried to construct "a tower that would reach into heaven" (Gen. 11:4), and just as the judgments on Babylon of old "reached to heaven" (Jere. 51:9), so the sins of religion "have piled as high as heaven" (18:5). God hates religion, and its sins will be judged! God's people (Hosea 2:23; Rom. 9:25; I Pet. 2:10), must get out, depart, exit and separate themselves from all religion. This has been God's command throughout history, to be seen especially in the Babylonian pre-figuring when God's people are told to "Go forth from Babylon," (Isa. 48:20), "Depart, depart, go out and touch nothing unclean" (Isa. 52:11; II Cor. 6:17), "Flee from the midst of Babylon" (Jere. 51:6), "forsake her" (Jere. 51:9), "come forth from her midst" (Jere. 51:45). Can it be any clearer that we are to extricate ourselves from any participation in the sins of religion? Only when we disassociate ourselves from religion will we avoid the judgments of God thereon.

After the judgments come upon the religious community, the heavenly voice explains that we should ***"rejoice over the destruction of religion, O heaven, and you saints and apostles and prophets, because God has pronounced judgment for you against her"*** (18:20). The entirety of the glorified church and the heavenly community will rejoice that God has justly judged religion by reversing the unjust judgments she has administered and administering the same unto her.

Hallelujah Chorus

Because the purpose of the Revelation is to encourage Christians to avoid being seduced into religion, and to instead recognize the victory that is in Jesus Christ alone so as to endure, persevere, overcome and remain "faithful unto death" (2:10), each of the panorama-visions concludes with a victory celebration. Each of the messages to the seven churches concluded with a

19:1,2

promise of victory (2:7,11,17,26,27; 3:5,12,21). The vision of the seals ended with victory (7:9-17), as did the trumpets (11:15-19), and the picture of the beasts (15:1-4). Now at the conclusion of the depiction of the fall of Babylon, we have another portrayal of victory (19:1-10), and we shall observe an extended celebration of victory after the demise of the devil in chapters 21 and 22. The risen Lord Jesus wants Christians to know of and participate in His victory over religion.

19:1 John records having heard *"a loud voice of a great multitude in heaven, saying, 'Hallelujah!'"* (19:1). The exclamation, "Hallelujah," is a Hebrew word meaning "praise to Jehovah." It is used many times in the Old Testament, but only four times within the New Testament, and all four of those usages are in the fourfold hallelujah expressions of this paragraph. The great multitude expressing their "praise to Jehovah" is surely the same "great multitude" referred to in 7:9. Again they are praising God for the salvation effected by the Savior, Jesus Christ, and by which men are "made safe" from the misuse and abuse of Satan in order to function as God intended by the restoration of God's life within humanity. The empowering for such functional humanity is the "power through His Spirit in the inner man" (Eph. 3:16), the working of which is unto His glory (Eph. 3:20,32). For such "salvation and power and

19:2 glory" they are praising God, and also because God's judgments upon *"the great harlot who was corrupting the earth with her immorality are true and righteous, for He has avenged the blood of His bond-servants upon the harlot"* (19:2) of the religious community. Their praise, like the "song of the Lamb" (15:3), coincides with the song of Moses and their praise for the deliverance of God's people and judgment upon the adversaries. "Rejoice, O nations, His people; for He will avenge the blood of His servants, and will render vengeance upon His adversaries" (Deut. 32:43).

A second time the multitude in heaven cries *"Hallelujah!"* (19:3). They praise God that the smoke of the burning (18:9,18) of the Babylon/harlot community of religion when she is "burned up with fire" (17:16; 18:8), continues to rise forever and ever, everlastingly tormenting "those who worship the beast and his image" (14:11).

19:3

"The twenty-four elders and the four living creatures" (4:4,6) are again seen to be worshipping God on the throne, saying, *"Amen, Hallelujah!"* (19:4). They are affirming the action of God's just judgment against the religious community, and praising Him for such.

19:4

A voice *"from the throne,"* from the presence of God, says, *"Give praise to God, all you His bond-servants, you who fear Him, the small and the great"* (19:5). The place of the creature is always to praise the Creator God, to reverence Him, and to recognize that though we may be "small or great" in the designations of the world, we are all equal in Christ (Gal. 3:28). True Christianity will not discriminate on the basis of position, class, culture or socio-economic criteria.

19:5

The great multitude again praises God, saying, *"Hallelujah! For the Lord our God, the Almighty, reigns"* (19:6). It was a thunderous sound like the sounds of many waters, as this innumerable multitude exclaimed the absolute and ultimate and eternal reign of the Lord God Almighty. This may be a fulfillment of what God said through Isaiah, "My people shall know My name,

19:6

19:7 that I am the One speaking, 'How lovely on the mountains are the feet of him who brings good news, who announces peace and brings good news of happiness, who announces salvation, and says to Zion, Your God reigns!'" (Isa. 52:6,7). It is the message that Christians of every age are to learn from the revelation that Jesus gave through John: In spite of any appearances to the contrary, God in Christ reigns and is victorious!

19:7 The great multitude in heaven continues to encourage rejoicing and gladness and glory unto God, *"for the marriage of the Lamb has come and His bride has made herself ready"* (19:7). The concept of God's people being a bride married to God was pre-figured in the Israelite people of the old covenant (Jere. 2:2; Hosea 2,3), who provided an inadequate picture by their unfaithfulness (Isa. 1:21; Hosea 2:5). The prophet declared that a time would come when God's people would be "betrothed to Him in righteousness and justice, in lovingkindness, compassion and faithfulness" (Hosea 2:19,20). That is fulfilled in the people of God in the new covenant, Christians who are joined spiritually with the Lord (I Cor. 6:17) and are considered to be the bride of Christ. In Biblical times the man and the woman were first betrothed in a legally binding agreement, and then after a period of time which was often a year or longer, they were wed in an elaborate ceremony and their union was consummated. Analogous to this, Christians are regarded as having been "betrothed to Christ" spiritually, and after a period of time when Jesus Christ returns, they will be collectively "presented to Him as a pure virgin" (II Cor. 11:2) at the marriage of the Lamb. The spiritual bride, the Christian community, "makes herself ready" by allowing the Spirit of Christ to "sanctify her" in order to "present

her to Himself in all her glory, holy and blameless" **19:8**
(Eph. 5:26,27). The bride of the Christian community
"clothes herself in fine linen, bright and clean, which is the righteous acts of the saints" (19:8), the character of Christ Himself, which is in sharp contrast to the gaudy garb of the prostitute of the religious community (17:4). When Christ returns the "marriage of the Lamb" will take place and all Christians will participate in the consummation of eternally unhindered matrimony and intimacy with Jesus Christ, the bridegroom. *"Blessed"* **19:9**
indeed *"are those who are invited to the marriage supper of the Lamb"* (19:9), for only Christians are invited who have "been blessed with every spiritual blessing in heavenly places in Christ Jesus" (Eph. 1:3) and have allowed themselves to be perfected (Phil. 1:6) in sanctification (Heb. 12:14), purity, holiness and righteousness.

The voice that John heard explained that what he had heard, and in particular the beatitude of blessing for *"those who are invited to the marriage supper of the Lamb,"* were definitely *"the true words of God"* (19:9). Christians down through the centuries have needed this assurance of the truth of God's words concerning our assured victory in Christ and our eternal union with Him.

For some reason John fell down to worship the one **19:10**
speaking to him (19:10). Perhaps he mistook him for Jesus, or perhaps he was so appreciative of being assured of ultimate victory and eternal union with Jesus that he fell down in worship. The one speaking to John said, *"Do not do that; I am a fellow servant of yours and your brethren who hold the testimony of Jesus"* (19:10). This is similar to the occasion when Cornelius fell at the feet of Peter to worship him, and Peter told

19:10

him to "Stand up; I too am a man" (Acts 10:25,26), as well as the situation when the people of Lystra tried to worship Paul and Barnabas, and they declared, "We are men of the same nature as you" (Acts 14:15). We are to "worship God" alone (Exod. 20:5), for He alone is worthy of our worship which should express the worth-ship of His worthy character.

The final words of the unidentified heavenly voice speaking to John are that *"the testimony of Jesus is the spirit of prophecy"* (19:10). The basis for Christian prophecy, of which this very Revelation is identified (1:3), is that the one thus engaging in proclamation be a witness of Jesus Christ willing to invest his or her life for the out-living of the life of Jesus Christ consistent with His character, even unto martyrdom. The observing of such a criterion would certainly diminish the misunderstanding of the false prophecies that have abounded in religious communities for centuries.

What is the emphasis that Christians are to gain from this panorama of the fall of Babylon? We are brought to the point of decision. Are we going to dwell in the religious community of Babylon identified with the harlotries thereof, or are we going to dwell in the community of the New Jerusalem identified with the character of God? Will we settle for religion, or will we abide in Christ? The heavenly voice says, "Come out of her, my people, that you may not participate in her sins and that you may not receive of her plagues" (18:4). Christians must choose to run from religion and disassociate from the diabolic dalliances therein.

19:10

Though religion is thoroughly exposed within the Revelation and so much of the text pertains to the judgment of God upon those involved in religion, we must ever remember that "Vengeance is Mine, says the Lord" (Rom. 12:19). The purpose of the Revelation is not to promote vindictiveness, but to promote faithfulness among Christians in every age, in order that they might persevere and participate in Christ's victory. We do not want to develop an emphasis of anti-religion to the extent that we fail to focus on Jesus Christ and His sufficiency in all things unto the very end. We must remember the words at the beginning of the book that this is "the revelation of **Jesus Christ**."

19:11 – 21:5

Religion Goes to Hell

Revelation 19:11 – 22:5

Christians in the first century and in every century since then have benefited from the pictorial representation of Christ's victory over diabolic forces as presented in the Revelation. In the "enigma of the interim" between the redemptive coming of Jesus Christ and His future coming in glory to consummate all things, Christians are encouraged by the verification of Christ's victory in the passion of His death, resurrection, ascension and Pentecostal outpouring, as well as the expectant hope of the culmination of His victory in the *parousia*. This final panoramic perspective of Christ's victory ties the accomplished victory of Christ in the past to the consummated victory of Christ in the yet future, giving us a glimpse of concluding realities.

Since this segment of the revelatory drama tends to bring things to a close in climactic fashion, and even to address the "end of time," it is increasingly important not to become myopic and attempt to interpret the vision with a microscope. The micro-interpretations that attempt to figure out every detail of the figurative symbols by identifying them with an earthly and historical counterpart, lose the perspective of the "big picture" of God's activity throughout human history. We must continue to employ a macro-cosmic interpretive viewpoint which attempts to transcend time and place in order to see the whole, and to recognize spiritual realities that take place "above history." This requires that we conceptualize abstractly, without seeking to tighten down every detail with concrete and tangible identifications of particular earthly events at precise periods of time.

Most of what John records having seen and heard throughout the Revelation vision, he carefully notes that he saw and heard happening "in heaven." This should alert us not to be too quick to equate these with events that happen "on earth." Our natural tendency, of course, is to attempt to fit everything into chronological parameters since finite thinking operates in the context of space and time. When we do so we lose the eternality of the divine perspective. As Christians who are "seated in the heavenlies" (Eph. 2:6), we must continually strive to keep the heavenly perspective of God's actions, and to recognize that the imagery of heavenly action that transpires in these panoramas does not require our connecting it with a particular historical event. The heavenly actions may or may not have particular earthly counterparts, and may have multiple historical manifestations identifiable by Christians in different generations, but the victory of Jesus Christ will be evident to all Christian readers in every age. (*See Addendum G*)

Victory and Defeat

19:11 Seeing *"heaven opened,"* John beheld a *"white horse, and He who sat upon it is called Faithful and True"* (19:11). Whereas the white horse and its rider referred to earlier in 6:2 seem to represent the religious pretense of power and victory as they go forth to conquer men, the white horse on which Jesus Christ is mounted in this pictorialization is no parody, but represents the reality of Christ's victory. Though Jesus rode a donkey into Jerusalem in the week prior to His crucifixion to illustrate that the means of His victory was not to be by the ways of men, this does not forestall the use of the symbol of a "white horse" to portray His victory over all evil forces.

That Jesus is the rider of the "white horse" is evident from the numerous descriptions provided in vss. 11-15. "He who sat upon the white horse is called Faithful and True" (19:11). The risen Lord Jesus identified Himself earlier as "the faithful and true witness" (1:5; 3:7,14). He is "the Truth" (John 14:6) personified. As the "Righteous" One, He "judges in righteousness" (19:11), having declared that His "judgment is just and true" (John 5:30; 8:16), just as Isaiah prophesied of the Messiah (Isa. 11:3-5). The eyes of Jesus are described as "a flame of fire" (19:12) as they were previously in 1:14 and 2:18. With penetrating gaze and knowledge, Jesus sees all things and knows all things; He cannot be deceived, therefore His judgment is always just. *"Upon His head are many diadems"* (19:12) representing His royal power as "ruler of the kings of the earth" (1:5). Though the dragon (12:3) and the beast (13:1) are pictured with diadems, they are but a pretentious parody of Him who is "King of kings and Lord of lords" (19:16), having such a title inscribed on His robe. In addition He had *"a name written which no one knows except Himself"* (19:12); " a name which is above every name" (Phil. 2:9), for the completeness of His character no man knows. The name of the rider of the white horse is called *"The Word of God"* (19:13). This typically Johannine designation refers to none other that the expressive agency of God in His Son, Jesus Christ. "In the beginning was the Word, and the Word was with

19:14,15

God, and the Word was God" (John 1:1). "The Word became flesh, and dwelt among us" (John 1:14). "What was from the beginning...the Word of Life" (I John 1:1). Who else other than Jesus Christ could be identified as "The Word of God, King of kings and Lord of Lords, Faithful and True, and the Righteous Judge" with omniscient awareness? No one!

Jesus is further described as a conquering victor. *"He is clothed with a robe dipped in blood"* (19:13). Some have identified this as His own redemptive blood, and others have interpreted it as the blood of the martyrs, but the context is best suited to an identification of the blood as that of those who have died in His righteous judgments. This is reminiscent of Isaiah's imagery of God's judgment where the red garments are the life-blood of those trampled in the wine press of God's **19:15** wrath (Isa. 63:1-6). In like manner Jesus is portrayed as *"treading the wine press of the fierce wrath of God, the Almighty"* (19:15), working out the judgment of God (cf. 14:20). *"From His mouth comes a sharp sword"* (cf. 1:16; 2:12,16; 19:21) indicating the cutting edge of His righteous judgment pronouncements wherewith He *"smites the nations,"* fulfilling Isaiah's prophecy that He would "strike the earth with the rod of His mouth" (Isa. 11:4), and consistent with Paul's expectation of Jesus "slaying the lawless one with the breath of His mouth" (II Thess. 2:8). In His victory Jesus *"rules the nations with a rod of iron"* (19:15) in fulfillment of the Messianic expectation of Psalm 2:9, already quoted in Rev. 2:27 and alluded to in 12:5.

19:14 Accompanying Jesus, also on *"white horses,"* are *"the armies which are in heaven, clothed in fine linen, white and clean"* (19:14). Note again that this is a heavenly scenario, not necessarily to be equated with any historical events. God's people, the followers of Christ, participate in His victory "conquering through Him" (Rom. 8:37), and express His character of purity, holiness and righteousness, represented by the clean, white garments of priesthood (3:5,18; 4:4; 6:11; 7:9,13; 14:4,13; 19:8,14).

A consequence of Christ's judgment is then viewed by John, as he sees *"an angel standing in the sun,"* that is the presence of God from whence all light comes, *"crying out with a loud voice to all the scavenging birds of prey which fly in the midheaven,"* calling them to *"Come, assemble for the great supper of God"* (19:17). Similar symbols are used by Ezekiel of the Son of Man speaking to every kind of bird, saying, "Assemble and come, gather...that you may eat flesh and drink blood" (Ezek. 39:17). Religionists serve as birds of prey upon mankind (8:13; 18:2), but in God's righteous judgment upon them they will suffer the indignity of being eaten by scavengers. The rotting flesh of religion and its adherents will be devoured. This is referred to as "the great supper of God," surely to be contrasted with "the marriage supper of the Lamb" mentioned just eight verses previous (19:9), wherein Christians celebrate their eternal and unhindered consummation of intimacy with Christ. The ungodly who have rejected Jesus Christ will also come to a supper, but they will not be feasting; rather they will be the fare. The birds of prey will *"eat the flesh of kings, commanders, mighty men, horses and their riders, and the flesh of all men"* who do not receive the Spirit of Christ regardless of their status, "free men and slaves, great and small" (19:18), but inevitably religious.

19:19-21

19:19 John then reports seeing what preceded and precipitated that grim feast, when *"the beast and the kings of the earth and their armies, assembled to make war against Him who sat upon the horse, and against His army"* (19:19). The beast of religion is allied with government as the primary agents of diabolic destruction, making war against Christ and those identified with Him. The battle that ensues does not require a particular identification with the final "war of the great day of God" (16:14), or the so-called "battle of Armageddon" (16:16), but it might have such an earthly counterpart in such a battle. Christ overcomes (John 16:33) and the

19:20 beast of religion (13:1-10) is captured (19:20) along with *"the false prophet"* who is identified with the other beast (13:11-18) as engaged in deceiving religious signs and wonders (13:13; 16:14). These two personified symbols of religion are then *"thrown alive into the lake of fire which burns with brimstone"* (19:20). The imagery for the "lake of fire and brimstone" may have come from the concept of Gehenna which is apparently derived from the garbage dump southwest of Jerusalem in the valley of Hinnom which was often burning and smoldering. Jesus referred to the "Gehenna of everlasting fire" (Matt. 18:8,9), the ultimate consequence for

19:21 all who refuse to accept and express Him. *"The rest"* (19:21) of those in the army of opposition to Jesus Christ, those who had identified with religion accepting *"the mark of the beast"* (19:20) and participating in the idolatrous worship of images other than God, along with the governmental militants, these *"were killed with the sword which came from the mouth of Him who sat upon the horse"* (19:21) and their flesh was devoured by the scavenger birds. God's judgment must come on all that is contrary to His character.

Getting deeper to the root source of all religion and all that is adversarial to God's objective for His creation through His Son Jesus Christ, the next vignette of the vision seen by John pictures the culminating defeat and demise of the devil. G.B. Caird explains that Rev. 20:1-10 is "a passage which, more than any other in the book, has been the paradise of cranks and fanatics on the one hand and literalists on the other,"[1] so we must tread carefully.

John indicates that he ***"saw an angel coming down from heaven"*** (20:1), which is not necessarily a cosmologically directional statement but explanatory of divine activity just as "born from above" (John 3:3,7). God is not locked in a dualistic battle with diabolic evil for an eternal standoff, but God is sovereignly omnipotent to effect the defeat, the limitation and ultimate demise of the satanic adversary. The heavenly messenger carries the "key" of divine authority (1:18) "over the abyss" (cf. 9:1) and has "a great chain in his hand" (20:1). Since Satan is a spirit (Eph. 2:2), he cannot be held by a physical chain, so we must recognize again the symbolism of this activity.

20:1

The angelic messenger ***"laid hold of the dragon, the serpent of old, who is the devil and Satan, and bound him for a thousand years"*** (20:2). Exercising superior divine strength and power, the angel captured the adversarial opponent of Christ, previously identified in like manner (12:9) as the dragon, the Genesis serpent, the devil and Satan. He is the Evil One (Matt. 13:13,38; Eph. 6:16; II Thess. 3:3; I John 2:13; 3:12; 5:19) whose very nature is the personified source of all evil contrary to the character of God, the one from whom all sin (I John 3:8) and religion (Rev. 13:1-18) is derived. The

20:2

20:2

failure to understand this theodicy causes Christians to berate themselves masochistically, to repudiate their humanity, and to focus their antagonism on human adversaries, even religionists, rather than on the Satanic adversary who energizes all that is in opposition to God. The first order for those engaged in warfare is to know their enemy.

In the picture that John draws for us the devil is ***"bound for a thousand years"*** (19:2). Keeping our heavenly perspective outside space and time, how is this to be interpreted? Should we attempt to identify any earthly counterpart to this action? Is this a future event that we should look forward to seeing fulfilled? Are we to apply earth-based time chronologies? Since Scripture is the best commentary on Scripture, can we discover any other occurrences where "binding" is applied to Satan? Yes we can. The Pharisees argued that Jesus was casting out demons by the power of Beelzebul because they did not want to admit that He was of God. Jesus explained that "Satan does not cast out Satan," and indicated that if He casts out demons, He has first gone into the "strong man's house" and "bound the strong man," Satan, and carried off his property, the demons (Matt. 12:24-29; Mark 3:22-27). Does this mean that Satan was incapacitated and rendered inoperable throughout the world because Jesus had "bound" him and cast out demons? No! Later Jesus told a parable about wheat and tares, the tares representing "sons of the evil one" who are to be bound and burned (Matt. 13:30). To His disciples Jesus gave divine authority in the "keys of the kingdom" so that "whatever they bind on earth shall have been bound in heaven" (Matt. 16:19; cf. 18:18). Avoiding the physical and tangible localization that is so often applied to the Satanic spirit, perhaps we can understand how limitations are imposed upon Satan's activity. When the seventy witnesses returned Jesus told them He "saw Satan fall from heaven like lightning" (Luke 10:17-19), indicating that a binding limitation was taking place. If one particular historical counterpart is to be identified with Satan being "bound," perhaps it would be the defeat of Satan when Jesus died on the cross. It was at that point that Satan was "cast out" (John 12:31), "disarmed" (Col. 2:15); "judged" (John 16:11); "thrown down" (Rev. 12:9,10,13); "rendered powerless" (Heb. 2:14), and his works "destroyed" (I John 3:8). Though it can obviously be argued that Satan is very active still today, "roaring and seeking to devour" (I Peter 5:8), "blinding" (II Cor. 4:4), counterfeiting (II Cor. 11:14), "capturing and ensnaring" (II Tim. 2:26), and "working" (Eph. 2:2), it must also be conceded that he is limited in his action. He does not have free reign, particularly in the lives of Christians.

The purpose of Satan's being "bound" is *"so that he should not deceive the nations any longer"* (20:3). When did Satan's deceiving of the nations begin? It commenced in the garden of Eden, and after the fall of man Satan's deception encompassed all of mankind, for "all the nations were permitted to go their own ways" (Acts 14:16). Satan reigned supreme as "the god of this world" (II Cor. 4:4). "The whole world lies in the Evil One" (I John 5:19). At the "tree of the knowledge of good and evil" in the garden, Satan defeated the first Adam (Gen. 3), but at the "tree" (Gal. 3:13) of the cross he could not defeat the second representative man, the "last Adam" (I Cor. 15:45), Jesus Christ. Rather, Christ defeated Satan, exclaiming from the cross, "It is finished!" (John 19:30), for the divine mission was accomplished and set in motion. The good news of the gospel

20:2,3

to "all the nations" (Matt. 28:19) from that time onward was that the life of God could be restored to man by receiving Jesus Christ (I John 5:12), that Satan's jurisdiction would thus be supplanted (Acts 26:18), and his ability to deceive the Christian limited and curtailed. Christians who do not understand the defeat of Satan at the cross, often live deficient Christian lives by selling themselves short of participation in the victory of Christ in the battle already won! They fail to attain the maturity whereby they are not tossed and carried about by the "deceitful scheming" (Eph. 4:14) of Satan and his religious efforts. The victory of Christ over Satan was accomplished at the cross. Satan was defeated and no longer has universal unlimited ability to deceive mankind. This does not mean that he was annihilated, incapacitated or rendered inoperable. He is still the "tempter "(I Thess. 3:5), the "accuser" (Rev. 12:10), and the "adversary" (I Peter 5:8). But in accord with the pictorial portrayal, Satan has been "thrown into the abyss," the bottomless pit of his underworld activities, and it has been "shut and sealed over him" (20:3) so that we are "protected by the power of God for a salvation ready to be revealed in the last time" (I Peter 1:5), "made safe" from Satan's right to rule over us and thus to abuse and misuse us and create deceptive dysfunction in us.

The parameter given for this restraining restriction and confining constraint of Satan is "a thousand years" (20:2,3). Let us not forget that we are viewing this panorama from a divine perspective beyond space and time, wherein "a day is as a thousand years, and a thousand years as one day" (Ps. 90:4; II Peter 3:8). T.F. Torrance notes, "we have no more right to take this thousand years literally than we have to take the ten-headed and seven-horned monster literally. It is entirely out of place therefore to bring down the thousand years out of its apocalyptic setting and place it on the ordinary plane of history, as if it could be handled by a worldly arithmetic and manipulated in calculations about the dispensations of time or about the end of the world. Such an intrusion into the secrets of God is utterly foreign to the Bible." [2]

We have noted throughout this study of the Revelation how numbers are employed figuratively and symbolically (ex. 3 1/2, 7, 10, 12, 24, 666, 144,000), rather than with base-ten human arithmetical designation. The number of "one thousand" seems to represent the "full scope," "comprehensiveness" or "completion" of that which is being described. Throughout the Scripture it is often used with this meaning. God is said to "keep His covenant and His lovingkindness toward men to the thousandth generation" (Deut. 7:9; I Chron. 16:15; Ps. 105:8). Does this mean that God's character of faithfulness and compassion ceases after the literal "thousandth generation" of mankind? No, it refers to the comprehensive and eternal completion of His character. Likewise the psalmist indicates that God possesses "the cattle on a thousand hills" (Ps. 50:10). Is He limited to a literal "thousand hills" of cattle? No, he possesses all the cattle in the world, and the number of "a thousand" is used to point out the complete comprehensiveness of God's control over His creation. Contemporary English usage still uses "thousand" in a figurative way, an example being, "I've told you a thousand times..." We must beware of limiting God by literalness of humanly defined interpretations. Symbolic and figurative interpretations are "literal" when they correspond to the literary intent of the literature, which is the case in this instance.

20:4

The Greek word translated "thousand" in these verses is the word *chilia*. The Latin word for "thousand" is *mille*, and when conjoined with the Latin word *annus* meaning "year" it forms the basis of the English word "millennium." The theories of those who interpret this thousand year period as an exact thousand calendar year expectation in the future have often been labeled as "chiliasm" or "millennialism." This interpretation which expects Christ's return to be prior to such a precise thousand year period is also called "premillennialism," as distinct from "postmillennialism" which expects Christ to return after a thousand year period of increasing evangelism, and the misnomer of "amillennialism" which does not mean "no millennium" as the etymology of the word implies, but interprets the thousand years to be a figurative period as we are doing in this study. It is most regrettable that millennial theories have become such a divisive issue among Christian peoples, and that some Christians have so focused on this "thousand year" period referred to only in this paragraph, Rev. 20:1-7, that they have superimposed it upon the rest of Scripture as a grid for all Scripture interpretation. (*See chart in Addendum H*).

20:4 In the midst of this comprehensive period of "a thousand years" which seems to have commenced in historical terms at Christ's victorious defeat of Satan on the cross, John **"saw thrones"** (20:4) in heaven with God's people "seated in the heavenlies" (Eph. 2:6). **"Judgment was given to them"** (20:4), just as Jesus indicated that His followers would "sit on thrones judging the twelve tribes of Israel" (Matt. 19:28; Luke 22:29), and Paul wrote that "the saints will judge the world" (I Cor. 6:2). John also saw those martyred **"because of the testimony of Jesus and because of the Word of God"**

(20:4). These were obviously Christians who endured physical death, knowing that spiritual life in Christ was of ultimate value. In addition, John saw *"those who had not worshiped the beast or his image, and had not received the mark upon their forehead or their hand"* (20:4), these being Christians who did not succumb to religion and its idolatry, disallowing religion to stamp their thinking and their activity. These Christians are represented as having *"come to life and reigned with Christ for a thousand years"* (20:4). Just as Jesus "was dead, and has come to life" (2:8), Christians have "come to life" passing "out of death into life" (I John 3:14). In so doing they "reign in life through Jesus Christ" (Rom. 5:17,21). To thus "reign with Christ" in His reign is to participate in "the kingdom of the beloved Son" (Col. 1:13), for the word "reign," *basileuo*, is the root of the word *basileia* which is translated "kingdom." The mistaken Jewish concept of a militaristic Messiah who would be a human king in a physical and nationalistic kingdom realm must not be transferred over into Christian interpretations of the kingdom reign of Christ during the "thousand year" period. Jesus explicitly said, "My kingdom is not of this world" (John 18:36); "the kingdom of God is within you" (Luke 17:20,21).

This *"coming to life"* and "reigning with Christ" is identified as *"the first resurrection"* (20:5). The physical resurrection of Jesus Christ was incorporative of the spiritual resurrection of all believers, for Jesus was "the first born from the dead" (Col. 1:18; Rev. 1:5) among "many brethren" (Rom. 8:29) who would likewise experience a birth (John 3:3,7; I Peter 1:3) unto spiritual life out of spiritual death. "As Christ was raised from the dead, so we too walk in newness of life,

20:6

...united in the likeness of His resurrection...alive to God in Christ Jesus" (Rom. 6:4,5,11); "raised up with Christ" (Col. 3:1); "made alive together with Christ and raised up with Him" (Eph. 2:5; Col. 2:12). The very resurrection-life of the risen Lord Jesus indwells Christian persons and is to be operative in their behavior. "Christ lives in me" (Gal. 2:20, Paul declares; "Christ is our life" (Col. 3:4). There is a pathetic paucity of understanding among those who posit the "first resurrection" as a future event and thus deprive Christians of recognizing the privilege of living by "the power of His resurrection" (Phil. 3:10), "reigning in life with Christ." Although a second resurrection is not mentioned in the text, some have speculated that it might be the bodily "resurrection from the dead" (I Cor. 15:12-57; Phil. 3:11).

20:6 *"Blessed and holy is the one who has a part in the first resurrection"* (20:6) declares the heavenly voice in another beatitude. Just as all Christians have participated in the "first resurrection," having "come to life" being "raised up with Christ," every Christian has thereby been "blessed with every spiritual blessing in heavenly places in Christ" (Eph. 1:3), and "made holy" (Col. 1:22; 3:12) by the presence of the Holy One (Acts 2:27; 3:14), Jesus Christ, in them. All Christians are *"priests of God and of Christ"* (20:6), a "holy priesthood" (I Peter 2:5), a "royal priesthood" (I Peter 2:9), "priests to God" (Rev. 1:6) who "reign upon the earth" (Rev. 5:10), "reigning with Him for a thousand years" (20:6) as kings and priests in the kingdom.

Over "these" Christians, John is told, *"the second death has no power"* (20:6). The death of Jesus "rendered powerless the one having the power of death, that is, the devil" (Heb. 2:14), but Christians on earth are still mortal and the "first death" of physical death still has power over them. "It is appointed for men to die once" (Heb. 9:27). The "second death" is clearly identified as the experience of "the lake of fire and brimstone" (20:14; 21:8). It is the everlasting consequence of remaining in spiritual death, absent from the life of God and in perpetuity of identification and union with Satan. Jesus befuddled the Jewish leaders when He said, "If anyone keeps My word, he shall never see death" (John 5:51,52), for He knew that He had come to "abolish death, and bring life and immortality to light through the gospel" (II Tim. 1:10), so that faithful Christians "will not be hurt by the second death" (Rev. 2:11).

The comprehensive and complete period of the *"thousand years"* will be *"completed"* (20:3,5,7). It will have a terminus, the timing of its counterpart on earth known by no man. It was "in the fullness of God's time" (Gal. 4:4) that Jesus came the first time in incarnation, and it will likewise be in the fullness of God's time when His objectives are completed, that Jesus will come again to conclude our reign with Him here on earth. At that time *"the rest of the dead"* who died during the "thousand year" period, other than those who have come to life spiritually in Christ during that period, *"will come to life"* (20:5) in what many call the "general resurrection," the "resurrection of the wicked" (Acts 24:15) and the "resurrection of judgment" (John 5:29).

Also at the conclusion of the "thousand year" period, *"Satan will be released from his prison"* (20:7) "for a short time" (20:3). His limitation of activity having been illustrated by the binding of a chain (20:1,2) and

20:8 the preventive custody of incarceration (20:3,7), but not indicating the incapacitation of inactivity, Satan is to be released to mount a final insurrection. He *"will come out to deceive the nations which are in the four corners of the earth, God and Magog, to gather them together for the war; the number of them is like the sand of the seashore"* (20:8). Consistent with his nature as the adversary, deceiver and the destroyer, Satan will attempt to influence unregenerate peoples from the nations of the earth, who have been functioning throughout the "thousand years," to oppose God and Jesus Christ. "Gog and Magog" are terms which were previously used in the vision of Ezekiel (Ezek. 38,39), and refer to the assemblage of ungodly, hostile nations and peoples. The war for which they are gathered, like that referred to in 19:19, may refer to a final "war of the great day of God" (16:14) and be equated with a "battle of Armageddon" (16:16), but does not require such a particular historical, if yet future, designation. Obviously the entire world of mankind is not going to become Christian, for the army assembled against the *"saints"* is innumerable and incalculable, *"like the sand of the*

20:9 *seashore."* This army assembled by the devil from the expanse and breadth of the earth *"surrounds the camp of the saints and the beloved city"* (20:9). The "camp of the saints" might seem to indicate an earthly scenario, since Christians as "citizens of heaven" (Phil. 3:20) are always in pilgrimage on earth, but "the beloved city" refers to the "New Jerusalem" (3:12), the "Jerusalem above" (Gal. 4:26), the "holy city" (11:2), the community of all who are identified with God through Christ, "beloved" as the Bride of Christ. This city cannot be localized geographically on earth, and cannot be equated with the ecclesiastical institution of the physical church.

The big question might be, "Why does God see fit to turn Satan loose to deceive the nations after the thousand year period?" Some have suggested that God's purpose is to expose that the nature of Satan has not been rehabilitated and that he remains evil and destructive despite the comprehensive period of captivity. Others suggest that the purpose is to reveal Satan's defeat and impotence; that he is a loser. In the similar imagery of Ezek. 38, God states His purpose as being, "I will magnify Myself, and make Myself known in the sight of many nations, and they will know that I am the Lord" (Ezek. 38:23). God can use the activity of Satan to bring people to Himself, and to bring glory to Himself.

God's judgment is then depicted as falling upon Satan and the army he assembles. *"Fire came down from heaven and devoured"* (20:9) those people who Satan had gathered together in his army, just as fire came upon those of Gog and Magog in Ezek. 38:22 and 39:6. "Our God is a consuming fire" (Heb. 12:29). Some interpret this with the yet future counterpart of Christ's second coming, for Paul writes that the "Lord Jesus shall be revealed from heaven in flaming fire" (II Thess. 1:7). The sovereign judgment of God upon the devil is illustrated by his being *"thrown into the lake of fire and brimstone, where the beast and the false prophet are also"* (20:10; 19:20). The final demise of the devil is here pictured, and from henceforth he is "out of the picture." That the "lake of fire and brimstone" is not referring to annihilation or cessation of being seems evident in the explanation that *"they will be tormented day and night forever and ever"* (20:10).

All that remains in the picture of Christ's over-all victory defeating all foes is the divine judgment on the personified consequences of the devil's activity in "death and hades," for "the one having the power of death is the devil" (Heb. 2:14). God "abolishes all rule and authority and power" (I Cor. 15:24) contrary to His character. John saw "a great white throne" (20:11) with a divine presence exercising His authoritative judgment thereon. This can be both "the judgment seat of God" (Rom. 14:10) and "the judgment seat of Christ" (II Cor. 5:10) at the same time. Jesus said, "I and the Father are one" (John 10:30).

20:11 *"Earth and heaven fled away"* from the presence of God, *"and no place was found for them"* (20:11). "Earth and heaven" could refer to the physical and material "heavens and earth," the creation of which is recorded in Genesis 1:1. On the other hand, since we are considering figurative and heavenly realities, the phrase "earth and heaven" could refer to the composite order of the "world system," the fallen and degenerative order, the realm which Satan developed as "the god of this world" (II Cor. 4:4) and in which the beast of religion operated. There is "no place" for this order in the presence of God, for they are mutually incompatible, and this world order will be obliterated and cease to exist. The "new heaven and new earth" (21:1) of God's new Christic order will exist eternally.

20:12 As "it is appointed for men to die once and after this comes judgment" (Heb. 9:27), John saw *"the dead, the great and the small, standing before the throne"* (20:12). These would appear to be equivalent to those identified as "the rest of the dead" in 20:5, the unregenerate who died during the "thousand year" period.

Whether their status be *"great or small"* no one is exempted or immune from facing judgment. These people's names were not to be found in *"the book of life"* (20:12), the heavenly register of the names of those who are identified with Jesus Christ, the Life (John 14:6). Rather they *"were to be judged from the things which were written in the books, according to their deeds"* (20:12). They had to face God on the basis of their behavior (Ps. 62:12; Jere. 17:10; Matt. 16:27; Rom. 2:6), all of which was contrary to the character of God, a total failure to function in accord with the purpose for which God created man (Isa. 43:7). The "fruit of our deeds" (Jere. 17:10) can always be traced to the root of spiritual source and identification (Matt. 12:33-35). "Whatever is not of faith is sin" (Rom. 14:23). "The one committing sin derives what he does from the devil" (I John 3:8). Who would want to face God's judgment with that record?

The judgment of God upon death continues as *"the sea gave up the dead which were in it"* (20:13). Are these the physical waters of earth, or is this the reservoir of evil (cf. 13:1), the murky depths of death and darkness from which monsters often come? If the "earth and heaven" of vs. 11 are interpreted as the physical cosmos of planet earth, then this would consistently be understood as the physical sea, but if "earth and heaven" are the fallen world order, then the sea is best understood figuratively. *"Death and hades also gave up the dead which were in them"* (12:13). When Satan is banished and the fallen and degenerative world order "flee away" (20:11) and vanish, then "death and hades" have no context in which to operate and hold people hostage. The effects of sin which began when "through one man sin entered into the world, and death through sin"

20:14 (Rom. 5:12), are now totally overcome. The unregenerate dead are *"judged according to their deeds"* (20:13), and the personified *"death and Hades are thrown into the lake of fire"* (20:14), alienated from the life of God. Paul wrote that "the last enemy that will be abolished is death" (I Cor. 15:26).

20:15 Everyone whose *"name was not found written in the book of life is thrown into the lake of fire"* (20:15). *"This is the second death"* (20:14), where if one's first physical death occurs while they are in a state of spiritual death, such spiritual death will be perpetuated after the judgment in everlasting death, in perpetuity of identification and union with Satan. They will be sent away "into the eternal fire which has been prepared for the devil and his angels" (Matt. 25:41), joined there by the devil (20:10), the beast and false prophet (19:20), and "death and hades" (21:14).

Reign of Life

As each of the panoramas of the Revelation wrap up with a scene of victory to provide an encouragement to Christians in every age (2:7,11,17,26,27; 3:5,12,21; 7:9-17; 11:15-19; 15:1-4; 19:1-10), so too does this final perspective. But this vision of victory is the most lengthy and conclusive of all of them as it moves from the ultimate defeat of the devil and death to the eternal reign of life in Christ Jesus.

21:1 John *"saw a new heaven and a new earth, for the first heaven and the first earth passed away, and there was no longer any sea"* (21:1). The temptation of our finite thinking is to visualize this in terms of concrete, tangible and corporeal entities of space and time, rather than retaining the abstract perspective of spiritual realities. Though it is true that the physical "heaven and earth" will "perish" (Ps. 102:26), "being reserved for fire" (II Peter 3:7), for the physical is not eternal, it is equally true that the fallen and degenerative world order which has so pervaded the physical universe as to be observable in the scientific "second law of thermodynamics," also "passes away" as noted in the previous chapter. The "first heaven and first earth" are included within "the first things" (21:4) which include Satan, sin, death, the beasts and Babylon, all of which "pass away" (21:1,4), along with the murky depths of Satan's operations in the reservoir of evil, the "sea" (21:1). Instead of participating in that degenerative world system, John sees God's people participating in the new, regenerative "heaven and earth" wherein God is "making all things new" (21:5), "transforming everything into the image of His glory" (II Cor. 3:18). Isaiah foresaw that God would "do something new" (Isa. 43:19) by "creating new heavens and a new earth" (Isa. 65:17). It is a "new creation" (Gal. 6:15) in which all new things in Christ are operative: a "new and living way" (Heb. 10:20), a "new covenant" (Heb. 8:13; 9:15; 12:24), a new birth (John 3:3,7), a "newness of life" (Rom. 6:4), a "new Spirit" (Ezek. 36:26), a "new man" (Eph. 4:24; Col. 3:10), the "new creature in Christ" (II Cor. 5:17) singing a "new song" (Rev. 5:9; 14:13). It is the "new heavens and new earth in which holiness and godliness and righteousness dwells" (II Peter 3:11,13).

Therein we see *"the holy city, the New Jerusalem"* (21:2), the "Jerusalem above" (Gal. 4:26), the "beloved city" (20:9), "the city whose architect and builder is God" (Heb. 11:10), "the city of the living God, the heavenly Jerusalem" (Heb. 12:22), the perfected com-

21:3

munity of God's people which we have been getting glimpses of throughout the Revelation (3:12; 11:2). This is not a geographical location, nor is it an institutional ecclesiastical entity. The essence of this city is the presence and character and activity of God by His Son Jesus Christ. It is contrasted with the cities which represent evil such as "Sodom, Egypt and Jerusalem of old" (11:8) and Babylon (18:2), the latter of which is also pictured as a "harlot" (17:1-6) in contrast to the spiritual city of "New Jerusalem" which is being "made ready as a bride adorned for her husband" (21:2), preparing to be "presented as a pure virgin" (II Cor. 11:2), "holy and blameless" (Eph. 5:27), at the coming "marriage supper of the Lamb" (19:9). Although the two contrasting "heaven and earth" orders are seen by John from the perspective of eternity wherein the "first order" is terminated, both the old and the new are present together in the "enigma of the interim" of the "thousand years." The "New Jerusalem" in "the new heaven and new earth" is not a reality that is reserved for the future. Christians participate in this "new creation" presently.

21:3   In verification of this *"a loud voice from the throne"* of God's divine presence, declares, *"Behold, the tabernacle of God is among men, and He shall dwell among them, and they shall be His people, and God Himself shall be among them"* (21:3). God's tabernacling among men was pre-figured in the physical tabernacle in the wilderness during the exodus when God's people constructed "a sanctuary that God might dwell among them" (Exod. 25:8; 29:45). God explained to the Israelites, "I will make My dwelling among you, ...I will be your God, and you will be My people" (Lev. 26:11,12). The disobedience of the old covenant peoples did not allow this relationship to transpire (Jere.

7:23), and Hosea illustrated this by naming his son "Lo-ammi, for you are not My people and I am not your God" (Hosea 1:9). The prophets went on to speak for God indicating that there would be an everlasting covenant wherein God could say, "My dwelling place will be with them, and I will be their God and they shall be My people" (Ezek. 37:27; Zech. 8:8; Hosea 2:23). That new "heaven and earth" order was introduced when "the Word became flesh, and tabernacled among us" (John 1:14). On the basis of His taking death on our behalf and giving us His "divine nature" (II Peter 1:4) and life, Paul indicates that "we are the temple of the living God; just as God said, 'I will dwell in them and walk among them; and I will be their God, and they shall be My people'" (II Cor. 6:16). We who "were not God's people" in the old covenant are "now God's people, ...sons of the living God" (Rom. 9:25,26), "a people for God's own possession" (I Peter 2:10), for we "are a temple of God, and the Spirit of God dwells in us" (I Cor. 3:16). The spiritual reality of this indwelling relationship is already the experience of every Christian, but the unhindered perfection of such relationship is yet to come.

The *"first things"* (21:4) of the "old heaven and earth" order have been superseded by "the new heaven and earth" order wherein "all things have become new" (II Cor. 5:17) and God *"is making all things new"* (21:5). We participate in the "better things" (Heb. 7:19,22; 10:34; 11:16,40). There is no longer any spiritual death within the "new creation" order for such cannot dwell where God's life dwells, but the physical consequences of the death process which began in Eden are still present in mortal men. We have been "delivered from the fear of death to which we were subjected

21:5,6

all our lives" (Heb. 2:15), but we will still "die once" (Heb. 9:27). Yet to come in the unhindered expression of the New Jerusalem, "death will be swallowed up in victory" (I Cor. 15:54). Isaiah indicated that God would "swallow up death for all time, and will wipe tears away from all faces" (Isa. 25:8) for "sorrow and sighing will flee away" (Isa. 35:10) and "mourning will be finished (Isa. 60:20). For such we yet wait in the anticipation of expectant hope when "he shall wipe away every tear from their eyes, and there shall no longer be any death; there shall no longer be any mourning, or crying, or pain" (21:4).

21:5 John is once again commissioned by the divine voice to *"write, for these words are faithful and true"* (21:5), as instructed previously (1:11; 19:9). "It is done" (21:6), God declares. Though some would point out that God does not say, "It will be done" in the future, we must admit that there is still a yet to be enacted consummation of that which is already accomplished from God's eternal perspective. Jesus declared from the cross, "It is finished" (John 19:30), and now the affirmation of completion and consummation is made, as was made in the final judgment of the seven bowls (16:17).

21:6 The divine voice identifies Himself by saying, *"I am the Alpha and the Omega, the beginning and the end"* (21:6). Through Isaiah, God said, "I am the first and the last, and there is no God besides Me" (Isa. 44:6; 48:12). In like manner Jesus identifies Himself as "the Alpha and the Omega, the first and the last" (Rev. 1:8; 22:13). Jesus constitutes all of what God has for man; everything from A to Z, and everything in between; everything that it takes for man to be man as God intended man to be.

Because He is such, He can *"give to the one who thirsts from the spring of the water of life without cost"* (21:6). Jesus said, "Whoever drinks of the water that I shall give him shall never thirst; but the water that I shall give him shall become in him a well of water springing up to eternal life" (John 4:14). "If any man is thirsty, let him come to Me and drink. He who believes in Me, from his innermost being shall flow rivers of living water" (John 7:37,38). "Blessed are those who hunger and thirst for righteousness, for they shall be satisfied" (Matt. 5:6). The innermost desires of man are fulfilled in Jesus Christ alone for time and eternity.

As Christians "we have obtained an inheritance" (Eph. 1:11), and we "share in the inheritance of the saints in light" (Col. 1:12; Eph. 1:18) with the indwelling "Holy Spirit as the pledge of our inheritance" (Eph. 1:14). We look forward to receiving "the reward of the inheritance" (Col. 3:24) "reserved in heaven" (I Pet. 1:4) for us, for *"he who overcomes shall inherit these things"* (21:7). We continue to overcome by identifying with the Overcomer (John 16:33), by allowing for faithful receptivity of His activity in our lives as Christians. Thus we continue in that relationship wherein God is our Father and we are "sons of God through faith in Christ Jesus" (Gal. 3:26), being "led by the Spirit of God" (Rom. 8:14).

21:7

Contrasted to this are the faithless, *"the cowardly and unbelieving and abominable and murderers and immoral persons and sorcerers and idolaters and all liars"* (21:8). These do not have a place in the New Jerusalem community of God for their behavior is contrary to the character of God; "uncleanness, abomination and lying, shall never come into it" (21:27). This

21:8

21:9,10

kind of behavior is indicative of the other community, the religious city of Babylon, wherein lying is derived from "the father of lies" (John 8:44). The Christians at the end of the first century and in every age thereafter have been tempted to take the cowardly course of self-preservation; to cower under the threat of persecution, suffering and death; to choose personal safety over faithfulness to Jesus Christ. Jesus said, "Whoever wishes to save his life shall lose it; and whoever loses his life for My sake and the gospel's shall save it" (Mark 8:35). Those who revert to religion, with which all these behaviors are identified, "their part will be in the lake that burns with fire and brimstone, which is the second death" (19:20; 20:6,10,14,15), the perpetuity of identification with Satan's destination (Matt. 25:41).

21:9 *"One of the seven angels who had the seven bowls full of the seven last plagues, came and spoke"* with John (21:9), as in 17:1, offering a fuller explanation of what he had seen. *"Come here, I shall show you the bride, the wife of the Lamb"* (21:9), was the invitation of the heavenly messenger. Controlled by the

21:10 Holy Spirit, John was carried *"to a great and high mountain"* (21:10), either for a better perspective and vantage point for viewing, or perhaps because the *"holy city"* of the "heavenly Jerusalem" is "Mount Zion, the city of the living God" (Heb. 12:22), the "mountain of the house of the Lord" (Isa. 2:2), the "city on the high mountain" (Ezek. 40:2). What John saw was the holy city of the New Jerusalem which is personified as "the bride, the wife of the Lamb," in contrast to the city of the old order, Babylon, which was personified as a harlot. Neither of them is to be construed as a tangible entity in a particular geographical location or as an individualized personage in history. The "Bride of Christ," the "New Jerusalem," is the collective community of God's people throughout time and eternity. The physical city of Jerusalem, the "city of peace," was to have been the pre-figuring of what God would do in the midst of the community of His people, but it became the center of the Judaic religion of the old covenant representative of the slavery of religion (Gal. 4:25). In fulfillment of God's intent, the New Jerusalem above represents the freedom (Gal. 4:26) of God's action in expressing His character within His creation unto His glory, for it *"comes down out of heaven from God, having the glory of God"* (21:11).

John continues his writing, attempting to describe this dynamic city which is already the experience of every Christian, but is yet to be experienced in unhindered consummation between Bridegroom and bride. What he saw is beyond human words; it is indescribable and inexplicable, as the dynamic presence and activity of God always is. How does one explain in human words the heavenly reality of a city which is not a place, and a bride who is not an individual person? The symbolic imagery that is employed is for the purpose of illustrating the inexpressible, by showing how impressive and immeasurable and invaluable and illuminative and inviolate and intimate and ideal this incredible heavenly reality really is.

The great value of God's presence is expressed as the *"brilliance of a very costly stone"* (21:11), and the splendor and radiance of His presence *"as a stone of crystal-clear jasper"* (21:11). When Isaiah saw a glorified Zion, he explained, "You will call your walls salvation, and your gates praise" (Isa. 60:18), indicating that the symbol of walls refers to spiritual realities.

21:12 John describes the immensity of ***"a great and high wall, with twelve gates"*** (21:12), allowing for abundant entrance of all the people of God. In conjunction with Ezekiel's vision (Ezek. 48:30-34), the twelve gates have ***"names written on them, which are those of the twelve tribes of the sons of Israel"*** (21:12), which shows an inclusivity of continuity with God's people in the old
21:14 covenant. ***"The wall of the city had twelve foundation stones, and on them were the twelve names of the twelve apostles of the Lamb"*** (2:14), similar to Paul's explanation of "God's household built on the foundation of the apostles and the prophets, Christ Jesus
21:15 Himself being the corner-stone" (Eph. 2:20). A ***"gold measuring rod"*** was used to ***"measure the city, and its gates and its wall"*** (21:15), all of which is to give us a measured understanding and discernment of this heavenly reality which is immeasurably immense and
21:16 infinite. The city was ***"laid out as a square"*** or a cube, ***"its length and width and height are equal"*** (21:16). This perfect symmetry was pre-figured in the Holy of Holies of the temple which was a perfect cube of "twenty cubits" each direction (I Kings 6:20). ***"Twelve thousand stadia"*** (21:16) is the human number given as a measurement of this heavenly city; twelve being symbolic of God's people, noted above as "twelve tribes" (21:12) and "twelve apostles" (21:14); a thousand representing the full complement thereof; a *stadia*, from which we get the English word "stadium," was the distance of a race course. So the measurement of this heavenly city was comprehensive of the full complement of God's people who run the race of life by God's provi-
21:17 sion. ***"One hundred and forty-four cubits"*** (21:17) is the measurement of the wall of the city. Whether this represents its height or its thickness, we do not know. Twelve (representing the number of the twelve tribes of

the old covenant) times twelve (representing the twelve apostles of the new covenant) times a cubit, which is the length of a man's forearm, is the symbolic number of the wall, and we are advised that a cubit is a cubit for angels also (21:17), for it is still a creature's attempt to measure God's immeasurable.

21:18 Though this city is not corporeal and material, John records that *"the material of the wall was jasper; and the city was pure gold, like clear glass"* (21:18), indicating the splendor and value and purity of what he saw. **21:19,20** *"The foundation stones of the city wall were adorned with every kind of precious stone"* (21:19,20), similar to the stones in the breastplate of the priests in the Old Testament (Exod. 28:17), and the parody of such in the King of Tyre (Ezek. 28:13), who apparently symbolized Lucifer. *"The twelve gates were twelve pearls"* **21:21** (21:21) representing great value (Matt. 13:45,46). *"The street of the city was pure gold, like transparent glass"* (21:21), pre-figured by the floor of the sanctuaries of the temple in the old covenant which were "overlaid with gold" (I Kings 6:30) wherever the priests walked. Now the new covenant "priests" move about on the purity and ultimate worth of God's character.

21:22 There was "no temple" in this heavenly city, though, *"for the Lord God, the Almighty, and the Lamb, are its temple"* (21:22). The purpose of the physical temple in the old covenant was to portray a "holy place" where God was represented as dwelling, which was "set apart" from all that was unclean, unholy and sinful. In this "holy city" (21:10) there is "nothing unclean" (21:27), so no need for such a temple. Religious institutions and buildings are superfluous. The inherent presence of God and Christ Jesus is pervasive throughout this city, so

21:23-27

that the entirety of it is a Theocentric and Christocentric "Holy of Holies" wherein "true worshippers shall worship the Father in spirit and in truth" (John 4:21).

21:23 The Shekinah glory of the divine presence illumines this city, and it *"has no need of the sun or of the moon to shine upon it"* (21:23). It "will have the Lord for an everlasting light" (Isa. 60:19). *"Its lamp is the Lamb"* (21:23), for Jesus Christ is "the light of the world" (John 8:12), the "light of men" (John 1:4), having "come into the world to enlighten every man" (John 1:9). The light of Christ enlightens all within this holy city. Isaiah foresaw that in the New Jerusalem, "nations will come to your light, and kings to the brightness of your rising" (Isa. 60:3). Earthly nations have indeed incorporated the concepts of God's kingdom, but any glory of royalty or government is subsumed and superseded by the glory of God, for God is only glorified by that which is derived from Him (Isa. 42:8; 48:11). "God is light, and in Him is no darkness at all" (I John 1:5),
21:25 so in the eternal day of the Lord *"there will be no night there"* (21:25; 22:5).

Jesus Christ is the "way" (John 14:6), having provided open access to this "holy city" by His substitutionary death. *"Its gates shall never be closed"* (21:25), just as Isaiah explained that "your gates will be open continually; they will not be closed day or night" (Isa. 60:11). No security measures are necessary, for "Jerusalem will dwell in security" (Zech. 14:11). "The glory and the honor of the nations" (21:26) will be transformed by the inter-relational character of Christ's life. The character of this city will remain inviolate and incorruptible,
21:27 for *"nothing unclean, abominable or false shall ever come into it"* (21:27). God will not tolerate anything

contrary to His character. Residency in this city is exclusive to those *"whose names are written in the Lamb's book of life"* (21:27), recorded in the heavenly register as having been identified and spiritually united with Jesus Christ.

John is describing "paradise regained." Just as there was "a river that flowed out of Eden" (Gen. 2:10), John sees *"a river of the water of life, clear as crystal, coming from the throne of God and of the Lamb"* (22:1). Ezekiel saw water flowing from the temple, and it was announced that "everything will live where the river goes" (Ezek. 47:1-12). Jesus provides that "water of life" (Rev. 7:17; 21:6), for He is the "well of water springing up to eternal life" (John 4:14) and His indwelling presence produces "rivers of living water" (John 7:38). The psalmist referred to this reality of "a river whose streams make glad the city of God, the holy dwelling places of the Most High" (Ps. 46:4). Just as "the tree of life was in the middle of the garden" (Gen. 2:9), so John sees the river "in the middle of the street, and on either side of the river was the tree of life" (22:2). Throughout Scripture the "tree of life" represents the abundance of the expression of the character of God. Jesus said, "I came that you might have life, and have it more abundantly" (John 10:10). This will involve the behavioral expression of "the fruit of the Spirit, which is love, joy, peace, patience, kindness, goodness, faithfulness, gentleness and self-control" (Gal. 5:22,23). *"The leaves of the tree were for the healing of the nations"* (22:2), John continues, for they abrogate the effects of the fall of man and restore God's intent for all of His creation.

22:1

22:2

22:3,4

22:3 In accord with Zechariah's prophecy that "there will be no more curse" (Zech. 14:11), John also indicates that in the "beloved city" the "curse" that came in the fall of man (Gen. 3:17) would no longer be present (22:3). Christ took the curse for us on the tree of crucifixion (Gal. 3:13), and Christians need not incur the curses for disobedience (Deut. 27,28) but may participate in the "blessings that are ours in Christ Jesus" (Eph. 1:3).

Within this heavenly community is *"the throne of God and of the Lamb"* (22:3) evidencing God's authority, in response to which God's "bond-servants shall serve Him." "God is not served with human hands, as though He needed anything" (Acts 17:22), but is "served" by our availability to His Lordship wherein we allow His character and activity to be expressed in our behavior. Thus we serve as "bond-servants of Christ" (Gal. 1:10).

22:4 The intimacy of this heavenly relationship that John is describing is indicated by the reference that we *"shall see God face to face"* (22:4). To Moses, God said, "You cannot see My face, for no man can see Me and live" (Exod. 33:20). In His sermon on the mount Jesus said, "Blessed are the pure in heart; for they shall see God" (Matt. 5:8). There is a sense in which we can "see God" as Christians, for "God has shone in our hearts to give the light of the knowledge of the glory of God in the face of Christ" (II Cor. 4:6), but we still look forward to "seeing Him just as He is" (I John 3:2) "face to face" (I Cor. 13:12). Meanwhile, like Moses, "we endure, as seeing Him who is unseen" (Heb. 11:27).

Those who reside in the spiritual and heavenly "city of peace" have *"His name on their foreheads"* (22:4), which seems to mean that they are identified with God in Christ as the character of God is evidenced in their thinking. *"They shall reign forever and ever"* (22:5). Though we "reign in life now through Christ Jesus" (Rom. 5:17,21) throughout the "thousand years" (Rev. 20:4,6), "if we endure, we shall continue to reign with Him" (II Tim. 2:12) eternally.

We must never forget that the Revelation was designed to serve as an incentive for Christians in all ages to endure and persevere during "the enigma of the interim" as they hope for the consummated victory of Jesus Christ. Christians must be willing to share in Christ's suffering even unto death, as they allow for the ontological out-living of the life of Jesus in their behavior. The emphasis of the Revelation is not on getting all the graphics figured out epistemologically, nor on charting future events eschatologically, but on the life and character of Jesus Christ lived out through us ontologically despite possible mistreatment and the temptation to revert to religious self-preservation.

This final panorama (19:11-22:5) of the victory of Jesus Christ over all religion (19:17-21), its satanic source (20:1-10), and its consequences (20:11-14), is timelessly applicable, being transgenerational and translocational. We must avoid pinning down God's heavenly realities to arbitrary humanly determined space and time parameters. When we do so, we miss the "big picture" of what God is doing in Jesus Christ, and draw the attention of Christians away from the privilege of present participation in Christ's victory.

22:5

Religious gnosticism is rampant in the varying contemporary interpretations of the Revelation. So many religious interpreters think they "know" the details and have "secret knowledge" about heavenly realities and future events. This last book of the Bible, which perhaps more than any other reveals the damnable character of religion, has been obscured by religious interpreters more than any other. Should we be surprised? Religionists certainly do not want to see or admit that it is they who are being exposed throughout the Revelation. They will never accept the message that "religion goes to hell" (19:20), along with its adherents and interpreters.

ENDNOTES

1 Caird, C.B., *A Commentary on the Revelation of St. John the Divine. (Black's New Testament Commentaries). London:* Adam and Charles Black. 1966. pg. 249.
2 Torrance, Thomas F., *The Apocalypse Today.* Grand Rapids: Wm. B. Eerdmans Publishing Co. 1959. pg. 133.

Epilogue of the Revelation

Revelation 22:6 – 22:21

After all of the imagery that John has recorded throughout this book, it is easy to lose sight of the original setting and objective that was noted in the prologue of this document. John was commissioned to write an account of the visions that he saw, and he was instructed to do so in the form of an encyclical epistle to seven churches in Asia (1:11). Now, after the various perspectives of the visions are concluded, John writes an epilogue to the document which also serves as an epistolary conclusion.

The expressions in the epilogue connect with several concepts introduced in the prologue. In the beginning John was told to write what he saw in a scroll (1:11), and now he is told not to seal up this scroll (22:10) and to indicate that the contents of the scroll are inviolable (22:18). The content of what John saw on Patmos was referred to as "the words of prophecy" (1:3), explaining the proclamatory intent of this document, and this is reiterated in the beatitude, "Blessed is he who heeds the words of the prophecy of this scroll" (22:7). The letter was intended to be read publicly in the churches to which it was addressed: "Blessed is he who reads and those who hear the words of the prophecy" (1:3), with a final caution to "everyone who hears the words of the prophecy of this scroll" (22:18). The imminence of the

22:6 "things which must take place" (1:1,19) for "the time is near" (1:3) or "at hand" is emphasized again *"as shortly taking place"* (22:6) "for the time is near" (22:10), referring to the ever-present conflict of God and Satan, Christianity and religion, the ordeals and judgments pictured throughout the different perspectives. Christ's expected physical return "coming in the clouds" (1:7) is announced again in the epilogue for the encouragement and hope of Christians in every age, with the promise that such an impending coming will be without undue delay (22:7,12,20). The prologue and the epilogue tie the whole of the Revelation together.

The heavenly messenger (21:9) explained to John that all of the foregoing words of the Revelation were *"faithful and true"* (22:6). They come from the risen Lord Jesus who is "Faithful and True" (3:14; 19:11), and therefore they are factually accurate and correspond with ultimate divine reality. *"The Lord, the God of the spirits of the prophets"* (22:6) is Himself the source of all valid prophetic proclamation as is declared in this Revelation, for "no prophecy is an act of human will, but men moved by the Holy Spirit speak from God" (II Peter 1:21). The purpose of this Revelation is that God *"sent His angel to show to His bond-servants the things which must shortly take place"* (22:6), the ever-imminent enactment of hostile encounters between the enemies of God within religion and the Christian people of God.

22:7 Speaking through the angel, the risen Lord Jesus declares, *"Behold, I am coming quickly"* (22:7). His impending return will come without unnecessary prolongation in God's "fullness of time," as was the timing of His first coming (Gal. 4:4). This does not imply an *imminence* that is calculably soon, but an *impending* return that all Christians can expect to take place "without delay."

Two of the seven beatitudes found in the Revelation are found here in the epilogue (22:7,14). Jesus says, **"Blessed is he who heeds the words of the prophecy of this book"** (22:7). This is similar to the beatitude expressed by Jesus during His earthly ministry, "Blessed are those who hear the word of God, and observe it" (Luke 11:28). These are not simply admonitions to "observe" and "heed" written propositions and directions from a book, but rather they inculcate a response to the Revelation predicated on our having "every spiritual blessing in heavenly places in Christ Jesus" (Eph. 1:3), the dynamic wherein we recognize the implications of the victory of Christ in our lives day by day. Every Christian is responsible to "heed" what Jesus tells us in this book in order to discern what is going on in the activities of historical events and to depend on the sufficiency of Christ's life in the midst of such.

John again attests that he is **"the one who heard and saw these things"** (22:8), and he records a second occasion when he mistakenly fell down to worship someone other than God. Previously he fell at the feet of a heavenly messenger to worship him (19:10) and was told not to do so for the one before whom he fell was "a fellow servant." Again John either mistakes the heavenly messenger for Jesus or is so overcome with the desire to worship that he is not discerning about the object of that worship, and falls before the angel. The angel says, **"Do not do that; I am a fellow servant of yours and of your brethren the prophets and of those who heed the words of this book"** (22:9). "I am just another worshipper like you," the angel says. God is the only legitimate object of our worship. Such worship may be expressed in physical prostration before God, but must also be expressed in the entirety of our behavior which expresses the worth-ship of God's character.

22:10 *"Do not seal up the words of the prophecy of this book"* (22:10), the angel declared. When Daniel received his vision, he was told to "seal up the scroll" (Dan. 12:4) to "keep the vision secret" (Dan. 8:26), but John is explicitly told not to seal the scroll on which the Revelation is written. Why? Because the revelation of how we are to live as Christians in the "enigma of the interim" is not to be closed, concealed or hidden. That is why the seals of the scroll were broken in chapters six and eight. The Revelation has a practical purpose for the discernment of how to deal with the conflict that Christians encounter in their daily lives. *"The time is near"* (22:10). The time for Christians to deal with these daily situations is now. "Now is the day of salvation" (II Cor. 6:2). Whether the Christian lives in the first century, the tenth century, or the twentieth century, the time is always "near at hand" to experience the life of Jesus Christ in the midst of the antagonism of the world and religion.

Contradictions in character will continue until all men face eventual judgment for their behavioral expressions.
22:11 *"Let the one who does wrong, still do wrong; and let the one who is filthy, still be filthy; and let the one who is righteous, still practice righteousness; and let the one who is holy, still keep himself holy"* (22:11). This is not to be construed as an encouragement of a laissez-faire attitude of abstention of concern for how people live. Rather, we are encouraged to recognize that

behavior modification and legislated morality will not suffice. It does no good to whitewash "filthy wrong-doing" with false piety. Men's behavior reveals the nature and character of the one who indwells them spiritually and/or empowers their behavior. The fruit must be traced back to the root. "The tree is known by its fruit. The good man out of a good treasure brings forth what is good; and the evil man out of an evil treasure brings forth what is evil" (Matt. 12:33,35). Spiritual condition of nature and identity will issue forth in the character expression of behavior. God created us as derivative men. We derive our nature, identity, and character from one spiritual source or the other, from God or Satan, "sons of God or sons of the devil" (I John 3:10). As we observe mankind, we let them be consistent with their spiritual nature, and this will evidenced in the character of their behavior. The "one who is righteous" is only "made righteous in Christ" (II Cor. 5:21) by the indwelling presence of "Jesus Christ, the Righteous" (I John 2:1), and can only "practice the righteousness that comes from God on the basis of faith" (Phil. 3:9). The "one who is holy" is only "holy and blameless" (Eph. 1:4) as Jesus Christ, the "Holy One" (Acts 2:27) dwells in the Christian spiritually, and manifests behaviorally "the holiness without which no man shall see the Lord" (Heb. 12:14). The dichotomy of character will become evident as we observe the behavior of men.

The eternal importance of this difference is recognized by the awareness that Jesus will return at a time which no man knows. *"Behold I am coming quickly,"* without delay (22:12), Jesus says. He will do so unexpectedly, unannounced "like a thief in the night" (16:15). At His return Jesus explains that *"My reward is with Me, to render to every man according to what he*

22:13

has done" (22:12). Isaiah likewise explained that "the Lord God will come with might, with His arm ruling for Him. Behold, His reward is with Him, and His recompense before Him" (Isa. 40:10). The judgment of God upon the deeds of men is not based on merit. It is based on the responsibility that all men have for the derivation of behavior from a spiritual source, expressing the nature and character of that spiritual personage. "Each man's work will become evident" (I Cor. 3:13). The deeds of the Christian will be judged in accord with the responsibility we have for being available to God in faith, allowing for receptivity of the activity of the character of the righteous and holy One who indwells us, in order to manifest the "fruit of the Spirit" (Gal. 5:22,23). As Christ is the only cause of His own character expression, He is also the "reward" for such as we develop appreciation for Who He is and what He does, in order to appreciate the worth-ship of His character for eternity.

22:13 Jesus is "the all in all" (Col. 3:11) for the Christian. He goes on to affirm, *"I am the Alpha and the Omega, the first and the last, the beginning and the end"* (22:13). The Alpha and the Omega were the first and last letters in the Greek alphabet. Jesus is everything from A to Z for the Christian. Christianity is Christ! Some important terms are employed in this self-designation of Jesus. When Jesus refers to Himself as the "last," the Greek term used is *eschatos*. This is the word from which we get the theological term "eschatology," often defined as the study of "last things." Many interpreters have thought that the document of the Revelation was intended to be an outline of "last things," and they have set about to make charts and calendars of futuristic "last things." They have missed the point, or should we say the **Person** of the Revelation. The Revelation does not reveal propositional statements about "last things," but the Person of the One who is "the first and the last." Jesus is the *Eschatos*! Genuine eschatology is not the study of the "last things" of future events, but it is the recognition that the "last word" of God for men is in His Son, Jesus Christ. The last thing God has to give to man is Jesus Christ. Jesus also identifies Himself as "the end," and the Greek word used is *telos*. Again, many interpreters have mistakenly thought that the Revelation was a forecast of "end times." The "end" is not in events of the future, but the "end" is the **Person** of Jesus Christ. Based on His accomplishing the end-objective of God when He exclaimed "It is finished" (John 19:30) from the cross, Jesus is the teleological personification of the divine intent. He is the "end (*telos*) of the Law" (Rom. 10:4). Jesus is the telos! We do not need to speculate on "end times." The *eschatos* and the *telos* are ontologically realized in the Person of Jesus Christ. We must not focus on the temporal *logos* of chronology, but on the eternal *Logos* of God in Christ.

"Blessed" are those who have experienced identification with and derivation from Jesus Christ is the essence of Christianity. In the last of seven beatitudes in the Revelation, Jesus says, *"Blessed are those who wash their robes, that they may have the right to the tree of life, and may enter by the gates into the city"* (22:14). In the "washing of regeneration and renewing of the Holy Spirit" (Titus 3:5), we have "put on Christ" and the robes of His righteous character. Having received the Spirit of His life in our spirit (Rom. 8:9), we have the right and privilege to receive of "the tree of life," which throughout Scripture represents the sanctifying process of partaking of the fruit of the character of God. In the garden Adam was encouraged to "eat freely" (Gen. 2:16) of the "tree of life" (Gen. 2:9), in order to allow for the divine out-working of the divinely in-breathed life of God (Gen. 2:7). He rejected such and was refused access to the "tree of life" (Gen. 3:22-24). Solomonic wisdom recognized that the "tree of life" represented the character expressions of wisdom (Prov. 3:18), righteousness (Prov. 11:30), fulfilled desire (Prov. 13:12) and gracious speech (Prov. 15:4). In the revelation of Himself in this last book of our Bible, Jesus ties the end to the beginning by explaining that the restoration of our *"right to the tree of life"* (22:2,14) is by the partaking of the character expression of His life in our behavior. Thereby we *"may enter by the gates into the city"* (22:14) wherein "nothing unclean dwells" (21:27). This "beloved" (20:9) and "holy city" (21:2,10; 22:19) is the New Jerusalem (21:2,10), the "city of the living God" (Heb. 12:22), the community of all God's people. Every Christian already participates in the glory of this heavenly community, the "Jerusalem above" (Gal. 4:26), but we also look forward in hope to the unhindered experience of that spiritual reality.

22:15 In contrast to the community of those "in Christ," are those who are *"outside"* (22:15) of the city of God's people. These are those who chose not to enter the city and "endure ill-treatment with the people of God, but rather to enjoy the passing pleasures of sin" (Heb. 11:25). They are identified as *"the dogs and the sorcerers and the immoral persons and the murderers and the idolaters, and everyone who loves and practices lying"* (22:15). These designations are applicable to the religionists who have been the warring opponents of God's people throughout the imagery of the Revelation.

Religion has historically engaged in the drug-induced hallucination of sorcery (9:21; 18:23; 21:8), the sensuous pleasures of immorality (9:21; 14:8; 17:2; 18:3; 19:2; 21:8), the cold-blooded murder of innocents (9:21; 11:7; 13:10; 21:8), the false worship of idolatry (9:20; 13:14; 21:8), and the practice of deceitful lying (21:8) derived from "the devil, the father of lies" (John 8:44). Clearer perhaps than any other writer in the New Testament, John points out the contrasts between God and Satan, Christianity and religion, light and darkness, life and death.

John then records that Jesus Himself explained that He had sent the angel *"to testify to you these things for the churches"* (22:16). All of the visionary perspectives are intended for the edification and encouragement of the seven churches which represent churches of all ages in all locations. Jesus identifies Himself again, saying, *"I am the root and the offspring of David, the bright morning star"* (22:16). The "I am.." statement indicates correlative identification with the "I AM" of Jehovah God as He identified Himself to Moses (Exod. 3:14). As the "root and offspring of David," Jesus provides continuity with the expectations of God's people in the old covenant for a successor to the throne of the Davidic kingdom. Paul documents the same connectivity by explaining that Jesus "was born of a descendant of David according to the flesh" (Rom. 1:3). Identifying Himself as "the bright morning star," Jesus indicates that a new day has dawned in "the new heaven and the new earth" (21:1) wherein there is "no night" (21:25; 22:5). Christians already know Jesus as the "bright morning star" of their spiritual lives, but still look forward to seeing the "morning star" (II Peter 1:19; Rev. 2:28) in the unadulterated environment of the eternal heavenly realm.

22:16

22:17-19

22:17 The invitation is still open for those who would "come" and receive Jesus Christ as their life. The Spirit of Christ and the Bride of Christ continue to say, *"Come"* (22:17). Those who receive Christ by faith repeat the invitation as witnesses, saying, "Come." *"Let the one who is thirsty come; let the one who wishes take the water of life without cost"* (22:17). Just as Isaiah invited "everyone who thirsts to come to the waters...without money and without cost" (Isa. 55:1), all who "hunger and thirst after righteousness" (Matt. 5:6) are invited to be satisfied in Christ. "The Lamb shall guide them to the springs of the water of life" (Rev. 7:16). Jesus promises to "give to the one who thirsts from the spring of the water of life without cost" (Rev. 21:6). He is that "living water" (John 4:10,11). "If any man is thirsty, let him come to Me and drink" (John 7:37), for "whoever drinks of the water I give shall never thirst" (John 4:14). Jesus fulfills the inner spiritual needs of mankind.

22:18,19

Knowing that the prophetic proclamation that he had recorded in this book had come from the Spirit of God and was therefore inviolable, John warns Christians not to distort the message which has been revealed by Jesus Christ. This is similar to Moses' warning, "You shall not add to the word I am commanding you, nor take away from it" (Deut. 4:2; 12:32). *"If anyone adds to the words of the prophecy of this book,"* John says, *"God shall add to him the plagues of judgment which are written in this book; and if anyone takes away from the words of the book of this prophecy, God shall take away his part from the tree of life and from the holy city, which are written in this book"* (22:18,19). In that Jesus does not utter false threats, it is obviously possible that one who has a part in "the tree of life" and "the holy city," i.e. a Christian, can have such identification and participation revoked, just as Jesus said earlier to the church in Thyatira, "He who overcomes, I will not erase his name from the book of life" (3:5). Man-made "eternal security" doctrines, advocating "once saved, always saved," establish a false security in the theological formulations of human logic, rather than in ontological oneness with Jesus Christ. Our only security is "in Jesus Christ" as we maintain dynamic union with Him. If we accept the encouraging words of this Revelation and continue to "overcome" by deriving all from the Overcomer (John 16:33), we need not concern ourselves with being alienated from the life of Jesus Christ. "The Spirit bears witness with our spirit that we are children of God" (Rom. 8:16).

The final testimony of Jesus is the third repetition within this epilogue (22:7,12,20) of His promise to come again without delay. We can be sure that Jesus is not "stalling" unnecessarily. He is not "dragging His feet" or delaying His return by indecision. The perfect purpose and patience of God are being fulfilled in the millennia between Christ's redemptive advent and His consummative advent, just as they were in the millennia between the fall of man and "the fullness of time when God sent forth His Son, born of a woman" (Gal. 4:4), the incarnate Messiah and Redeemer. *"Yes, I am coming quickly"* (22:20), Jesus says. John's response is, *"Amen. Come Lord Jesus."* John is desirous that Jesus should come and consummate His victory. His plea is similar to the Aramaic word that Paul employed when he said, *"Maranatha"* (I Cor. 16:22). Knowing that Jesus is the divine "I AM," John uses the word "Amen" to express his certainty that God will act in accord with Who He is. It is much more that a final punctuation to

22:21

a prayer, for it is freighted with the ontological understanding of God's Being and His sure activity in accord with His character.

22:21   That very reality of God's activity in accord with His character is John's final affirmation and admonition to the readers of the Revelation. *"The grace of the Lord Jesus be with you all"* (22:21). At the outset of the letter John extended "Grace to you and peace" (1:4), and now he concludes with a call for "grace" again. Grace is God's activity "realized through Jesus Christ" (John 1:17). There is no functionality of Christ's life apart from grace. There is no Christianity and no Christian living except by the dynamic of the grace activity of God in Jesus Christ. There could be no encouragement to endure and persevere unless it were by "the grace of the Lord Jesus," so there could be no more fitting conclusion to the Revelation.

Application of the Revelation

The Christocentric-Triumphalist interpretation that has been employed in this study of the Revelation allows the entirety of the book to remain timelessly applicable. A Christian in any time period and in any place can observe and discern what the risen Lord Jesus has revealed, and the implications of such for their life as the life of the Lord Jesus is lived out through them in their present situation. The Revelation is never "out of date." From beginning to end the images of the Revelation portray situations that are "bound to happen" throughout Christian history for "the time is near" (Rev. 1:3; 22:10) when these things "must shortly take place" (1:1,19; 22:6). The inevitability of such remains valid for every Christian in every age.

Recognition of the spiritual conflict between God and Satan is essential for every Christian. To fail to understand such is to be constantly baffled by all that is going on in the universe around us, and to be vulnerable to espousing every new theory proffered for the resolution of world problems. There is far more going on than what is visible on the earthly plane, and the Christian has the unique indwelling resource of "the mind of Christ" to ascertain and discern such invisible "spiritual things" (I Cor. 2:10-16). The dichotomies of the spiritual realm must be recognized. "God is Spirit" (John 4:24), but there is also the Satanic "spirit that works in the sons of disobedience" (Eph. 2:2). The "children of God" and the "children of the devil" (I John 3:10) must obviously be differentiated. This "either/or" contrast is so apparent in the imagery of the Revelation. The di-

Application

abolic "dragon" (12:9) is opposed to the Messianic Lamb (5:6; 13:8). The army of the "beast" (11:7; 19:19) makes war (17:14) against the army of the "Word of God" (19:13,14). The "great city of Babylon" (18:2) is contrasted with "the holy city of the New Jerusalem" (21:2), the community of religion versus the community of God's people, a contrast that many Christians have failed to understand. The "harlot" (17:1) of religion is set in contradiction to the "Bride" of Christ (19:7; 21:2). Religion will be the fare of scavenging birds at "the great supper of God" (19:17), whereas Christians will feast together with Christ at "the marriage supper of the Lamb" (19:9). When these heavenly and spiritual contrasts are obscured, religion is able to counterfeit itself as the work of God, as Christianity (II Cor. 11:13-15).

Paul Minear cautions against the

> "hasty classification of Christianity under the category 'religion,' so that we assume that it is 'harmless,' ...the notion that religion is on the whole a conservative, innocuous, self-protective force, applicable to man's inner life but not to the powers which control historical destiny.
>
> The Church has so emasculated the Gospel that it threatens no other power-structures. The Church no longer arouses hostility among the elites and to the same degree as in the first century, but this is due not so much to a change in the operation of the power-structures as to the Church's betrayal of the Gospel itself. ...In reading Revelation, we may discover that the prophet was alive to that very betrayal in the churches of Asia and that he traced such betrayal to Satan's deceptions. This is why he describes the Great Prostitute as he does, because he discovers whoredom among Christians themselves. This is why his parodies are so caustic and cutting: the Prostitute as a parodic image of the church, Babylon as parody of the New Jerusalem, the Beast as parody of the Lamb, the slaves of the Beast as parody of the slaves of Christ. Such an interpretation of John brings him

Application

within the succession of the great prophets, like Isaiah, Jeremiah and Ezekiel, whose vocation under God was to make God's people aware of their own apostasy"[1]

It is imperative that Christians understand that religion is part of the old order of the "first things" (21:4) which have been defeated by Christ. We are to function in the "new creation" (Gal. 6:15) of the "new heavens and new earth" (Rev. 21:1) in the "newness of life" (Rom. 6:4) that we have in Jesus Christ. The old degenerative, sinful and fallen order has been defeated and superseded by the new regenerative, redemptive and restorative order that is ontologically encompassed in the life of the risen Lord Jesus. Failing to discern such, many who call themselves Christians coalesce with the misnomer of "Christian religion," engaging in the activities of Satan's world system. Their apostasy is revealed by the Revelation.

Christianity is the dynamic indwelling and out-living of the life and character and ministry of Jesus Christ in the behavior of Christians. It is the restoration of the very presence of God within man by the presence of His Son, Jesus Christ. "If any man does not have the Spirit of Christ, he is none of His" (Rom. 8:9). We must not allow the dynamic of Christ's life in us to be devitalized in religious institutionalism and relativism. This will be the constant temptation of Satan for Christians in every age.

Throughout the figurative "thousand years" (20:1-7) of the "enigma of the interim" between the physical advents of Jesus Christ to earth, Christians will "reign with Christ" (20:4,6), but will also continue to be assailed by the religious assaults of Satanic temptation. They must live in the recognition of Christ's victory accomplished in the past on the cross (John 19:30), despite apparent visible evidences to the contrary on the physical plane in the present, all the while looking forward in hope

Application

to the unhindered experience of that victory in the future. Jesus reveals His victory and sufficiency to Christians in the Revelation. No matter how tough the going gets, Christians are called upon to manifest the character of Christ in their behavior, to endure and persevere (2:2,3,19; 3:10; 13:10; 14:12) in the midst of animosity, hostility, mistreatment, persecution, tribulation (1:9; 7:14) and suffering (2:10) which may lead even unto physical death (11:7; 12:11; 14:13; 17:6; 20:4).

Are we willing to allow Jesus Christ in us to continue to be unjustly treated, to be persecuted, to be subject to death? Are we willing to die as Christ died? Are we willing to pay that ultimate physical price in what Dietrich Bonhoeffer called "the cost of discipleship"?[2] In the Revelation the risen Lord Jesus explains that such tribulation is the inescapable consequence of being part of His kingdom, just as Paul noted that "through many tribulations we must enter the kingdom of God" (Acts 14:22). G.B. Caird correctly indicates that "the one imminent event which John expected was persecution."[3]

In the midst of the difficulties Christians are to discern "what the Spirit is saying" (2:7,11,17,29; 3:6,13,22) in order to "listen under" His direction in obedience. Our response to religion must be to "come out" (18:4) of any involvement therein, and to "repent" (2:5,16,21,22; 3:3,19) of such failure to derive all from Christ. We must "remember what we have received" (3:3) in Christ, and the sufficiency of His grace provision (1:4; 22:21), in order to "overcome" (2:7,11,17,26; 3:5,12,21) by relying on the divine Overcomer (John 16:33). Recognizing the adequacy of Christ's life, we continue to pray (8:3,4), to witness (1:2,9; 6:9; 11:3; 12:17; 19:10; 20:4), and to praise God (7:10; 14:2; 15:3,4; 19:1-7) in the confident expectation of hope that the victory of Jesus Christ over all forces of evil will be consummated in an unhindered heavenly eternity.

Application

If ever there was a message that was "the need of the hour" for Christians in every age, and particularly in our age, it is the message of the Revelation. It is a most practical message for ever-present Christian living in the context of the physical world prior to Christ's return. The Revelation is not primarily an historical document wherein one can study the details of how the pictorial images fit historical circumstances of the first century or intervening centuries. Neither is it a puzzling predictive prophecy of the future on which to speculate about possible details and dates of events which are yet to transpire. In fact, very little is mentioned in the Revelation concerning future events, despite popular interpretations of late to the contrary. There is no mention of the rapture, no mention of a seven year tribulation, and even the few allusions to Christ's return to earth (1:7; 3:3,11; 22:7,12,20) are so general as to provide no details of information concerning such, but they merely provide an assurance to Christians of the confident expectation of hope they are to have for the consummation of Christ's victory. The foremost message of the Apocalypse pertains to the practical implications of how the Christ-life is to be evidenced in Christian lives throughout the period between His earthly advents, with the willingness to sacrifice physical life, as did the Lord Jesus, for the ultimate value of the spiritual and eternal life in Christ.

We must never forget that this is "the revelation of **Jesus Christ**" (1:1). Our interpretation and application must remain Christocentric, and go beyond the static belief-systems of epistemology to the dynamic ontological implications of the Being of Christ in believers. It is a Person that is being revealed in the Revelation, not prophecy; the Being of the Savior, not a belief-system. When interpretations of the Revelation fail to focus on Jesus Christ and His dynamic life in Christians, they inevitably end up with a deified revelatory document alleged to reveal theological and eschatological data to those having

Application

the interpretive "key." They fail to understand that the "Word of God" (19:13) who is the Victor is Jesus Christ, a spirit-Person to be received in faith, rather than a prophetic outline to be believed; a life to be lived, rather than a book to be interpreted.

ENDNOTES

1. Minear, Paul. *I Saw a New Earth: An Introduction to the Visions of the Apocalypse*. Washington D.C.: Corpus Books. 1968. pgs. 210, 211.
2. Bonhoeffer, Dietrich, *The Cost of Discipleship*. New York: Collier Books. 1949.
3. Caird, G.B., *A Commentary on the Revelation of St. John the Divine*. (Black's New Testament Commentary series). London: Adam & Charles Black. 1966. pg. 291.

ADDENDA

Addendum A
Geography of the Revelation.................................. 317

Addendum B
Outline of the Revelation...318

Addendum C
Balancing Our Perspective of Christ's Victory.....319

Addendum D
Structure of the Letters to the Seven Churches....320

Addendum E
Varying Interpretations of the Revelation 321

Addendum F
**The Interpretive Placement of the
Varying Perspectives of the Revelation** 322

Addendum G
The Interpretive Tensions of the Revelation 323

Addendum H
Millennial Theories 324

Addendum A

Geography of the Revelation

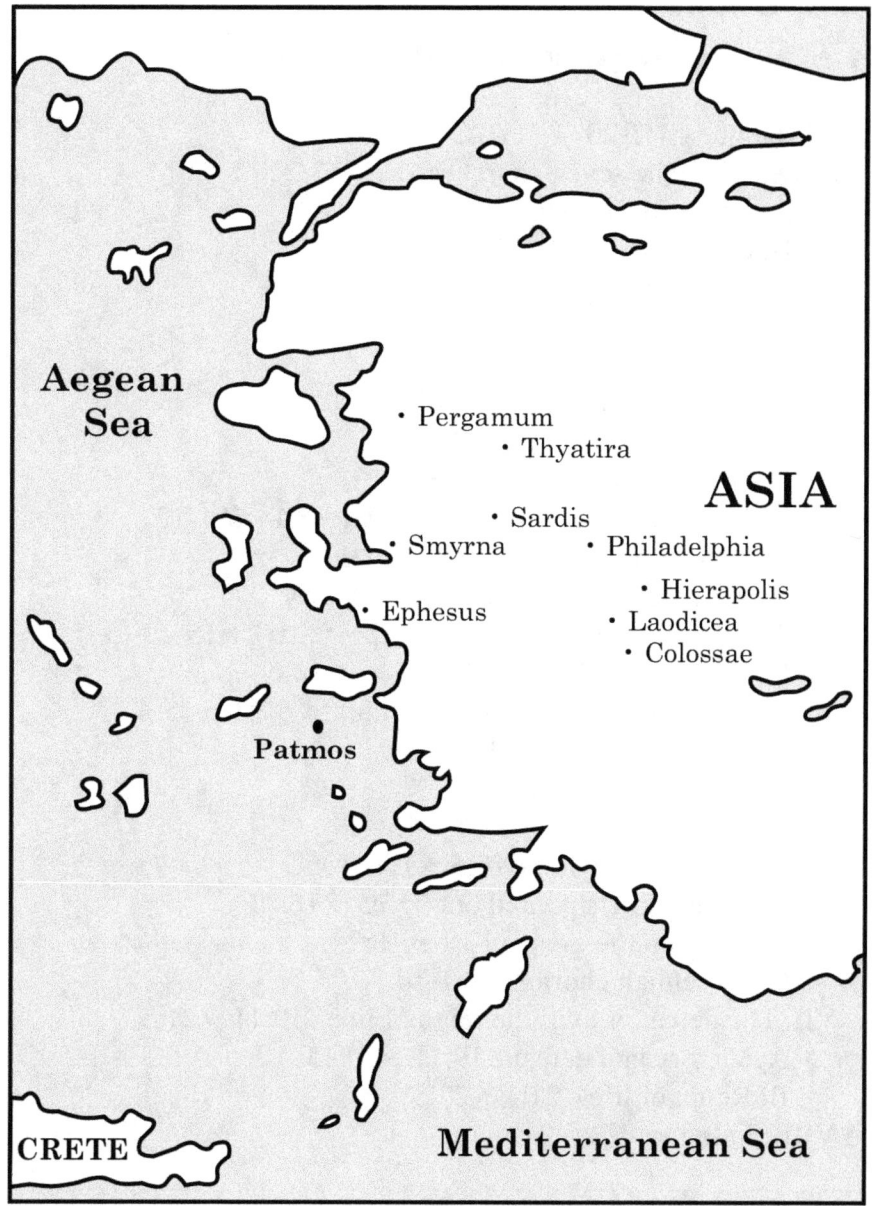

©1996, 2013 by James A. Fowler. All rights reserved.

Addendum B

Outline of the Revelation

I. Prologue - 1:1-20
II. Letters to the seven churches - 2:1 ¬ 3:22
    A. Letter to Ephesus - 2:1-7
    B. Letter to Smyrna - 2:8-11
    C. Letter to Pergamum - 2:12-17
    D. Letter to Thyatira - 2:18-29
    E. Letter to Sardis - 3:1-6
    F. Letter to Philadelphia - 3:7-13
    G. Letter to Laodicea - 3:14-22
III. Breaking of the seals - 4:1 ¬ 8:1
    A. The heavenly throne-room - 4:1 ¬5:14; 7:1-17
    B. Seven seals broken - 6:1-17; 8:1
IV. Sounding of the trumpets - 8:2 ¬ 11:19
    A. Seven trumpets sounded - 8:2 ¬ 9:21; 11:15-19
    B. Interlude - 10:1 ¬ 11:14
V. The Dragon, the Beasts and the Lamb - 12:1 ¬ 15:4
    A. The Dragon - 12:1-17
    B. The Beasts - 13:1-18
    C. Christian victors - 14:1 ¬ 15:4
VI. The fall of Babylon - 15:5 ¬ 19:10
    A. Seven bowls poured out - 15:5 ¬ 16:21
    B. Babylon the great - 17:1 ¬ 18:24
    C. Hallelujah chorus - 19:1-10
VII. The defeat of evil; the reign of life - 19:11 ¬ 21:5
    A. Victory and defeat - 19:11 ¬ 20:15
    B. Reign of life - 21:1 ¬ 22:5
VIII. Epilogue - 22:6-21

©1996, 2013 by James A. Fowler. All rights reserved

Addendum C

BALANCING OUR PERSPECTIVE OF CHRIST'S VICTORY

"The Enigma of the Interim"

Past	Present	Future
The Victory Accomplished	The Victory Enacted	The Victory Consummated
"Already"	"Now"	"Not Yet"
Redemption of Christ	Reign of Christ	Return of Christ
Over-emphasis: Passivism	Over-emphasis: Activism	Over-emphasis: Futurism

©1996, 2013 by James A. Fowler. All rights reserved

Addendum D

STRUCTURE OF THE LETTERS TO THE SEVEN CHURCHES
Revelation 2:1 – 3:22

	Ephesus	Smyrna	Pergamum	Thyatira	Sardis	Philadelphia	Laodicea
Commission and Address	2:1a	2:8a	2:12a	2:18a	3:1a	3:7a	3:14a
Personal Identity	2:1b	2:8b	2:12b	2:18b	3:1b	3:7b	3:14b
Observations	2:2,3,6	2:9	2:13	2:19	3:1c	3:8	3:15-17
Charges	2:4	None	2:14,15	2:20-23	3:2-4	None	3:15-18
Commands	2:5	2:10	2:16	2:24,25	3:2,3	3:11	3:18,19
Call to Discernment	2:7a	2:11a	2:17a	2:29	3:6	3:13	3:22
Promises	2:7b	2:11b	2:17b	2:26-28	3:4,5	3:12	3:20,21

©1996, 2013 by James A. Fowler. All rights reserved.

Addendum E

VARYING INTERPRETATIONS OF REVELATION

Interpretive Methods	A.D. 100	1517	1900	Second Coming	Eternity
Preterist (from Latin *Praeter* = past)	*Rev. 1-20* First century *Rev. 1-22* Spiritualize				
Historicist (Western Church)	*Rev. 1-3* Ephesus Smyrna	*Rev. 1-3* Pergamum Thyatira Sardis	*Rev. 1-3* Philadelphia Laodicea	*Rev. 19-22* (overthrow papacy)	*Rev. 21-22*
	←———————— Teaching value ————————→				
Futurist	*Rev. 1-3* Ephesus Smyrna Pergamum Thyatira Sardis Philadelphia Laodicea			*Rev. 10* Reformation ←— Teaching value —→ *Rev. 4-22*	*Rev. 10* Millennium
Triumphalist (Symbolic or Idealist)	*Rev. 1-22* ←———— Message of conflict between good and evil, between Christianity and "religion." Jesus Christ, the Victor ————→				

©1996, 2013 by James A. Fowler. All rights reserved.

Addendum F

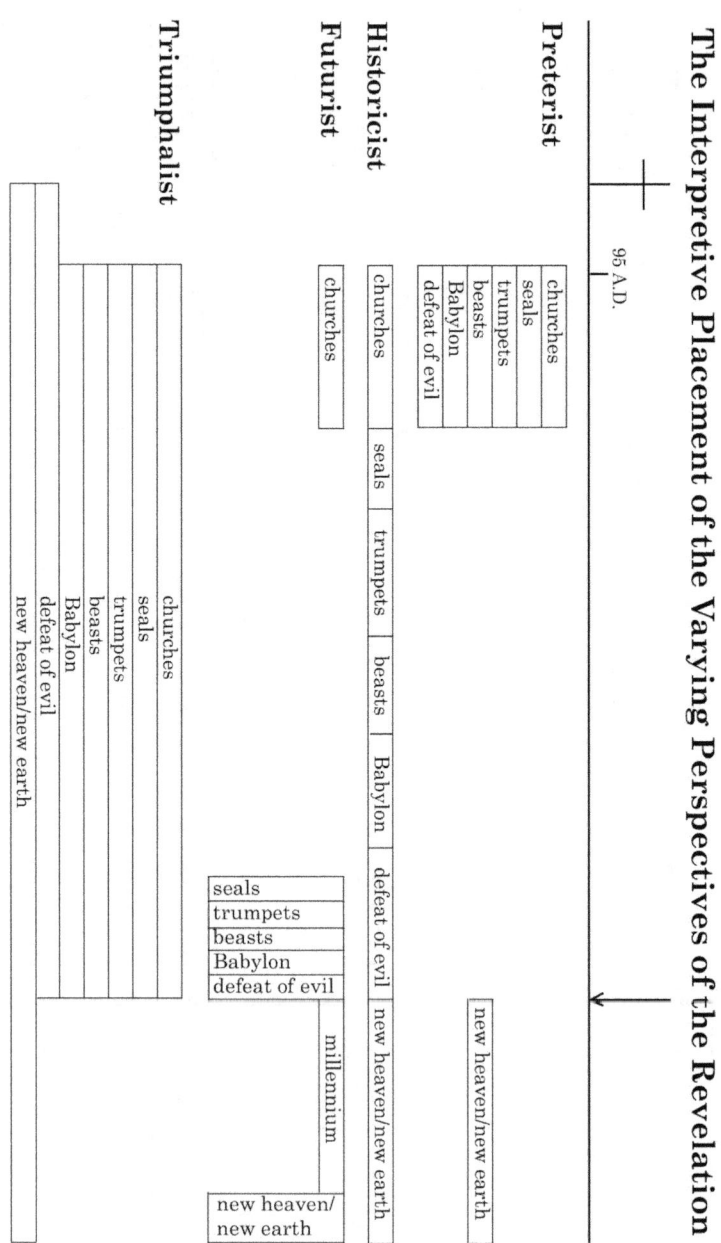

©1996, 2013 by James A. Fowler. All rights reserved.

Addendum G

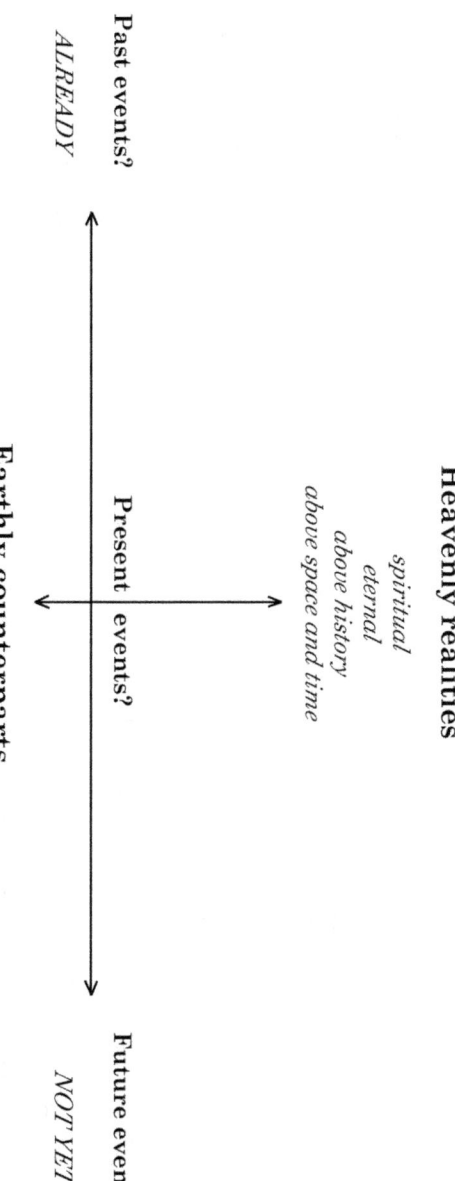

Addendum H

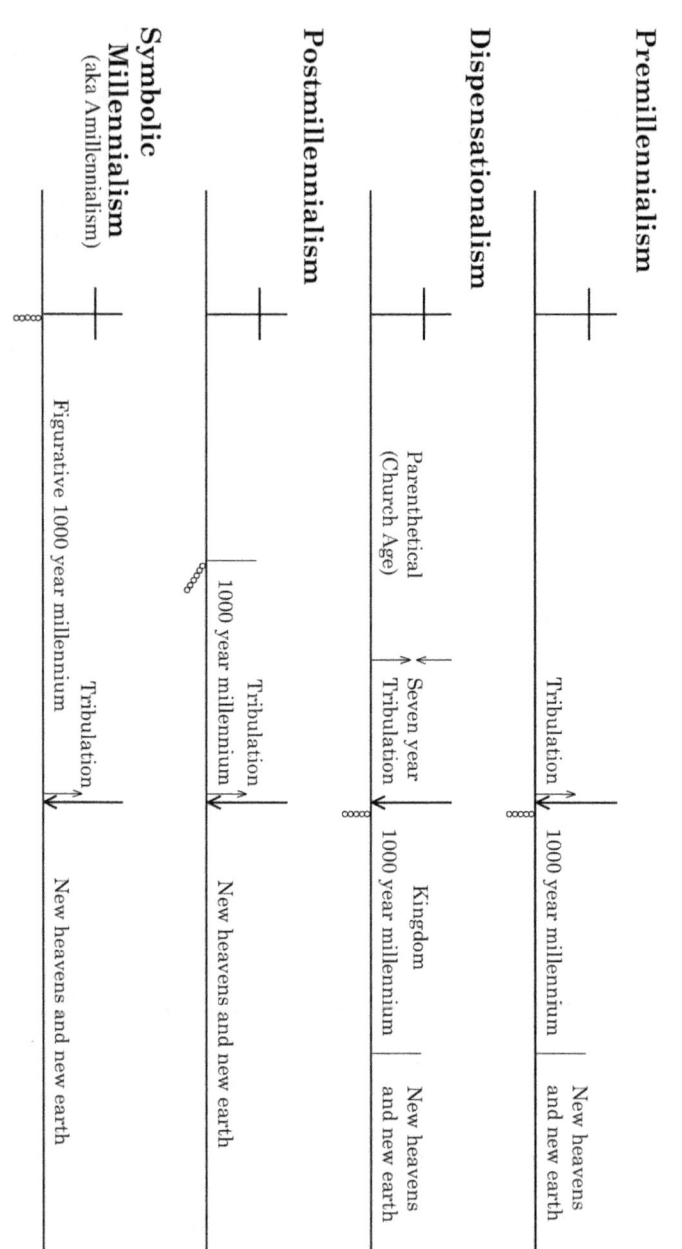

BIBLIOGRAPHY

(All of the books noted are in author's personal theological library.)

Adams, Jay, *The Time is at Hand*. Presbyterian and Reformed Pub. 1976.
Albrecht, Greg, *Revelation Revolution: The Overlooked Message of the Apocalypse*. Nashville: World Pub. 2005.
Allen, Cady H., *The Message of the Book of Revelation*. Nashville: Cokesbury Press. 1939.
Allis, Oswald T., *Prophecy and the Church*. Phillipsburg: Presbyterian and Reformed Pub. 1945.
Anderson, Roy Allan, *Unfolding the Revelation: Evangelistic Studies*. Mountainview: Pacific Press Pub. Assoc. 1953.
Anonymous, *Five Visions of the Revelation*. London: A.R. Mowbray. 1906.
Aune, David E., *Revelation*. Word Biblical Commentary series. (3 vols.), Nashville: Thomas Nelson. 1998.
Ashcraft, Morris, *Revelation*. Broadman Bible Commentary series. Nashville: Broadman Press. 1972.
Baldinger, Albert H., *Preaching From Revelation*. Grand Rapids: Zondervan Publishing House. 1960.
Balyeat, Joseph R., *Babylon: The Great City of Revelation*. Sevierville: Onward Press. 1991.
Barber, Michael, *Coming Soon: Unlocking the Book of Revelation*. Steubenville: Emmaus Road Pub. 2005.
Barclay, William, *Letters to the Seven Churches*. London: S.C.M. Press. 1957.
Barclay, William, *The Revelation of John*. The Daily Study Bible. 2 vols. Philadelphia: Westminster Pr. 1959.
Barnes, Albert, *Notes on the New Testament Explanatory and Practical: Revelation*. Grand Rapids: Baker Book House. 1949.

Bauckham, Richard, *The Climas of Prophecy: Studies on the Book of Revelation*. Edinburgh: T&T Clark. 1993.

Bauckham, Richard, *The Theology of the Revelation*. New Testament Theology series. Cambridge Univ. Press. 1993.

Beale, G.K., *The Book of Revelation: A Commentary on the Greek Text*. The New International Greek Text Commentary series. Grand Rapids: Wm. B. Eerdmans. 1999.

Beasley-Murray, G.R., *The Book of Revelation*. New Century Bible series. Greenwood: Attic Press. 1974.

Beasley-Murray, G.R.; Hobbs, Herschel; Robbins, Ray Frank, *Revelation: Three Viewpoints*. Nashville: Broadman Press. 1993.

Beckwith, Isbon T., *The Apocalypse of John: Studies and Introduction with a Critical and Exegetical Commentary*. Grand Rapids: Baker Book House. 1919.

Blaney, Harvey J.S., *Wesleyan Bible Commentary* Vol. VI. Grand Rapids: Wm B. Eerdmans Pub. 1972.

Bleek, Friedrich, *Lectures on the Apocalypse*. Edinburgh: Williams and Norgate. 1875.

Blunt, Henry, *Practical Expositions of the Epistles of the Seven Churches of Asia*. Philadelphia: Hooker & Claxton. 1839.

Boatman, Russell, *What the Bible Says About the End Time*. Joplin: College Press Pub. 1980.

Cock, Emil, *The Apocalypse of St. John*. London: Christian Community Press. 1957.

Boettner, Loraine, *The Millennium*. Phillipsburg: Presbyterian and Reformed Pub. 1957.

Boring, Eugene M., *Revelation*. Interpretation Series. Louisville: John Knox Press. 1989.

Brown, David, *Christ's Second Coming: Will it be Premillennial?* Grand Rapids: Baker Book House. 1983.

Caird, G.B., *A Commentary on the Revelation of Saint John the Divine*. Black's New Testament Commentary series. London: Adam and Charles Black. 1966.

Carpenter, W. Boyd, *The Revelation*. Layman's Handy Commentary Series. Grand Rapids: Zondervan. 1957.

Carter, Charles W., *The Wesleyan Bible Commentary*. Grand Rapids: Eerdmans Pub. 1966.

Charles, R.H., *A Critical and Exegetical Commentary on the Revelation of Saint John*. International Critical Commentary Series. 2 vols. Edinburgh: T&T Clark. 1920.

Chilton, David, *The Days of Vengeance: An Exposition of the Book of Revelation*. Fort Worth: Dominion Press. 1987.

Christie, T.W., *The Book of Revelation*. London: Edward Howell. 1892.

Clark, David S., *The Message from Patmos: A Postmillennial Commentary on the Book of Revelation*. Grand Rapids: Baker Book House. 1989.

Clarke, Adam, *Clarke's Commentary*. Nashville: Abingdon Press. n.d.

Clouse, Robert G., *The Meaning of the Millennium: Four Views*. Downers Grove: Inter-Varsity Press. 1977.

Cohen, Gary G., *Revelation Visualized*. Chicago: Moody Press. 1971.

Coleman, Robert E., *Songs of Heaven: A New Perspective on Revelation*. Old Tappan: Revell. 1980.

Court, John M., *Revelation*. New Testament Guides series. Sheffield Academic Press. 1994.

Cox, William E., *Biblical Studies in Final Things*. Nutley: Presbyterian and Reformed Pub. 1977.

Cumming, John, *Apocalyptic Sketches: Lectures on the Book of Revelation*. Philadelphia: Lindsay & Blackiston. 1856.

Davidson, I.E., *Readings in Revelation*. Kent: Barbican Book Room. 1969.

DeHaan, M.R., *Revelation: Thirty-five Simple Studies on the Major Themes in Revelation*. Grand Rapids: Zondervan Pub. 1946.

Dods, Marcus, *The Epistles of Our Lord to the Seven Churches of Asia*. Edinburgh: John Maclaren. 1869.

Dusterdieck, Friedrich, *Critical and Exegetical Handbook to the Revelation of John*. Winona lake: Alpha Pub. 1883.

Eller, Vernard, *The Most Revealing Book of the Bible: Making Sense out of Revelation*. Grand Rapids: Eerd. Pub., 1974.

Ellicott, Charles John, *The Revelation*. Layman's Handy Commentary series. Grand Rapids: Zondervan Pub. 1957.

Ellul, Jacques, *Apocalypse: The Book of Revelation*. New York: Seabury Press. 1977.

Epp, Theodore H., *Christ Speaks to the Church*. Lincoln: Back to the Bible Pub. 1960.

Erdman, Charles R., *The Revelation of John*. Philadelphia: Westminster Press. 1966.

Ewert, David, *And Then Comes the End*. Scottsdale: Herald Press. 1980.

Ezell, Douglas, *Revelations on Revelation: New Sounds from Old Symbols*. Waco: Word Books. 1977.

Fairbairn, Patrick, *Prophecy Viewed in Respect to its Distinctive Nature, its Special Function, and Proper Interpretation*. Grand Rapids: Baker Book House. 1976.

Farrer, Austin, *The Revelation of Saint John the Divine*. Oxford: Clarendon Press. 1964.

Fausset, A.R., *A Commentary, Critical, Experimental and Critical*. Grand Rapids: Eerdmans Pub. 1978.

Ferrar, W. J., *The Apocalypse Explained for Readers of Today*. London: SPCK. 1936.

Ford, Desmond, *Crisis: A Commentary on the Book of Revelation* (2 vols). Newcastle. 1982.

Ford, J. Massyngberde, *Revelation: A New Translation with Introduction and Commentary*. Anchor Bible Series. New York: Doubleday. 1975.

Ford, W. Herschel, *Simple Sermons on the Seven Churches of Revelation*. Grand Rapids: Zondervan. 1959.

Foster, Lewis, *Revelation*. Standard Bible Studies series. Cincinnati: Standard Publishing. 1980.

Gentry, Kenneth L. Jr., *Before Jerusalem Fell: Dating the Book of Revelation*. Tyler: Institute for Christian Economics. 1989.

Gill, John, *Gill's Commentary*. Grand Rapids: Baker Book House. 1980.

Goldsworthy, Graeme, *The Lamb and the Lion: The Gospel in Revelation*. Nashville: Thomas Nelson Pub. 1984.

Gordon, S.D., *Quiet Talks About the Crowned Christ*. London: Fleming H. Revell. 1914.

Graham, Billy, *Approaching Hoofbeats: The Four Horsemen of the Apocalypse*. Minneapolis: Grason Pub. 1983.

Grant, F.W., *The Revelation of John: An Exposition*. London: Hodder & Stoughton. 1880.

Greene, Oliver B., *The Revelation: A verse by verse study*. Greenville: The Gospel Hour. 1922.

Gregg, Steve (ed), *Revelation: Four Views, A Commentary*. Nashville: Thomas Nelson. 1997.

Grenz, Stanley J., *The Millennial Maze: Sorting out Evangelical Options*. Downers Grove: Inter-varsity Press. 1992.

Gundry, Stanley N. (ed), *Four Views on the Book of Revelation*. Counterpoint series. Grand Rapids: Zondervan. 1998.

Guthrie, Donald, *The Relevance of John's Apocalypse*. Grand Rapids: Wm. B. Eerdmans Pub. 1987.

Gutzke, Manford George, *Plain Talk on Revelation*. Grand Rapids: Zondervan Pub. House. 1979.

Guyon, Geanne, *Christ Our Revelation*. Gardiner: Christian Books Pub. House. 1985.

Hailey, Homer, *Revelation: An Introduction and Commentary*. Grand Rapids: Baker Book House. 1979.

Hardie, Alexander, *A Study of the Book of Revelation*. Los Angeles: Times Mirror Pr. 1926.

Harrington, Wilfred J., *The Apocalypse of St. John: A Commentary*. London: Geoffery Chapmen. 1969.

Harrison, L. Sale, *The Wonders of the Great Unveiling: The Remarkable Book of the Revelation*. Harrisburg: Evangelical Press. 1930.

Hartingsveld, L. von, *Revelation, A Practical Commentary, Text and Interpretation*. Grand Rapids: Eerdmans Pub. 1985.

Hastings, James, *The Great Texts of the Bible*. Edinburgh: Charles Scribners and Sons. 1915.

Havner, Vance, *Repent or Else! The Seven Churches of Revelation*. Westview: Fleming H. Revell. 1958.

Hendricksen, William, *Three Lectures on the Book of Revelation*. Grand Rapids: Zondervan. 1949.

Hendriksen, William, *More Than Conquerors: An Interpretation of the Book of Revelation*. Grand Rapids: Baker. 1939.

Hengstenberg, E.W., *The Revelation of Saint John Expounded for those who Search the Scriptures*. New York: Robert Carter and Brothers. 1852.

Henry, Matthew, *Commentary on the Whole Bible*. Wilmington: Sovereign Grace Pub. 1972.

Hinds, John T., *A Commentary on the Book of Revelation*. Nashville: Gospel Advocate Co. 1973.

Hoekema, Anthony A., The Bible and the Future. Grand Rapids: Eerdmans Pub. 1979.

Hoeksema, Herman, *Behold He Cometh: An Exposition of the Book of Revelation*. Grand Rapids: Reformed Free Pub. Assoc. 1969.

Hort, F.J.A., *The Apocalypse of Saint John: The Greek Text with Introduction, Commentary and Additional Notes*. London: Macmillan Co., 1908.

Hoyt, Edyth Armstrong, *Studies in the Apocalypse of John of Patmos: a Non-interpretive and Literary Approach to the Last Book of the English Bible*. Ann Arbor: Edward Brothers Pub., 1956.

Hughes, Philip Edgcumbe, *The Book of the Revelation*. England: Inter-Varsity Pr. 19990.

Huntingford, Edward, *A Practical Interpretation of the Revelation of Saint John the Divine*. London: Bickers and Son. 1900.

Ironside, H.A., *Lectures on the Revelation with Chart*. Waterloo: Cedar Book Store. n.d.

Johnson, Alan F., *Revelation*. Expositor's Bible Commentary series. Grand Rapids: Zondervan Pub. 1981.

Johnson, B.W., *A Vision of the Ages: Lectures on the Apocalypse*. Delight, Ark.: Gospel Light Pub. Co., n.d.

Kallas, James, *Revelation: God and Satan in the Apocalypse*. Minneapolis: Augsburg Pub. 1973.

Kiddle, Martin, *The Revelation of Saint John*. Moffat New Testament Commentary Series. London: Hodder & Stoughton, 1940.

Kistemaker, Simon J., *Revelation*. New Testament Commentary series. Grand Rapids: Baker Books. 2001

Kovacs, Judith; Rowland, Christopher, *Revelation*. Blackwell Bible Commentaries series. Oxford: Blackwell Pub., 2004.

Krodel, Gerhard A., *Revelation*. Augsburg Commentary series. Minneapolis: Augsburg Pub. House. 1989.

Kuyper, Abraham, *The Revelation of Saint John*. Grand Rapids: Wm. B. Eerdmans Pub. 1935.

Lange, John Peter, *Lange's Commentary on the Holy Scriptures*. Grand Rapids: Zondervan Pub. n.d.

Lee, William, *The Bible Commentary*. Grand Rapids: Baker Book House. 1981.

Lenski, R.C.H., *The Interpretation of Saint John's Revelation*. Minneapolis: Augsburg Pub. 1943.

Lindsey, Hal, *There's a New World Coming: A Prophetic Odyssey*. Irvine: Harvest House Pub. 1973.

Little, C.H., *The Explanation of the Book of Revelation*. Saint Louis: Concordia Pub. House, 1950.

Lubbers, George C., *The Bible Versus Millennial Teachings: An Exegetical Critique*. Grand Rapids: 1989.

Macarthur, Jack, *Expositional Commentary on Revelation*. Eugene: Certain Sound Pub. 1973.

Maclaren, Alexander, *Expositions of Holy Scripture*. Grand Rapids: Baker Book House. 1974.

Maier, Harry O., *Apocalypse Recalled: The Book of Revelation After Christendom*. Minneapolis: Fortress Pr. 2002.

Martin, Hugh, *The Seven Letters*. Philadelphia: Westminster Press. 1956.

Mauro, Philip, *The Gospel and the Kingdom with an Examination of Modern Dispensationalism*. Sterling: Grace Abounding Ministries. 1988.

Mauro, Philip, *The Seven Weeks and the Great Tribulation*. Swengel: Reiner Pub. n.d.

Mauro, Philip, *Things Which Soon Must Come to Pass: A Commentary on the Book of Revelation*. Sterling: G.A.M. Pub., 1990.

Maxwell, Marcus, *Revelation*. Doubleday Bible Commentary series. New York: Doubleday. 1998.

McCarrell, William, *Christ's Seven Letters to His Church: Expository Study of Revelation chapters two and three*. Grand Rapids: Zondervan Pub. 1936.

McConkey, James H., *The Book of Revelation: A Series of Outline Studies in the Apoclypse*. Pittsburgh: Silver Pub. Society. 1921.

McDowell, Edward A., *The Meaning and Message of the Book of Revelation*. Nashville: Broadman Press. 1951.

McGee, J. Vernon, *Revelation*. 3 vols. Pasadena: Thru the Bible Books. 1979.

McGee, J. Vernon, *Reveling Through Revelation*. 2 vols. Pasadena: Thru the Bible Books. 1962.

McGuiggan, Jim, *The Book of Revelation*. Let the Bible Speak series. West Monroe: William C. Johnson Inc., 1976.

McKnight, William J., *The Apocalypse of Jesus Christ: John to the Seven Churches*. Boston: Hamilton Brothers. 1927.

Metzger, Bruce M., *Breaking the Code: Understanding the Book of Revelation*. Nashville: Abingdon Press. 1993.
Milligan, William, *Discussions on the Apocalypse*. London: Macmillan and Co., 1893.
Minear, Paul S., *I Saw A New Earth: An Introduction to the Visions of the Apocalypse*. Washington: Corpus Books. 1968.
Minear, Paul S., *New Testament Apocalyptic*. Interpreting Bible Texts series. Nashville: Abingdon Press. 1981.
Morris, Leon, *The Revelation of Saint John: An Introduction and Commentary*. Tyndale New Testament Commentary Series. Grand Rapids: Wm. B. Eerdmans Pub. 1969.
Morris, S.L., *The Drama of Christianity: An Interpretation of the Book of Revelation*. Grand Rapids: Baker Book House. 1928.
Mounce, Robert H., *Revelation*. New International Commentary on the New Testament series. Grand Rapids: Wm. B. Eerdmans.
Mounce, Robert H., *What Are We Waiting For? A Commentary on Revelation*. Grand Rapids: Eerdmans. 1992.
Mulholland, Robert Jr., *Revelation: Holy Living in an Unholy World*. Grand Rapids: Francis Asbury Press. 1990.
Newell, William R., *The Book of the Revelation*. Chicago: Moody Press. 1935.
Nicoll, Robertson (ed), *Revelation*. The Expositor's Greek Testament. Grand Rapids: Eerdmans Pub. 1970.
Niles, D.T., *As Seeing the Invisible: A Study on the Book of Revelation*. New York: Harper and Brothers Pub., 1961.
Noe, John, *The Apocalypse Conspiracy*. Brentwood: Wolgemuth and Hyatt Pub. 1991.
O'Leary, Stephen D., *Arguing the Apocalypse: A Theory of Millennial Rhetoric*. Oxford: Oxford Univ. Press. 1994.
Osbourne, Grand R., *Revelation*. Baker Exegetical Commentary on the New Testament series. Grand Rapids: Baker Academic. 2002.

Palmer, Earl F., *Revelation*. The Communicator's Commentary series. Waco: Word Books. 1982.
Parker, Joseph, *Preaching Through the Bible*. Grand Rapids: Baker Book House. 1987.
Peake, Arthur S., *The Revelation of John*. London: Holborn Pub. n.d.
Philips, John, *Exploring Revelation*. Chicago: Moody Press. 1974.
Plumptre, J.H., *A Popular Exposition of the Epistles to the Seven Churches of Asia*. London: Hodder & Stoughton. 1984.
Poellet, Luther, *Revelation*. Concordia Classic Commentary series. St. Louise: Concordia Publishing House. 1962.
Poole, Matthew, *Commentary on the Holy Bible*. McLean: MacDonald Pub. n.d.
Preston, R.H., and Hanson, A.T., *Revelation, the Book of Glory*. Torch Bible Series. London: S.C.M., 1949.
Ramsay, William, *Letters to the Seven Churches of Asia and their place in the plan of the Apocalypse*. New York: Hodder and Stoughton. n.d.
Ramsey, James B., *Revelation: An Exposition of the first Eleven Chapters*. Geneva series. Pennsylvania: Banner of Truth Trust. 1977.
Rattan, James J.L., *The Apocalypse of St. John: A Commentary on the Greek Text*. London: R & T Washbourne. 1915.
Richardson, Donald W., *An Interpretation of the Revelation of Jesus Christ*. Atlanta: John Knox Press. 1976.
Rist, Martin, *The Interpreter's Bible*. New York: Abingdon Press. 1957.
Robbins, Ray Frank, *The Revelation of Jesus Christ: A Commentary on the Book of Revelation*. Nashville: Broadman Press. 1975.
Robertson, A.T., *Word Pictures in the New Testament*. Nashville: Broadman Press. 1933.
Rolls, C.J., *The Book of Revelation: the Unveiled Christ*. Spartanburg: Norm Burleson Bookseller. n.d.

Rolls, C.J., *The Christ We Think We Know, Identified and Interpreted.* Spartanburg: Norm Burleson Bookseller. n.d.

Rosenthal, Marvin, *The Pre-wrath Rapture of the Church.* Nashville: Thomas Nelson Pub. 1990.

Rossing, Barbara R., *The Rapture Explained: The Message of Hoope in the Book of Revelation.* Boulder: Westview Pr. 2004

Rushdoony, Rousas John, *Thy Kingdom Come: Studies in Daniel and Revelation.* Fairfax: Thoburn Press. 1978.

Russell, D.S., *Prophecy and the Apocalyptic Dream: Protest and Promise.* Peabody: Hendriksen Publisher. 1994.

Ryrie, Charles C., *Revelation.* Everyman's Bible Commentary. Chicago: Moody. 1968.

Sadler, M.F., *The Revelation of St. John the Divine.* London: George Bell & Sons. 1898.

Sale-Harrison, L., *The Wonders of the Great Unveiling: The Revelation.* London: Stationers Hall. 1930.

Scott, Anderson C., *Revelation.* Century Bible series. London: T.C. and E.C. Jack. n.d.

Seiss, J.A., *The Apocalypse: Lectures on the Book of Revelation.* Grand Rapids: Zondervan Pub. House. 1973.

Simcox, William Henry, *The Revelation of Saint John the Divine with Notes and Introduction.* Cambridge Bible for Schools and Colleges series. Cambridge: Camb. Univ. Press. 1890.

Simcox, William Henry, *The Revelation of Saint John the Divine with Notes and Introduction.* Cambridge Greek Testament series. Cambridge: Cambridge Univ. Press. 1893.

Simpson, Albert B., *Revelation.* The Christ in the Bible Commentary series. Camp Hill: Christian Publications. 1994.

Sleeper, C. Freeman, *The Victorious Christ: A Study of the Book of Revelation.* Louisville: Westminster John Know Press. 1996.

Smith, J.B., *A Revelation of Jesus Christ: A Commentary on the Book of Revelation.* Scottdale: Herald Press. 1961.

Smith, Uriah, *The Prophecies of Daniel and the Revelation.* Nashville: Souther Publishing Assoc. 1944.

Spencer, Duane, *The Seven Epistles of Jesus: Word-Keys Which Unlock Revelation.* San Antonio: Word of Grace. 1967.

Stott, John R.W., *What Christ Thinks of the Church.* Wheaton: Harold Shaw Pub. 1990.

Strauss, James, *The Seer, The Saviour, The Saved.* Bible Study Textbook series. Joplin: College Press. 1963.

Summers, Ray, *Worthy is the Lamb: An Interpretation of Revelation.* Nashville: Broadman Press. 1951.

Swedenborg, Emanuel, *The Apocalypse Revealed.* Philadelphia: Lippincott. 1925.

Sweet, J.P.M., *Revelation.* Westminster Pelican Commentary series. Philadelphia: Westminster Press. 1979.

Swete, Henry Barclay, *The Apocalypse of Saint John: The Greek Text with Introduction, Notes and Indices.* Grand Rapids: Eerdmans Pub. Co. 1954.

Swete, J.P.M., *Revelation.* Westminster Pelican Commentary series. Philadelphia: Westminster Press. 1979.

Talbert, Charles H., *The Apocalypse: A Reading of the Revelation of John.* Louisville: Westerminster John Knox. 1994.

Tenney, Merril C., *The Revelation of Jesus Christ.* Scottdale: Herald Press. 1961.

Terry, Milton S., *Biblical Apocalyptics: A Study of the Most Notable Revelations of God and Christ.* Grand Rapids: Baker Book House. 1988.

Thompson, Leonard L., *The Book of Revelation: Apocalypse and Empire.* Oxford: Oxford Univ. Press. 1990.

Tooley, Dale, *All Things New.* New Zealand: Hasten the Light Ministries. 1983.

Torrance, Thomas F., *The Apocalypse Today.* Grand Rapids: Eerdmans Pub. Co. 1959.

Trapp, John, *A Commentary or Exposition on the Books of the New Testament.* Grand Rapids: Baker Book House. 1981.

Travis, Stephen, *I Believe in the Second Coming of Jesus.* Grand Rapids: Eerdmans Pub. 1982.

Trench, Richard Chenevix, *Commentary on the Epistles to the Seven Churches in Asia: Revelation.* Minneapolis: Klock and Klock. 1897.

van Hartingsveld, L., *Revelation*: A Practical Commentary. Grand Rapids: Wm. B. Eerdmans. 1985.

Vaughan, C.J., *Lectures on the Revelation of Saint John.* 2 vols. London: Macmillan. 1875.

Wainwright, Arthur W., *Mysterious Apocalypse: Interpreting the Book of Revelation.* Nashville: Abingdon Press. 1993.

Wall, Robert W., *Revelation.* New International Biblical Commentary series. Peabody: Hendrickson Pub. 1991.

Webber, E.F., *A Study in the Revelation.* Fort Dodge: Walterick Printing Co. n.d.

Weeber, George G., *The Consummation of History: a Study on the Book of Revelation.* 1978.

Weidner, Revere F., *Annotations on the Revelation of St. John the Divine.* New York: Christian Literature Pub., 1898.

Weinrich, William C., *Revelation.* Ancient Christian Commentary on Scripture series. Downers Grover: InterVarsity Press. 2005.

Westcott, Brooke Foss, *The Revelation of the Risen Lord.* New York: Macmillan. 1891.

Wilcock, Michael, *The Message of Revelation.* Bible Speaks Today series. Downers Grove: Inter-Varsity Press. 1975.

Witherington, Ben III, *Revelation.* New Cambridge Bible Commentary series. Cambridge Univ. Press. 2003.

Yeager, Randolph O., *The Renaissance New Testament.* Gretna: Pelican Pub. 1985.

www.ingramcontent.com/pod-product-compliance
Lightning Source LLC
LaVergne TN
LVHW051822080426
835512LV00018B/2688